Contemporary Issues of Urban Development in 21st Century: Planning and Practices

Contemporary Issues of Urban Development in 21st Century: Planning and Practices

Edited By:

Dr. Indrajit Roy Chowdhury

M.Sc. (Geography), Ph.D. (Geography)
Assistant Professor
Department of Geography & Applied Geography
University of North Bengal (Accredited by NAAC with Grade A)
Raja Rammohanpur, Darjeeling, West Bengal, India

RAJESH PUBLICATIONS

NEW DELHI - 110 002

Contemporary Issues of Urban Development in 21st Century: Planning and Practices

Published by :
Sanjay Gupta
RAJESH PUBLICATIONS
1, Ansari Road, Darya Ganj, New Delhi - 110002
Ph.: 011-23274550, 43084725
Website : www.rajeshpublications.com
Email : rajeshpublications@gmail.com,
rajeshpubdelhi@gmail.com

First Published in India 2022

ISBN : 978-93-91139-48-3

Printed in India by :
Aryan Digital Press
Delhi - 110002

Dedicated

to

My Beloved Parents

Prof. (Dr.) Ranjan Basu, Ph.D.
Professor (Retd.)

Foreword

It's a great pleasure to get the book entitled *Contemporary Issues of Urban Development in 21st Century: Planning and Practices* introduced amid the domain of the intelligentsia. This edited volume containing as many as fourteen articles contributed mainly by the new generation geographers representing different States and academic institutions of India, is the brain child of a young and energetic teacher of the University of North Bengal, Dr. Indrajit Roy Chowdhury and has been launched by a Delhi based renowned publisher. Such an academic initiative deserves accolade especially from the court of veteran geographers.

It is indeed a matter of regret that because of Covid-19 induced pandemic situation the decadal census could not be conducted in India as per schedule in the year 2021. Consequently, after one hundred year of deadly Spanish Flue – the preceding pandemic that shook the Indian subcontinent challenging the health infrastructure and ended up in a negative growth of population in 1921, the demographic profile of the country has remained under an opaque cover. Such a data constraint is of course painful for the scholars engaged in research in any branch of social sciences.

Under such circumstances, it becomes inevitable for the research workers to opt for other sources of data available from National Sample Survey Organization and various reports prepared by the relevant Government department/s along with municipal bodies and regional development authorities. Herein lies the importance of generating primary data based on field investigation followed by application of quantitative or qualitative techniques for analysis of the result obtained. Such empirical studies bear the testimony of time specific ground reality of a given space or area under study. Most of the articles in this edited book are case studies of a certain geographical unit reflecting the dynamics of urban growth and development thus altering the cultural landscape on one hand and raising a series of economic as well as environmental issues to be addressed by the powers that be.

Articles published in this edited volume have been placed under two different sections: I) Issues of urban infrastructure – Planning and practices and II) Urban environment, sustainability and climate change issues. As many as four authors have concentrated on Calangute town or beach of Goa highlighting the issues ranging from urban planning to status of health and from beach tourism to municipal solid waste management. Other four authors have devoted their attention on another coastal city Visakhapatnam and have dealt with the status of health, strategies of smart city development, sustainable management of solid waste and environmental challenges of road traffic congestion. Material wellbeing of the selected urban agglomerations, dynamic nature of urban landscape and panorama of transit in the cultural capital of India has come under the investigative lens of three other scholars from the State of West Bengal. Satellite data have been used to study the impact of land use /land cover change on land surface temperature in Assam apart from temporal change in land use surrounding the lacustrine environment in Bangladesh. Designing green building in Kerala has also come under the focus of another scholar.

In fact the issues involving sustainable management of the urban landscape are multidimensional which of course differ from the coastal areas to the mountainous terrain, from the center of pilgrimage to the proximity of the forest clad land cover or river bank location, from the lake oriented existence to the wetland-side built environment and from the mining –industrial belt to the centers of tourism or sanatoriums. The program of Providing Urban Amenities to the Rural Areas (PURA) has failed miserably at least in West Bengal. Urban greeneries and ponds are vanishing rapidly in the name of urban development. Urban expansion with erection of housing complexes and high rise buildings are taking toll in the form of either ground water depletion or arsenic contamination of the earthen source of water in the vulnerable areas. Providing Basic Services for the Urban

Poor (BSUP) under the Jawaharlal Nehru National Urban Renewal Mission (JNNURM) is notorious for its sluggish achievement. Slum development and economy housing for the people below the poverty line as well as provision of safe tap water with sanitation for them and the pedestrians (*Sulov Souchalay* for *Amjanata*) is still eluding the urban dwellers. The complex problems of hawker rehabilitation, safe disposal of municipal-medical-industrial waste, water logging, traffic congestion and road accidents, deteriorating quality of ambient air, the menace of ever increasing noise coupled with formation of urban heat island are yet to find an acceptable remedial measure despite fatty budget proposals. The role of efficient and rapid mass transit with adequacy of road space having under pass and flyovers with feeder roads, proper planning for hassle-free movement of the commuters apart from recognizing the problem of the difference between the diurnal and nocturnal population of an urban unit are still waiting for a state-of-the-art pragmatic redressal.

I'm rather optimistic that new generation geographers will realize the importance of interdisciplinary research appreciating the role of a mix of quantitative and qualitative approaches with emphasis on digital cartography and analytical style of writing adopting a suitable style of referencing to do justice on temporal and spatial variation of physico-cultural landscape on one hand and the sequence of the major issues and events with their cause and effect relationship on the other.

Kolkata
23rd May, 2022

Prof. Ranjan Basu, Ph.D.
Professor (Retd.) of Geography,
University of Calcutta and
Former ICSSR Senior Fellow,
Institute of Development Studies Kolkata

Professor (Dr.) Ranjan Roy, Ph. D.
Professor & Head

Foreword

Urbanisation brings the, economic, social, demographic and environmental changes over the space through time. The manifestations of those changes are going to be positive and negative as well. It a quite obvious fact that, the process of urban development offer job opportunities, provide better infrastructure, promote social and economic mobility and their impact is explored in improving the various indicators of urban quality of life such as good standard of living, infrastructural development, betterment of urban policy, but on the other hand, rapid growth of urban population has resulted differential and unstable environmental conditions throughout the globe. Rapid and unplanned urban development suffer from acute housing shortages, environmental degradation, water and power shortages, and crowdedas well as inefficient transport network. Generally pace of urbanisation and developmental issue leads to decline the area of agricultural land, forest and wetlands which leading to food insecurity and damage to the global and urban ecological balance. According to the various Census report, it is found that the number of urban agglomeration in India was reported 1827 in 1901 but in 2011, the number have increased in 7935 which has indicated almost 20.32 percent growth of urban population during 110 years span period. A very remarkable fact has stated that in view of urban development, during pre-independence there were only two places are recognized as metropolitan cities, such as Calcutta (1911) and Bombay (1941), but after independence the number of metropolitan cities have increased to 12 during 1981 and doubling effect has pointed out that is the number have increased to 53 in 2011, so this fact shows the tremendous pace not only in the number of cities but also an increase in rate of urban population decade after decade. This developmental stage of urbanisation in India and associated SAARC nation is leading to exploitation in the perspective of environmental resources. There is an urgent need to growing awareness of these issues among environmentalist, scholars and urban planners at all levels and to provide both better information on which to base national and international policies and a policy framework against which to interpret this information.

I am truly admiring the venture of Dr. Indrajit Roy Chowdhury, one the successful academicians who have paid constant unflagging cares to identify the issue of urban development especially in the context of India and Bangladesh too. The present edited volume is structurally divided into two parts. The first part with sub theme "Issues of Urban Infrastructure: Planning and Practices" contains eight contributed chapters, the second part about "Issues of Urban Environment and Sustainability" entails six chapters.

The first chapter entitled "Assessment of Material Wellbeing of Selected Urban Agglomerations, West Bengal India" and the chapter has contributed by Dr. Anindya, Adrija Bhattacharya and Sudarshana Sinha which has enlightened on Material wellbeing Index in connection with the selected urban Agglomerations in West Bengal.

The second chapter highlighted "Challenges and Mitigation Strategies of Urban Health Status: A Study on Calangute Beach Town: North Goa" and the chapter has written by Bikram Basak and the author has tactfully stated the several health issues of North Goa, India followed by some policy matters in view of the improvement of health concern of the selected Study area.

The third chapter entitled "Study on Health Status in Visakhapatnam City of Andhra Pradesh: Challenges and Prospects" and it has written by Bandana Sarkar and she has rightly pointed out the issues of health risk inVisakhapatnam city where the author has focused on the water and vector borne diseases with measurement of improving health quality.

The fourth chapter entitled "A Geo-critical Narrative on the Monumental Makeover in the Panorama of Transit within the Cultural Capital of India" which has written by Dr. Ayan Das Guptahas stated the urban development along the peri urban areas of the Cultural Capital of India with the provision of basic infrastructural System.

The fifth chapter enlightened on "Geo-Cultural Study on Beach Tourism and its Prospects in Calangute Town, North Goa, India" and the chapter has written by Suity and she has taken the Geo-Cultural issues of Beach Tourism in North Goa and they have mainly focused on the crime issue like child sextourism in the city and obviously it should be an emerging social crime in the study area too.

The Sixth chapter entitled "Dynamic Nature of Urban Landscape of Selected Urban Centres in Nadia District, West Bengal" and the chapter has been contributed by Iman Sk which has discussed about the demographic changes of Nadia district in Connection with the newly emerged urban centers with the available facilities of urban infrastructure.

The Seventh chapter focused on the "Geographical Study on Urban Planning of Calangute Town, North Goa, India" and this chapter has written by Ruchika Saha and she has stated about the Sustainable policy measures of urban planning where the author mainly highlighted on the management issues of solid Waste in Calangute Town of North Goa.

The eight chapter entitled on "Strategies of Smart City Development: A Study in Visakhapatnam City, Andhra Pradesh, India" which has written by Amlan Maitra and he has discussed about the planning strategies of future Smart city development in connection with Visakhapatnam city and suggested some improvement strategies for fulfilling the basic amenities of the proposed smart city.

The Ninth chapter entitled "Temporal Land Use Change Pattern of Kaptai Lake and surrounding area using Remotely Sensed Data, Bangladesh" and the chapter has written by Md Mujibor Rahman and Md Al Amin and the authors rightly stated the temporal change of land use pattern of Kaptai lake with some possible remedies to control the effect of landuse changes on the environment.

The tenth chapter entitled on "Assessing the impact of land use/land cover change on land surface temperature by using satellite data: a case study of Guwahati city, Assam" and the chapter has been authored by Chandana Sarkar, Bhalindar

Singh and Dr. Bimal Kumar Kar and they have pointed out the very emerging issue like the impact of land use change on changing trend of Land Surface Temperature (LST) in Guwahati city and they have also highlighted the fact that growth of urbanisation leading the creation of Urban Heat Island in the city.

The Eleventh chapter enlightened "Towards eco-sustainability: scope and significance of designing green buildings for urbanizing Kerala, India" and the chapter has written by Dr. T. K. Prasad & Jishnu J.S and they have rightly stated the relevant issues like importance of green technology in reducing Carbon emission in Kerala city.

The Twelve chapter entitled "Geo-Environmental Study on Solid Waste and its Management in Calangute Beach Town, North Goa, India" and the chapter has written by Subhanita Ghosh and she has pointed out the geo-environmental issue of Solid waste management in North Goa where the author mainly focused on the sustainable technological implication for Solid waste management in the Study area.

The Thirteenth chapter entitled "Status of Solid Waste Generation & Sustainable Management in Visakhapatnam Municipal Corporation, Andhra Pradesh, India" and the chapter has written by Barnali Biswas and Reetuparna Das and the authors have focused on the management procedures of Solid waste in the proposed Smart City like Visakhapatnam, Andhra Pradesh.

The Fourteenth chapter entitled "Road Traffic Congestion and its Environmental Challenges: A Study in Visakhapatnam City, Andhra Pradesh, India" and this chapter has written by Mouli Sarkar and Dr. Indrajit Roy Chowdhury and the authors have carefully pointed out the impact of road traffic Congestion onenvironment of Visakhapatnam City with some methodological measures in order to improve the situation.

I strongly belief that the papers incorporated in this edited volume will definitely cater the need of the readers, academicians, young researchers related with Contemporary Issues of Urban Development in 21st Century: Planning and Practices.

At the end, I feel to acknowledge that I am really honored in writing the foreword of the edited volume, "Contemporary Issues of Urban Development in 21st Century: Planning and Practices". I post my heartfelt thanks to Dr. I.R. Chowdhury for his excellent endeavor in the arena of Urban Geography.

Siliguri
31st May, 2022

Professor (Dr.) Ranjan Roy, Ph. D.
Professor & Head
Department of Geography & Applied Geography
University of North Bengal
(Accredited by NAAC with Grade A)
Raja Rammohunpur, Darjeeling, West Bengal, India
Email: royranjangeo@gmail.com

Preface

Contemporary issues of urban development are the utmost relevant matter of discussion where much awaited challenges in connection with urban development in 21st century have been narrated in the field of urban geography. Urbanisation and process of urban development brings about the variety of spatial, economic, social, demographic and environmental changes. The domain of urbanisation and associated issues of urban development is the primarily matter of discussion where the subjective discussion may be crossed the boundary of India and encompasses the multi domain issues in connection with urban development from other south Asian countries like Bangladesh too. It is very much evidential fact that usually urban centres provide better job opportunities, good infrastructures, promote social and economic mobility and their impact is revealed in improving several indicators of health such as life expectancy, infant child and maternal mortality rate, on the other hand urban development leads several emerging issues such as acute land and housing shortages; environmental degradation, shortages of water and power, shanty slums, overcrowding and insufficient of transport network planning, which leads more congestion along the traffic intersection points and it creates environmental degradation. Thus the issues of urban development lead to decline the area under agriculture, forest and wetlands leading to food insecurity and destroy urban ecology as well. However the urban areas provide enough opportunities to the dwellers but instead of the advantages it creates more constraint about sustainable urban development which is the pertinent issues of discussion. Therefore the title of the book "**Contemporary Issues of Urban Development in 21st Century: Planning and Practices**" is very much relevant in view of previous discussed background score.

This book is divided into two parts. The first part describes about several issues of urban infrastructure in the perspective of urban development followed by Planning and Practices. In this section, the first chapter has been contributed by Dr. Anindya Basu, Adrija Bhattacharyya and Sudeshna Sinha on a very relevant discussion such as assessment of material wellbeing of selected urban agglomerations of West Bengal where they highlighted that standard of living in any urban area cannot be judged only on the basis of economic indicators where the availability of urban infrastructures and basic amenities are the actual keys for urban development. In this chapter by using the techniques like Material wellbeing Index (MWI) has been stated an extra advantages in order to calculate two broad domains like Housing Index (HI) and Basic Amenities index (BAI). The next chapter contributed by Bikram Basak highlighted on the very relevant issue like the challenges of urban health status of Calangute Beach town of North Goa where he examined the matters like child and maternal health care issue and he took the initiative of mitigation strategies regarding the improvement of implied health policies followed by several management ideas which has been improvised the health issues of this selected urban case. The next chapter states on the same issue like urban health but the area of study has been selected in Visakhapatnam city where the author again highlighted the health related issues like water and vector borne diseases followed by some strategic measures to improve the health condition of the city. Dr. Ayan Das Gupta has expressed the new venture of urban development where he discussed about the panorama of transit within the cultural capital of India, where he highlighted on the development of the city limit in connection with inside and outside peripheral area and decided to provide the basic priority like roads, drainage and public transport system. The next chapter contributed by Suity Ghosh, narrates the Geo-cultural study on Beach Tourism and its prospect in Calangute Town, North Goa where she focused a new venture such as child sex tourism which is threatening as a darker side of Goa tourism, however she highlighted the socio-economical part of the study area where tourism potentiality makes the city economy more viable and upgraded. The next chapter on dynamic nature of urban landscape in the selected urban centres of Nadia District, West Bengal and here the author again put forward the statistical implication through which he suggested that the equilibrium location of mean centre of urban population and uniform distribution of urban centres are suggested for considering a demographic change of the district. Another author Ruchika Saha has highlighted the issues related to environmental degradation, absences of sewage and sanitation network, lack of solid waste management of Calangute town of North Goa followed by some sustainable mechanism of urban planning which may reduce the problem of the cities in future. Amlan Maitra has written on the topic such as smart city development and he has taken study area like Visakhapatnam city where he also highlighted the hindrance of urban planning and put forward some suggestive measures on the improvement of sanitation, solid waste management, sewage system, Public health facilities of the said study area. The second part of this book discussed about urban environmental issues and sustainability under this part first chapter contributed by Prof. Mujibur Rahaman from Bangladesh where he established the temporal changes of land use pattern of Kaptai lake using remotely sensed data, where the study highlights a small prevailing effort to look into the land cover Change pattern of Kaptai sub-basin which might be useful as a starting point for further in depth spatial study of the problem to figure out possible remedies. The next chapter highlighted on the impact of land use and Land cover change on land surface temperature of Guwahati city where the authors stated the fact that increase in temperature of growing urban areas induced by rapid urbanisation and fast transformation of land use and Land cover creates the urban heat island of the city. The next chapter contributed by T.K. Prasad and Jishnu J.S. where they discussed about the relevant issues like eco-sustainability and they suggested the designing of green buildings for urbanisations of Kerala, therefore the authors have proposed engineered bamboo and wood as a replacement material that has less amount of carbon emission and will contribute to the sustainable aspect of Kerala. Subhanita Ghosh has worked on geo-environmental study on Solid waste of Calangute town, north Goa where she tried to find out the various sources of solid waste in the city and suggested a systematic improvement of institutional arrangement and appropriate technological implications for solid waste management in the city. The next chapter contributed by Barnali and Reetuparna Das discussed about the same issue but the study area is in Vishakhapatnam city, Andhra Pradesh, where they focused on the management procedures of solid waste in the study area. The last chapter contributed by Mouli Sarkar and Dr. Indrajit Roy Chowdhury on road traffic congestion and environmental challenges of Vishakhapatnam city where they discussed the impact of nodal traffic congestion on environmental degradation followed by some technical measures to solve it.

Therefore the edited volume entitled **"Contemporary Issues of Urban Development in 21st Century: Planning and Practices"** will definitely create a harmonistic platform for the future research scholars who will resolve their challenging task in the field of scientific research in connection with the border themes of multi-dimensional issues of urban geography.

June, 2022
Raja Rammohunpur

Dr. Indrajit Roy Chowdhury
Editor
M.Sc. (Geography), Ph.D. (Geography)
Assistant Professor
Department of Geography & Applied Geography
University of North Bengal, Raja Rammohunpur,
Darjeeling, West Bengal
Email: ndrjt.roychoudhury@gmail.com

Acknowledgement

I would like to extend my deepest sense of gratitude to all the contributors who have shared their insightful thoughts in the multidimensional perspective of contemporary issues of urban development in 21st century in view of global and national level.

I would like to give special thanks to Dr. Subiresh Bhattacharaya, Honourable Vice-Chancellor of University of North Bengal, Prof. (Dr.) Pranab Ghosh, (offg.) Registrar, University of North Bengal for their valuable suggestions to complete this book successfully.

I would like to express my sincere thanks to Prof. (Dr.) Ranjan Roy, Head, Department of Geography & Applied Geography, Prof. Subir Sarkar, Prof. Sushma Rohatgi, Prof. Deepak Kumar Mandal, Dr. Indira Lepcha, Dr. Sudip Kumar Bhattacharya, Dr. Snehasish Saha, Dr. Arindam Basak, Dr. Rupak Kumar Paul, Dr. Riti Moktan and Dr. Suryapada Paul of Department of Geography & Applied Geography, University of North Bengal and Prof. Lakshmi Sivaramakrishnan, Department of Geography, Jadavpur University and Prof. Pradip Chouhan, Department of Geography, University of Gour Banga for their inspiration and encouragement that motivated me to take up this work. I am also indebted to my other colleagues who has helped me to publish this edited volume into the pragmatic reality .

I also extend my high gratitude to my beloved research scholars Debanjan Basak, Arghadeep Bose, Prosenjit Kayal, Suranjan Majumder, Debarati Chowdhury, Subham Roy and Guneswar Barman and Subham Mustafi for their extensive hard work to edit and arrange all the chapters and make the book in its final shape. I would like to thank to the

Department of Geography & Applied Geography, University of North Bengal for providing me the platform to compile this edited volume completely.

I am also thankful to my Ph.D. Supervisor, Prof. (Dr.) Sukla Bhaduri (Retired) and my sir Prof. (Dr.) Ranjan Basu (Retired), Department of Geography, University of Calcutta, who has always helped me by providing valuable suggestions to reach to my goals always.

Further, I extend my thanks to Mr. Sanjay Gupta, for making the volume into final shape and did all necessary corrections to make the manuscripts into the final book form.

Above all, I must pay my sincere thanks to my parents for their inspiration and encouragement.

June, 2022
Raja Rammohunpur

Dr. Indrajit Roy Chowdhury
Editor
M.Sc. (Geography), Ph.D. (Geography)
Assistant Professor
Department of Geography & Applied Geography
University of North Bengal, Raja Rammohunpur,
Darjeeling, West Bengal
Email: ndrjt.roychoudhury@gmail.com

List of Contributors

Dr. Anindya Basu is working as Assistant Professor in Department of Geography, Diamond Harbour Women's University since 2017. Previously, from 2011 she served as an Assistant Professor in Women's Christian College, Kolkata. She has been a rank-holder in Bachelor's and Master's degree programme in Geography from University of Calcutta and UGC-JRF recipient. She has also done PG Diploma in RS-GIS from Jadavpur University. She has interest in Socio-political Geography, Gender studies and Tourism Geography. She presented a number of papers in national and international conferences and seminars. She has also published several research papers in various reputed journals.

Adrija Bhattacharjee is an ex post graduate student of Department of Geography. She has secured first class in both her Bachelor's and Master's degree programme from University of Calcutta and Diamond Harbour Women's University respectively. She has interest in Environmental and Social Geography. She presented papers in national and international conferences and seminars. She has also published several research papers in various reputed journals.

Sudarshana Sinha is pursuing her Ph.D. from the Department of Humanities and Social Sciences, Indian Institute of Technology, Kharagpur. She is interested in Social Geography, Urban studies and Gender studies. She has presented a number of papers in national and international conferences and has also published papers in various reputed journals.

Bikram Basak is a former student of Department of Geography and Applied Geography of North Bengal University. He has completed Post Graduation in 2021. He is interested in various aspects of social geography, regional development, urban-environmental issues, urban planning and transport geography.

Bandana Sarkar has completed her master's from University of North Bengal in Geography and Applied Geography and working as Ph.D. Research Scholar in University of North Bengal. She has done his project work and Dissertations on Physical Geography and Urban Geography. She has a lot of interest in the subject, especially on urban geography, environmental geography, Pedology, Climatology, Bio geography and Remote Sensing & GIS.

Dr. Ayan Das Gupta has completed his Ph.D. from CU in 2014 on Urban Geographical Management and Planning and he has given total service of 14 years in the Postgraduate Departments of two reputed Government Colleges in WB, one of which is the Krishnagar Government College, Nadia and the rest one is the Chandernagore Government College, Hugli. He has to his credit, total 16 publications including writings in Journals and Books of National and International Reputes. One Minor Research Project he has completed and Grant was received then, from the esteemed end of the University Grants Commission. Right now he is carrying on one Major Research Project and that's received from the State DSTBT, Govt. of W.B. He has supervised total 55 Master-level Theses or Dissertations till date. He has extended lectures in total 62 Seminars and Symposiums of National and International Levels. He has Life-membership and Editorial Membership of total 6 National and International Level Journals.

Suity Ghosh is a former Post Graduate student of Department of Geography and Applied Geography, University of North Bengal. She has completed her Masters in the year of 2020 from the same institute. She has keen interest in the fields of Tourism Geography, Urban development and Socio-Cultural Geography.

Iman Sk has completed his Graduation in Geography Honours from Surendranath College, Kolkata, 2009 and M.Sc. in Geography from Chhatrapati Sah Ji Maharaj University, Kanpur, 2011. Presently, he is an Assistant Teacher in Geography at Chakdiknagar Tarakdas Memorial High School, Krishnanagar, Nadia, West Bengal. Earlier he taught as Guest Lecturer in Geography at Kalinagar Mahavidyalaya, North 24 Pargana, West Bengal and an Assistant Teacher in Geography at Vivekananda Palli Kishore Bharati High School, Behala, Kolkata. He has already been published 7 research papers in the leading National and International level geographical journals and edited books. He has presented over 4 seminar papers in National and International Seminar and Conferences.

Ruchika Saha is a Former Post Graduate Student of Department of Geography and Applied Geography, University of North Bengal. Presently, she is pursuing Bachelor of Education (B.Ed.) from Antony B.Ed. College under WBUTTEPA University.

Amlan Maitra Currently working as PGT Geography in Children's Academy School (A CBSE affiliated school), Lakhimpur Kheri, Uttar Pradesh. Has done his Master's degree in Geography and Applied Geography from University of North Bengal, 2017-19. Taught previously as a contractual Assistant professor of Geography at North Bengal St. Xavier's College. Followed by Regent Research, a research based firm, upto 2021. Has a fair bit of knowledge of the subject in general and GIS/RS in specific.

Professor (Dr.) Md Mujibor Rahman Professor of Environmental Science Discipline, Khulna University, Bangladesh having PhD in GIS application, received Post Graduate Diploma in GIS and Remote Sensing and Land Information System Training course from Indian Institute of Remote Sensing (IIRS) Dehradun India. Also completed PG and UG in Geography and Environmental Studies, supervised several numbers of PhD, Master and UG students.

Attending various national and International seminar and conferences home and abroad and also published more than 100 articles in national and international level and 08 book chapters in national and international level. Completed more 20 research projects national and international level GIS, Remote Sensing, Disaster Management and Environmental aspects. Current research interest is GIS, Remote Sensing, Physical Environment, Disaster Management and Environmental Planning & Management.

Md Al-Amin Research Associate of Environmental Science Discipline, Khulna University, Bangladesh also completed Post Graduate and Under Graduate degree in Environmental Science Discipline, Khulna University, Bangladesh. Attending various national and International seminar, conferences home and abroad.

Ms. Chandana Sarkar is a Doctoral Student in Department of Geography, Gauhati University, Assam. She has completed Master's Degree in Geography from Banaras Hindu University with specialization in urban geography. She has keen interest in various aspects of social geography, urban environmental issues, urban planning and health geography. She has presented a number of papers in both national and international conferences and seminars. She has also published research papers and book chapters.

Bhalindar Singh is working as Assistant Professor in Department of Geography, Kampur College, Assam since 2021. He is also pursuing Ph.D. in Geography from Department of Geography, Gauhati University. He has completed master's degree in Geography from Gauhati University with specialization in Geoinformatics. His research interests include application of remote sensing and GIS in ecological studies, river geomorphology and urban studies. He has presented a number of papers in both national and international conferences and seminars. He has also published research papers and book chapters.

Professor (Dr.) Bimal Kumar Kar working as a professor in Department of Geography, Gauhati University since 2010. He was a former Head, Department of Geography, and Gauhati University. He has been a gold medallist in Master's degree programme in Geography from Gauhati University. He has keen interest in population and geographic issues, social and urban geographic issues, and development dynamics. He has presented a number of papers in both national and international conferences and seminars. He has also published research papers and book chapters.

Dr. T K Prasad completed Graduation and post-graduation from Calicut University, Kerala with first rank. He is specialised in geomorphology and urban geography. His Ph.D. was under the supervision of Prof. G.R. Parthasarathy from Madhurai Kamaraj University on the topic "Geographic analysis of changing landuse pattern of Kannur district in Kerala with special reference to laterite mining." He has many publications in reputed journals and presented papers in different conferences. Presently working as Associate professor and head of Dept. of geography of Kannur University.

Jishnu J.S. from Thiruvananthapuram is currently a post graduate student under Dr. T. K. Prasad. He had completed his graduation from Kerala University. His area of interest is sustainable urban development and environmental geography.

Subhanita Ghosh is a teacher trainee in Siliguri B.Ed. College, West Bengal under University of Teachers' Training, Education Planning and Administration. She is a Former Post Graduate Student in the Department of Geography and Applied Geography, University of North Bengal.

Barnali Biswas has completed her Master's from University of North Bengal in Geography & Applied Geography and her Post Graduate Diploma in Applied Geoinformatics from Jadavpur University. Presently she is doing Ph.D. in

Geography from University of North Bengal. She has done her project work & Dissertation on Physical Geography and Urban Geography. She has a lot of interest in Urban Geography, Regional planning, Cartography, Geoinformatics, Environmental Geography.

Reetuparna Das has done her graduation from Southfield College, Darjeeling in geography and completed her master's from University of North Bengal in geography and applied geography. She has done her project work and dissertation in urban geography and Pedology. She has a lot of interest in urban geography, regional geography, social geography, Pedology.

Mouli Sarkar has completed her Post Graduation from University of North Bengal in Geography & Applied Geography. She has done her project works and dissertation on Urban Geography. She also attended so many national seminars in geography. She has great interest in Urban Geography, Population geography, regional planning and Geoinformatics.

Dr. Indrajit Roy Chowdhury obtained his higher secondary from Garfa D.N.M. High School, Kolkata in 2002, Graduation in Geography honours from Asutosh College, Kolkata, 2005, M.Sc. in Geography in 2007 and Ph.D. Degree in Geography from University of Calcutta in 2015. Presently, he is an Assistant Professor in the Department of Geography & Applied Geography, University of North Bengal, Darjeeling, West Bengal. He specialized in Urban Geography, Regional Planning, Transport Geography, Environmental Geography, GIS and Remote Sensing in Geography. He has already been published 53 research papers in the leading National and International level geographical journals and edited books.

Contents

Part-II
ISSUES OF URBAN ENVIRONMENT AND SUSTAINABILITY

Part-I
Issues of Urban Infrastructure: Planning and Practices

1

Assessment of Material Wellbeing of Selected Urban Agglomerations, West Bengal, India

Dr. Anindya Basu[1], *Adrija Bhattacharya*[2] *and Sudarshana Sinha*[3]

Abstract: The gradual global urbanizing trend is being mirrored in developing countries like India too, where the strong rural-urban migration is creating pressure on the existing urban fabric and infrastructure. Standard of living, in urban areas cannot be judged only on the basis of economic indicators but availability of urban infrastructure and basic amenities are the actual keys. This paper concentrates on West Bengal which is one of the highly urbanized state and focuses on 25 Urban Agglomerations (UAs) i.e. continuous urban spreads having population 1 lakh and above, as per Census of India, 2011. It tries to determine what extent availability of housing and basic amenities vary across the leading UAs of West Bengal and whether there is any significant difference in material wellbeing. For calculating the composite score i.e. Material Wellbeing Index (MWI) two broad domains of Hosing

[1]Assistant Professor, Department of Geography, Diamond Harbour Women's University, West Bengal, India.
Email: Basu_anindya2004@yahoo.com (Corresponding Author)
[2]Ex-Post Graduate Student, Department of Geography, Diamond Harbour Women's University, West Bengal, India. Email: adrija866@gmail.com
[3]Ph.D. Research Scholar, Indian Institute of Technology, Department of Humanities and Social Sciences, Kharagpur, West Bengal, India. Email: sudarshanasinha1@gmail.com

Index (HI) and Basic Amenities Index (BAI) were considered where sub-indicators like Material of the walls, floors and roofs along with latrine facilities within premises, usage of clean fuel like LPG/ PNG, availability of drinking water within premises, availability of closed drainage system, provision of electricity were taken into account respectively. For the index calculation the secondary data has been used and scale equivalence technique has been used to standardize the unit-free indicators for better interpretability. Smaller, compacts UAs like Chakdaha, Jalpaiguri and Puruliya show high values of MWI than the voluminous UAs like Kolkata, Asansol and Siliguri. Bivariate analysis depicts a strong positive correlation between housing parameter i.e. concrete roof with the parameters of basic amenities for all the UAs. It can be highlighted that the governmental initiatives for urban development in UAs have to be focused towards newly constituted census towns, outgrowths and slum areas which are deprived from basic urban facilities so that the inter and intra level disparities can be addressed.

Keywords: *Basic Amenities Index (BAI), Housing Index (HI), Material Wellbeing Index (MWI), Quality of living, Urbanization*

1.1 Introduction

Over the last few decades there has been a mass migration of people from rural to urban areas across the world (Ritchie and Roser, 2018). It has been estimated that by 2050, more than two-thirds of the world will live in urban areas United Nations (2018a). Since 1911, the urbanization tend is India is going on unabashed; in 2011 the percentage of urbanization was 31.16%. The recent report of United Nations (2018b) "World Urbanization Prospects 2018" corroborated similar trend where in 2018 rate of urbanization was 34 percent of its total population. The availability of urban amenities greatly influences the quality of life and degree of urban development (Murray, 1988). Infrastructure is intrinsically connected to provision of basic amenities to all residents ensuring a healthy standard of living and infrastructure is broadly categorized into physical, social and economic (Ghosh and De 1998).Only through economic indicator, quality of living cannot be gauged; it is a complex and multi-dimensional issue (Kironji 2008) which involves accessibility to proper housing facilities, availability of basic services and provision of healthy food (Kitchen and Muhajarine 2008).

In developing countries like India, where urban population density is very high, providing improved urban amenities for areas like water supply, drainage systems etc to all is a cause of serious concern (Kumar, 2015) leading to social deprivation, decrease of quality of urban life and affects the ecological sustainability too (Das and Das 2019). In some developed countries too along the lines of racial and ethnic diversity housing inequality can be perceived (Krivo and Kaufman, 2004; Elmelech, 2004). On the other hand, in developing countries social status and economic footings affects the access to better housing facilities (Kundu et al., 1999; Ahmad, 2012). and at times even leads to deprivation in basic amenities (Srinivasan and Mohanty, 2004) As per as Census of India, 2011, 43 percent of the total urban population resides in class I towns having population more than 1 lakh and it is likely to clock 87 percent in 2030. The mega-city centric urbanization in India faced a sea change (Kundu, 2014; Kundu & Saraswati, 2012) as there was a great increase in the number of Census Towns (CT) - an increase of 2532 CTs (have a population of over 5,000; density of at least 400 people per square kilometer; and more than 75% percent of the male working population is engaged in non-agrarian employment [Government of India, 2017]) initiating substantive urbanization (Pradhan, 2013). Situation was similar for West Bengal where over 500 CTs emerged and most of them are in close vicinity to major cities in per-urban belt (Guin & Das, 2015); 47 percent of the CTs are within 50 km radius of Kolkata, leading to larger UAs.

So, to ensure the quality of urban life, residential amenities of the crowded urban centers which are centers of growth as well needs to be taken care of. Gottlieb (1995) regarded residential amenities to be place specific goods or services which assist in utility functions of residents directly and it was mirrored by Howie et al. (2010), who believed urban residential amenities are important to a household's sense of place. To tackle the unprecedented urban growth in the Class I cities due to rural-urban migration and the resultant pressure on the existing infrastructure, huge investment to increase the infrastructural base is needed which will take care of the urban civic amenities (Sarkar 2011). Das and Mistri (2013) believed housing condition, basic amenities and asset possessions were the crucial elements to determine the social condition. The provision of universal coverage of basic services remains a challenge for the government (Shaw 2007) and out of all water and sanitation were taken to be the prime targets in the 12th Five Year Plan (Planning Commission of India 2013) and this accessibility to basic amenities is related to the physical and mental wellbeing (Kumar, 2014).

In case of West Bengal, the size distribution of urban population for Class I cities showed few varying trends - in 1951 it represented 75.12 percent while in 1991 it rose to 81.71 percent and declined to 63.38 percent in 2011 (Census of India, 2011). From this, it can be stated that even in present times, fewer number of larger urban centers houses a significant number of people reflecting the attraction for the greater economic opportunities, but the smaller sized urban centers have come up in a big way decreasing the share of population to some extent. In this context, one can refer to the traditional theories like - Growth Pole Theory (Perroux, 1952) which states that growth appears at different points with varying intensity and then gradually spreads affecting the entire economy; the gradual spread of economic growth from centre to peripheral areas has been termed as 'spread effect' (Myrdal, 1957) and 'trickle-down effect' (Hirschman, 1958) which seem to be very relevant even in present context. For West Bengal the healthy economic growth of 6 percent (World Bank 2017) has ushered a positive impact on the general quality of living (Dey, 2015). The gradual growth in the number of CTs in the peripheral areas of West Bengal have definitely played an important role in the state's urbanization scenario (Guin and Das, 2015).

The provision for critical determinants of urban amenities needs to be ensured for the UAs which suffers from squatters, pollution and crowding (Ali and Rahman 2004) and this has been recognized by the government too (Planning Commission, 2008). Now, India has been striving hard to achieve the Sustainable Development Goals aiming to further improve the availability of basic amenities and earlier while pursuing the Millennium Development Goals India was able to progress in terms of access to safe drinking water and sanitation facilities (Government of India, 2014). So, there is a need for suitable urban governance and planning strategies to ensure balanced infrastructural development in all the UAs.

1.2 Literature Review

Partridge et al. (2007) explained how provision of urban amenities guarantees locational advantage ensuring greater economic activities. Deb (2008) highlighted the rural-urban divide both in terms of economic and non-economic dimensions involving health, education and basic amenities across the states of India and reported a wider gap in terms of basic amenities provision. Rappaport (2008) on the other hand emphasized how the accessibility of the basic urban amenities determines the quality of life. Bhagat (2011) attempted to show how basic amenities like access to electricity, safe drinking water, toilet facility, and clean fuel like LPG varied across states with different levels of urbanization and also by the size class of cities and towns and expected that the provision of basic services is directly related to the size of urban centres. Pal et al. (2015) addressed the inequality in housing and basic amenities in India (2009-12) and brought out income as the determining factor. It concluded that economic background of the households has a positive relation with the accessibility and usage of basic amenities. Mahajan (2016) presented an account of status of basic amenities across major states of urban India on the basis of factors like housing conditions, electricity, drainage, sanitation, drinking water and the leading states were Gujarat, Karnataka and Andhra Pradesh, while West Bengal ranked twelfth out of the total seventeen taken into account.

Haque (2016a) by examining the city-level infrastructural data realized that access to basic amenities did not improve much over time and the schemes proposed were mostly targeted towards the larger ones ignoring the medium and smaller ones leading to inter-city disparity. Haque (2016b) dealt with assessment of West Bengal's basic urban services and amenities through selection of 19 indicators for several classes of towns located within and outside Kolkata Metropolitan Area. Van Duijne et al (2020) through the article created a geo-database of the CTs of West Bengal and tried to link the urban growth with road infrastructure. Mondal (2020) tried to understand the spatial pattern of household quality of living taking into account the locational attributes of various urban centers of West Bengal and for that selected the criteria like quality of housing, asset ownership of the household and access to basic amenities. The results implicated that the quality of living is better in areas of greater urban influence than the ones having peripheral rural areas. For formulating sustainable urban planning strategies proper assessment of the quality life of the urban people of the region needs to made (Lee 2008). India has been able to reduce poverty to great extent but the access to core public services remains quite low even when compared with the other BRIICS countries and to improve such situation government-initiated schemes like PM Awaas Yojana, Nirmal Bharat Abhiyan etc. (Deb, 2018).

1.3 Objectives

The paper concentrates on Urban Agglomerations (UAs) in West Bengal having population 1 lakh and above, as per Census of India, 2011 and tries to address some basic areas -

a) To determine at what extent availability of housing and basic amenities vary across the leading UAs of West Bengal.
b) To find out whether there is any significant difference across the UAs in terms of material wellbeing?

1.4 Method and Methodology

To assess the level of material wellbeing 25 UAs of West

Bengal was taken into account, 8 sub-indicators under two broad domains were considered. The brief summarisation about the methodology is stated (Fig. 1).

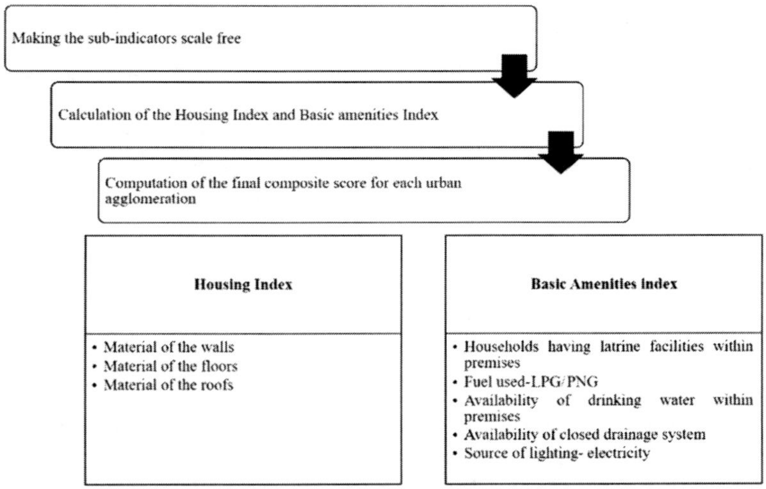

Fig. 1: Showing the methodological framework and details about the domains selected to assess the material wellbeing of Urban Agglomerations (UAs) having population more than 1 lakh in West Bengal, India

The housing index analyses the material used for the construction of the houses, among the various materials used only cement was chosen for the analysis owing to its high durability. The Housing index was calculated using–

$$\text{Housing index} = [\Sigma(X_a X_b + X_c)/N_{\text{indicators}}]$$

where,

- X_a = Materials used in the construction of walls.
- X_b = Materials used in the construction of floors.
- X_c = Materials used in the construction of roofs.

The basic amenities index analyses the availability of various amenities which are required by individuals to lead to a healthy life. Under this domain, firstly, households having the availability of latrine facilities within the premises were selected because it is considered to be more hygienic and safe for the all members; secondly, availability of LPG/PNG was selected as a medium of fuel used as it has been categorized as a cleaner fuel in comparison to firewood; thirdly, it is very important to have clean and safe drinking water within the premises as it ensures the reduction in the occurrence of various diseases, hence this sub-indicator was chosen for the study; fourthly, the availability of closed drainage facility is important to emit the waste water from the households, the availability of this facility is considered as an important indicator of good sanitation facility and hence was included in the study; lastly, electricity was chosen as the chief source of the available lighting with the house. The basic amenities index was calculated using the formula–

$$\text{Basic Amenities Index} = [(X_d+X_e+X_f+X_g+X_h)/N_{indicators}],$$

where,

- X_d = Households having latrine facilities within premises
- X_e = Availability of LPG/PNG facilities
- X_f = Availability of drinking water within premises
- X_g = Availability of closed drainage system
- X_h = Availability of electricity

1.4.1 Standardization of Indicators

Owing to the huge variance in the values of the variables scale equivalence is important. In the scale equivalence technique, the values of the variables are transformed within the range of 0 to 1, where 0 represents the minimum and 1 represents the maximum value. It was applied to the sub-indicators to make all of them unit free. It was conducted with the help of the equation–

$$Xic = [(Xij - Xij_{min})/(Xij_{max} - Xij_{min})]$$

where,

- Xic = Scale equivalence,
- Xij = Observed value in a array,
- Xij_{max} = highest value in the same array,
- Xij_{min} = lowest value in the same array

1.4.2 Correlation Analysis

Pearson correlation coefficient was calculated–

$$r = [N\Sigma xy-(\Sigma x)*(\Sigma y)]/\Sigma\{[N\Sigma x^2-(\Sigma x)^2]\ [N\Sigma y^2-(\Sigma y)^2]\}$$

where,

- r = Pearson correlation,
- N = number of pairs of scores,
- Rxy = sum of the products of paired scores,
- Rx = sum of x scores,
- Ry = sum of y scores,
- Rx^2 = sum of squared x scores,
- Ry^2 = sum of squared y scores

1.4.3 Construction of the Composite Score

The composite score was constructed to measure the level of development among the various UAs. The variables were selected based on their theoretical construct and the availability of data for constructing the composite index score (Table 1).

Table – 1

Selection of the Sub-Indicators for Construction of Housing Index (HI) and Basic Amenities Index (BAI) for Urban Agglomerations (UAs) having Population more than 1 lakh in West Bengal, India

Housing Index (HI)	
Concrete roof	Kingdon and Knight (2006), Bohnke (2008), Li et al. (2010)
Concrete wall	
Cement floor	
Basic Amenities Index (BAI)	
Availability of drinking water within premises	Haq and Zia (2008), Siddiqui (2008), Haq et al. (2010), Bhagat (2011), Zorondo-Rodri´guez et al. (2012), Das and Mistiri (2013), Muhammad and Sabo (2017)
Electricity availability	
Availability of latrine within premises	

Closed Drainage
LPG as source of fuel

Source: Compiled by authors from various sources

1.4.4 Data Source and Software Used

The work is entirely based on secondary data sources. Some of the notable ones are Census of India records and district statistical handbooks for 2011. Statistical analysis was performed using SPSS v27 and the mapping was performed using Arc GIS v10.3.

1.5 Study Area

Urbanization in West Bengal is primarily driven by the city of Kolkata, which has a rich colonial legacy since the days of the British (Dasgupta 1987). However, the present trend of urbanization shows a refreshing change with increasing number of Class I cities which depicts that urbanization is only limited to Kolkata and its suburbs but several new urban centres have come up (Das et al., 2021). This notion is corroborated by the presence of 25 UAs having population more than 1 lakh spread across the state (Fig. 2 and Table–2). The continuous urban spread having town/towns and adjoining urban outgrowths together is referred as UA.

Table – 2

Detailed list of the Urban Agglomerations (UAs) having Population more than 1 lakh in West Bengal, India in Aascending Order Based on Total Population (Municipal Corporation-MC, Municipality-M, Census Town-CT and Out Growth-OG)

S.No.	Urban Agglomerations (UAs)	Corresponding District	Number and Type of Constituent Units
1	Kolkata	Kolkata and South 24 Parganas	4 MCs, 38 Ms, 75 CTs and 6 OGs
2	Asansol	Paschim Barddhaman	1 MC, 3 Ms, 12 CTs and 1 OGs
3	Siliguri	Siliguri	1 MC and 4 CTs
4	English Bazar	Maldah	2 Ms, 3 CTs

5	Durgapur	Paschim Barddhaman	1 MC and 2 CTs
6	Barddhaman	Purba Barddhaman	1 M and 3 CTs
7	Berhampur	Murshidabad	1 M and 9 CTs
8	Habra	North 24 Parganas	2 Ms and 4 CTs
9	Kharagpur	West Medinipur	1 M and 2 CTs
10	Santipur	Nadia	1M, 6 CTs and 4 OGs
11	Dankuni	Hooghly	1 M, 21 CTs
12	Raiganj	Uttar Dinajpur	1M, 2 CTs
13	Dhulian	Murshidabad	1 M, 9 CTs
14	Ranaghat	Nadia	2 Ms, 10 CTs and 1 OG
15	Krishnanagar	Nadia	1 M, 3 CTs
16	Nabadwip	Nadia	1 M, 6 CTs
17	Jalpaiguri	Jalpaiguri	1 M, 1 CT
18	Balurghat	Dakshin Dinajpur	1 M, 2 CTs and 1 OG
19	Basirhat	North 24 Parganas	1 M, 3 CTs
20	Alipurduar	Alipurduar	1 M, 6 CTs
21	Chakdaha	Nadia	1 M, 5 CTs
22	Darjeeling	Darjeeling	1 M, 2 CTs
23	Puruliya	Puruliya	1 M, 1 CTs

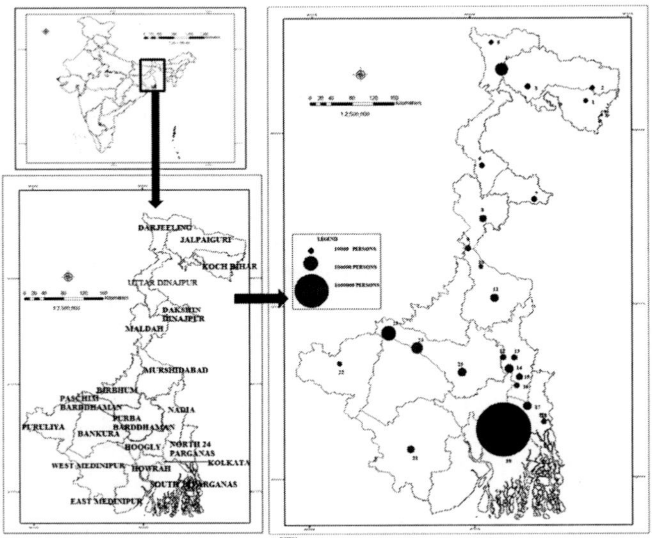

KEY

1- Koch Bihar UA	2- Alipurduar UA	3- Jalpaiguri UA	4- Silliguri UA
5- Darjiling UA	6- Raigunj UA	7- Balurghat UA	8- English Bazar UA
9- Dhuliyan UA	10- Jangipur UA	11- Barhampur UA	12- Nabadwip UA
13- Krishnanagar UA	14- Shantipur UA	15- Ranaghat UA	16- Chakdaha UA
17- Habra UA	18- Basirhat UA	19- Kolkata UA	20- Dhankuni UA
21- Kharagpur UA	22- Puruliya UA	23- Asansol UA	24- Durgapur UA
25- Barddhaman UA			

Fig. 2: Location map showing the Urban Agglomerations (UAs) having population more than 1 lakh in West Bengal, India

24	Jangipur	Murshidabad	1 M, 3 CTs
25	Koch Bihar	Koch Bihar	1 M, 2 CTs

Source: Census of India, 2011.

1.6 Results and Discussion

1.6.1 Housing Index (HI)

Puruliya UA has highest percentage of households (49.92%) with concrete roof, Darjeeling with highest percentage of households (40.07%) with concrete wall and Krishnanagar UA has highest percentage of households (77.86%) with cement floor where Santipur with 1.461 percent of households with concrete roof is lowest among 25 UAs, Raiganj has lowest percentage of households (1.00%) with concrete wall and Dhulian has the lowest percentage of households (29.70%) with cement floor. From Table 3 it is observed that in all the UAs highest percentage of households has cement floor followed by households with concrete roof and concrete wall.

1.6.2 Basic Amenities Index (BAI)

Koch Bihar has the highest percentage of households (93.32%) with latrine facility within premise and Puruliya has the lowest (63.05%). Darjeeling UA has highest percentage of households (84.92%) where LPG/PNG is used as fuel for cooking. Berhampur UA has highest percentage of households (84.31%) with drinking water within premise. Dhulian has the lowest percentage (5.33%) of households with LPG/PNG used for cooking and households with drinking water within premise (2.21%). Kolkata UA has highest percentage of households (39.51%) with waste water outlet connected to closed drainage system where Alipurduar has the lowest (4.08%). Kolkata has the highest percentage of households (93.99%) with electricity as source of lighting where Dhulian has the lowest (37.02%). It can be seen (Table 3) that in all the 25 UAs most of the households have latrine facility within premise and has electricity as source of lighting whereas least percentage of households possess waste water outlet connected to closed drainage system.

Table – 3
Calculation of Domains–Housing Index (HI) and Basic Amenities Index (BAI) for Urban Agglomerations (UAs) having Population more than 1 lakh in West Bengal, India

S.No.	Urban Agglomerations (UAs)	Housing Index (HI)			Basic Amenities Index (BAI)				
		Households with concrete roof (%)	Households with concrete wall (%)	Households with cement floor (%)	Households with drinking water within premises (%)	Households with electricity (%)	Households having latrine facility within premises (%)	Households where waste water outlet connected to closed drainage system (%)	Households where LPG/PNG used for cooking (%)
1	Kolkata	18.08	8.68	76.00	64.73	94.00	93.32	39.51	61.37
2	Asansol	6.63	9.77	67.91	26.53	83.01	65.45	12.59	28.21
3	Siliguri	4.12	11.86	70.47	70.70	80.36	87.27	8.71	60.11
4	English Bazar	3.44	5.07	64.85	72.34	82.55	88.83	23.66	53.70
5	Durgapur	7.45	11.40	72.91	54.90	81.68	77.84	31.08	54.10
6	Barddhaman	3.47	5.42	78.64	70.48	89.01	83.61	15.16	53.18
7	Berhampur	2.65	3.82	71.35	81.02	81.92	88.54	13.59	49.52
8	Habra	1.90	3.14	68.06	66.11	81.42	95.83	9.00	37.55
9	Kharagpur	2.74	4.19	75.64	60.26	80.79	80.02	10.67	63.12
10	Santipur	1.46	2.97	49.44	84.31	78.24	93.35	6.46	23.93
11	Dankuni	3.70	6.53	74.86	44.31	94.03	88.02	17.73	35.31
12	Raiganj	38.54	1.00	55.09	5.81	69.02	83.90	9.90	48.17
13	Dhulian	25.92	3.32	29.70	2.21	37.02	44.71	4.44	5.33
14	Ranaghat	46.42	4.96	65.73	8.30	78.72	91.46	7.33	33.70
15	Krishnanagar	65.47	2.06	77.86	19.72	86.69	95.51	15.97	57.90
16	Nabadwip	44.39	5.77	57.90	5.68	73.83	92.72	5.41	26.30
17	Jalpaiguri	36.98	4.25	63.83	21.21	75.91	85.03	6.38	55.60
18	Balurghat	50.45	4.34	68.51	6.04	85.45	94.51	15.03	58.74
19	Basirhat	49.12	6.93	64.22	5.07	74.99	91.24	10.30	35.99
20	Alipurduar	17.85	2.41	54.74	6.86	81.08	86.28	4.08	49.56
21	Chakdaha	48.42	3.44	69.34	19.04	84.97	95.00	9.94	54.56
22	Darjeeling	43.49	40.08	68.37	22.28	95.75	76.27	23.68	84.92
23	Puruliya	49.92	11.54	65.52	8.88	74.53	63.06	10.20	42.30
24	Jangipur	54.58	12.74	62.00	13.34	75.90	67.04	7.76	25.41
25	Koch Bihar	35.57	2.60	75.60	21.45	88.51	94.84	6.03	69.16

Source: Computed by the authors from the data obtained from Census of India, 2011

1.6.3 Material Wellbeing Index (MWI)

With the help of HI and BAI values MWI values has been calculated (Table 4) and according to the results the UAs have been divided into three broad zones i.e. UAs with MWI values less than 0.25 are stated as Low Zone, values ranging from 0.25 to 0.50 are stated as Medium Zone and UAs with MWI values greater than 0.50 are stated as High Zone (Table 5). Chakdaha, Jalpaiguri and Puruliya UAs have MWI values greater than 0.50, thus marked as UAs with high MWI values, Kolkata, Barddhaman, Habra, Kharagpur, Raiganj, Ranaghat, Krishnanagar, Nabadwip, Balurghat, Basirhat, Alipurduar, Darjeeling, Jangipur and Koch Bihar UAs have MWI values ranging from 0.25 to 0.50 are in medium category and Asansol, Siliguri, English Bazar, Durgapur, Berhampur, Santipur, Dankuni and Dhulian are the UAs which have MWI values less than 0.25 fall in low category.

It is interesting to note that the larger UAs like Kolkata, Asansol, Siliguri - the three leading ones do not indicate a high MWI; as these have a number of municipalities, census towns and outgrowths under their belt all of which have not been equally endowed with material infrastructure like the main municipal corporation(s) and that might be the reason that they are lagging behind than the smaller, comparatively compact UAs like Chakdaha, Jalpaiguri and Puruliya.

Table – 4
Calculation for Material Wellbeing Index for Urban Agglomerations (UAs) having Population more than 1 lakh in West Bengal, India

S.No.	Urban Agglomerations (UAs)	Housing Index (HI)	Basic Amenities Index (BAI)	Material Wellbeing Index (MWI)
1	Kolkata	0.38	0.29	0.33
2	Asansol	0.08	0.11	0.09
3	Siliguri	0.23	0.24	0.23
4	English Bazar	0.24	0.25	0.24
5	Durgapur	0.34	0.01	0.17

6	Barddhaman	0.26	0.26	0.26
7	Berhampur	0.26	0.11	0.18
8	Habra	0.36	0.29	0.32
9	Kharagpur	0.39	0.43	0.41
10	Santipur	0.19	0.22	0.2
11	Dankuni	0.12	0.15	0.13
12	Raiganj	0.34	0.32	0.33
13	Dhulian	0.16	0.06	0.11
14	Ranaghat	0.13	0.47	0.3
15	Krishnanagar	0.35	0.5	0.42
16	Nabadwip	0.16	0.36	0.26
17	Jalpaiguri	0.83	0.66	0.74
18	Balurghat	0.01	0.55	0.28
19	Basirhat	0.26	0.41	0.33
20	Alipurduar	0.22	0.46	0.34
21	Chakdaha	0.33	0.7	0.51
22	Darjeeling	0.34	0.41	0.37
23	Puruliya	0.83	0.38	0.6
24	Jangipur	0.28	0.22	0.25
25	Koch Bihar	0.35	0.53	0.44

Source: Computed by the authors from the data obtained from Census of India, 2011

Table – 5
Zoning of Urban Agglomerations (UAs) having Population more than 1 lakh in West Bengal, India on the Basis of Material Wellbeing Index (MWI) Values

Zones		
High (greater than 0.50)	**Medium (0.25-0.50)**	**Low (less than 0.25)**
Chakdaha, Jalpaiguri and Puruliya	Kolkata, Barddhaman, Habra, Kharagpur, Raiganj, Ranaghat, Krishnanagar, Nabadwip, Balurghat, Basirhat, Alipurduar, Darjeeling, Jangipur and Koch Bihar	Asansol, Siliguri, English Bazar, Durgapur, Berhampur, Santipur, Dankuni and Dhulian

Source: Computed by the authors from the data obtained from Census of India, 2011.

1.6.4 Bivariate Analysis depicting correlation between housing parameter and basic amenities parameters

Bivariate Pearson Correlation has been calculated to measure the strength and direction of linear relationships between the pairs of selected parameters of Housing Index and that with selected parameters of Basic Amenities Index. Among the three parameters of Housing Index (i.e. Condition of Roof- Concrete, Condition of wall- Concrete and Condition of floor- Cement) Condition of Roof- Concrete has been selected to measure its correlation with the parameters of Basic Amenities Index (i.e. LPG/PNG used for cooking, availability of latrine within premises, availability of drinking water within premises, waste water outlet connected to closed drainage system and source of lighting- electricity).

In the selected 25 UAs it can be seen that there are a considerable number of households which have either concrete wall or cement floor but number of households with concrete roof are much less than the other two parameters which indicates the households with concrete roof are already facilitated with other two parameters. The values of correlation coefficient are ranging from 0.757 to 0.999, which indicates concrete roof has strong positive correlation with the parameters of basic amenities (Table 6). Maximum correlations are significant at 0.01 significance level with only a few are at 0.05 significance level and the variables in different UAs with p-values less than .001 (.005 in case of .05 significance level) indicates statistically significant correlation.

1.7 Conclusion

The access to basic amenities varies with the level of urbanization of selected UAs of West Bengal. According to housing parameters desirable percentage of households have cement floor but the percentage households with concrete roof is still much low from the percentage desired. The constituent units where presence of slum population is occupying a considerable part of the total population is one of

Table – 6

Bivariate Analysis Depicting Correlation between Housing Parameter and Basic Amenities Parameters for Urban Agglomerations (UAs) having Population more than 1 lakh in West Bengal, India

S. No.	Urban Agglomerations (UAs)	Concrete roof	Households where LPG/PNG used for cooking	Households having latrine facility within premises	Households with drinking water within premise	Households where waste water outlet connected to closed drainage system	Households with electricity
1	Kolkata	Pearson Correlation	.928**	.956**	.964**	.997**	.926**
		Sig. (2-tailed)	.000	.000	.000	.000	.000
2	Asansol	Pearson Correlation	.997**	.985**	.976**	.999**	.988**
		Sig. (2-tailed)	.000	.002	.004	.000	.000
3	Siliguri	Pearson Correlation	.997**	.983**	.991**	.994**	.995**
		Sig. (2-tailed)	.000	.000	.000	.000	.000
4	English Bazar	Pearson Correlation	.999*	.964**	.975**	.998**	.985
		Sig. (2-tailed)	.000	.008	.005	.000	.000
5	Durgapur	Pearson Correlation	.999**	.993*	.997*	.999*	.997**
		Sig. (2-tailed)	.000	.018	.013	.011	.000
6	Barddhaman	Pearson Correlation	.998**	.999**	.999**	.996**	.999**
		Sig. (2-tailed)	.000	.001	.001	.000	.000
7	Berhampur	Pearson Correlation	.900**	.759*	.757*	.804**	.921**
		Sig. (2-tailed)	.000	.011	.011	.005	.000
8	Habra	Pearson Correlation	.969*	.894*	.817*	.619*	.968*
		Sig. (2-tailed)	.000	.016	.047	.190	.000

S. No.	Urban Agglomerations (UAs)	Concrete roof	Households where LPG/PNG used for cooking	Households having latrine facility within premises	Households with drinking water within premise	Households where waste water outlet connected to closed drainage system	Households with electricity
9	Kharagpur	Pearson Correlation	.949**	.957**	.927**	.992**	.962**
		Sig. (2-tailed)	.014	.188	.245	.081	.009
10	Santipur	Pearson Correlation	.984**	.937**	.937**	.901**	.979**
		Sig. (2-tailed)	.000	.001	.001	.002	.000
11	Dankuni	Pearson Correlation	.972**	.855**	.854**	.626**	.981**
		Sig. (2-tailed)	.000	.000	.000	.002	.000
12	Raiganj	Pearson Correlation	.999**	.999**	.998**	.998**	.998
		Sig. (2-tailed)	.000	.028	.044	.040	.000
13	Dhulian	Pearson Correlation	.993**	.979**	.968**	.972**	.992**
		Sig. (2-tailed)	.000	.000	.000	.000	.000
14	Ranaghat	Pearson Correlation	.997**	.957**	.969**	.974**	.986**
		Sig. (2-tailed)	.000	.000	.000	.000	.000
15	Krishnanagar	Pearson Correlation	.996**	.996**	.998**	.999**	.999**
		Sig. (2-tailed)	.000	.011	.008	.008	.000
16	Nabadwip	Pearson Correlation	.998**	.999**	.999**	.998**	.997**
		Sig. (2-tailed)	.000	.000	.000	.000	.000
17	Jalpaiguri	Pearson Correlation	.999**	.995**	.987**	.989**	.978*
		Sig. (2-tailed)	.001	.004	.000	.000	.022
18	Balurghat	Pearson Correlation	.999**	.993**	.986**	.989**	.999**
		Sig. (2-tailed)	.000	.002	.003	.002	.000

S. No.	Urban Agglomerations (UAs)	Concrete roof	Households where LPG/PNG used for cooking	Households having latrine facility within premises	Households with drinking water within premise	Households where waste water outlet connected to closed drainage system	Households with electricity
19	Basirhat	Pearson Correlation	.995**	.999**	.999**	.983**	.980**
		Sig. (2-tailed)	.000	.000	.001	.000	.000
20	Alipurduar	Pearson Correlation	.996**	.996**	.990**	.926**	.987**
		Sig. (2-tailed)	.000	.000	.000	.008	.000
21	Chakdaha	Pearson Correlation	.999**	.997**	.995**	.974**	.999
		Sig. (2-tailed)	.000	.000	.000	.001	.000
22	Darjeeling	Pearson Correlation	.995**	.986**	.979**	.996**	.998**
		Sig. (2-tailed)	.000	.015	.015	.005	.000
23	Puruliya	Pearson Correlation	.999**	.993**	.989**	.994**	.959**
		Sig. (2-tailed)	.000	.000	.000	.000	.000
24	Jangipur	Pearson Correlation	.995**	.997**	.998**	.999**	.983**
		Sig. (2-tailed)	.000	.000	.002	.001	.000
25	Koch Bihar	Pearson Correlation	.994**	.988**	.987**	.993**	.981**
		Sig. (2-tailed)	.000	.101	.004	.008	.003

**Correlation is significant at the 0.01 level (2-tailed)

*Correlation is significant at the 0.05 level (2-tailed)

Source: Computed by the authors from the data obtained from Census of India, 2011 the primary reasons for low housing index (i.e. Kolkata) as the slum areas are deprived from basic urban facilities. Most of the UAs are presently facilitated with electricity and have latrine facility within their premise but do not have closed drainage system as waste water outlet system. It is observed that the UAs which have old municipal corporations or municipal towns more than newly constituted census towns are more developed in both terms of housing and basic amenities. With expanding nature of urbanization number of constituent units under different urban agglomerations is increasing but they are still seeking government attention for urban infrastructural development. The availability of rudimentary urban infrastructure like decent shelter, improved sanitation, cleaner fuel etc for the urban units are the basic necessities otherwise the initiatives like smart cities, clean and green cities will almost go in vein. Thus, appropriate government plans and schemes are most needed to remove the disparities of material wellbeing among intra as well as inter UAs of West Bengal.

References

Ahmad, S. (2012). Housing Inequality in Socially Disadvantaged Communities: Evidence from Urban India, 2009. Environment and Urbanization ASIA. 3(1), 237-249.

Ali, Osman, Z.M. and Rahman, M.R.A. (2004) 'The Effect of Urbanisation on the Health of Urban Residents', Akademika, 65, 111-124.

Bhagat, R. B. (2011). Urbanisation and access to basic amenities in India. Urban India, 31(1), 1-13.

Bohnke, P. (2008). Does society matter? Life satisfaction in the enlarged Europe. Social Indicators Research, 87, 189-210.

Census of India. (2011). Rural urban distribution of population. Available at http://censusindia.gov.in/2011-prov-results/paper2/data_files/india/Rural_Urban_2011.pdf. Accessed on 24.12.2021

Das, A., Das, M., & Barman, H. (2021). Access to basic

amenities and services to urban households in West Bengal: Does its location and size of settlements matter? GeoJournal, 86(2), 885-913.

Das, M., & Das, A. (2019). Dynamics of Urbanization and its impact on Urban Ecosystem Services (UESs): A Study of a Medium Size Town of West Bengal, Eastern India. Journal of Urban Management, 8(3), 420-434.

Das, B. and Mistri, A. (2013). Household Quality of Living in Indian States: Analysis of 2011 Census. Environ Urban Asia 4(1): 151-71.

Deb, S. (2018). Globalization and the Rural-Urban Divide: An Inquiry on the Health, Education and Basic Amenities in India. Globalization, 31, 07.

Dey, S. (2015). Regional inequality of West Bengal: a district level study. Bangladesh Dev Stud 38(01):101-117.

Elmelech, Y. (2004). Housing Inequality in New York City: Racial and Ethnic Disparities in Homeownership and Shelter-Cost Burden. Housing, Theory and Society. 21(4), 163-175.

Ghosh, B. and P. De. (1998). 'Role of Infrastructure in Regional Development: A Study over the Plan Period', Economic and Political Weekly, 33 (47-48): 3039-48.

Gottlieb, P. D. (1995). Residential amenities, firm location and economic development. Urban Studies, 32(9), 1413-1436.

Government of India. (2014). Millennium Development Goals– India Country Report 2014. Ministry of Statistics and Planning Implementation. New Delhi. India.

Government of India. (2017). Census of India metadata. Office of the Registrar General & Census Commissioner.

Guin, D., & Das, D. N. (2015). Spatial perspectives of the New Census Towns, 2011: A case study of West Bengal. Environment and Urbanization ASIA, 6(2), 109-124.

Haque, I. (2016). Infrastructure development and access to basic amenities in Class-I cities of West Bengal, India: Insights from census data. Journal of Infrastructure Development, 8(1), 36-84.

Haq, R., Ahmed, A., & Shafique, S. (2010). Variation in the quality of life within Punjab: Evidence from MICS, 2007-2008. The Pakistan Development Review, 49(4), 863-879.

Haq, R. & Zia, U. (2008). Dimensions of well-being and millennium development goals. The Pakistan Development Review, 47(4), 851-876.

Hirschman, AO. (1958). The strategy of economic development. Yale University Press, United states of America, New Haven.

Howie, P., Murphy, S. M., & Wicks, J. (2010). An application of a stated preference method to value urban amenities. Urban Studies, 47(2), 235-256.

Kingdon, G. G., & Knight, J. (2006). Subjective well-being poverty vs. income poverty and capabilities poverty? The Journal of Development Studies, 42(7), 1199-1224.

Kironji, E. (2008). Measuring quality of life in South Africa: a household-based development index approach. University of Pretoria. https://hdl.handl e.net/2263/25060

Kitchen, P. and Muhajarine, N. (2008). Quality of life research: new challenges and new opportunities. Soc Indic Res 85(1): 1-4.

Krivo, L.J. and Kaufman, R.L. (2004). Housing and Wealth Inequality: Racial-Ethnic Differences in Home Equity in the United States. Demography. 41(3), 585-605.

Kumar, A. (2015). Indian urban households' access to basic amenities: Deprivations, disparities and determinants. The Journal of Applied Economic Research, 9(3), 278-305.

Kundu, A. Bagchi, S. and Kundu, D. (1999). Regional Distribution of Infrastructure and Basic Amenities in Urban India: Issues Concerning Empowerment of Local Bodies. Economic and Political Weekly. 34(28), 1893-1906.

Lee, S.-Y. (2008). Drivers for the participation of small and medium-sized suppliers in green supply chain initiatives. Supply Chain Management: An International Journal, 13(3), 185-198.

Mahajan, S. K. (2016). Status of Basic Amenities across Major States of Urban India. North Eastern Economic Review, 17.

Mondal, S. (2020). Modeling the spatial pattern of household quality of living in West Bengal: an approach of hotspot and cluster analysis. Modeling Earth Systems and Environment, 1-19.

Muhammad, S. & Sabo, A. (2017). The Impact of Material Wellbeing and Safe Drinking Water on Quality of Life in Africa. International Journal of Novel Research in Marketing Management and Economics, 4 (2): 1-7.

Murray, P. (1988). Marx's theory of scientific knowledge. Atlantic Highlands: Humanities Press.

Myrdal, G. (1957). Economic theory and under-development regions. Gerald Duckworth, London.

Pal, R., Aneja, N., and Nagpal, D. (2015). Inequality in housing and Basic Amenities in India. MPRA Paper No. 61994. https://mpra.ub.uni-muenchen.de/61994/

Partridge, M., Olfert, M. R., & Alasia, A. (2007). Canadian cities as regional engines of growth: Agglomeration and amenities. Canadian Journal of Economics/Revue canadienne d'e´conomique, 40(1), 39-68.

Perroux, F. (1952). Note sur les coûts de l'homme. Économie appliquée, 1(5), 139-150.

Planning Commission of India. (2008). Eleventh Five-Year Plan (2007-12), Social Sector, Vol II, New Delhi: Oxford University Press, p.163.

Planning Commission of India. (2013). Urban development. In Twelfth five-year plan (2012-2017), New Delhi, pp 318-61.

Pradhan, K. (2017). Unacknowledged urbanisation: The new Census Towns in India. In E. Denis, & M. H. Zérah (Eds.), Subaltern urbanisation in India: An introduction to the dynamics of ordinary towns (pp. 9-66). Springer.

Rappaport, J. (2008). Consumption amenities and city

population density. Regional Science and Urban Economics, 38(6), 533-552.

Ritchie, H. and Roser, M. (2018). Urbanization. Available at https://ourworldindata.org/urbanization Accessed on 23.12.2021

Sarkar, A. (2011). 'Urbanization and City Size Distribution of West Bengal, India 1901-2001', Indian Journal of Regional Science, 43 (1): 9-16.

Shaw, A. (2007). Basic amenities in urban India: analysis at state and town level. in ninth Asian urbanisation conference, Chuncheon, pp 1-33.

Srinivasan, K. and Mohanty, S. K. (2004). Deprivation of Basic Amenities by Caste and Religion: Empirical Study Using NFHS Data. Economic and Political Weekly. 39(7), 728-735.

United Nations. (2018a). UN World Urbanization Prospects, Population Division of the UN Department of Economic and Social Affairs. Available at https://esa.un.org/unpd/wup/Download/. Accessed on 23.12.2021

United Nations. (2018b). The revision UN World Urbanization Prospects, Population Division of the UN Department of Economic and Social Affairs. Available at: https://esa.un.org/unpd/wup/Download/. Accessed on 20.12.2021

Van Duijne, R. J., Choithani, C., & Pfeffer, K. (2020). New urban geographies of West Bengal, East India. Journal of Maps, 16(1), 172-183

World Bank. (2017). West Bengal-Indicators at a Glance. In: World Bank Brief, Washington DC, United States. https ://www.worldbank.org/en/count ry/india /brief /india -state s-brief s-west-Bengal

Zorondo-Rodr?´guez, F., Go´mez-Baggethun, E., Demps, K., Ariza-Montobbio, P., Garc?´a, C., & Reyes- Garc?´a, V. (2012). What defines quality of life? The gap between public policies and locally defined indicators among residents of Kodagu, Karnataka (India). Social Indicators Research, 115(1), 441-456.

2

Challenges and Mitigation Strategies of Urban Health Status: A Study on Calangute Beach Town: North Goa

Bikram Basak

Abstract: Good health throughout the life span of human being is basically dependent upon life style and intake of nutritious food. Among other factors in life health is very important thing as without good health proper activity cannot be expected, so everyone needs to keep maintaining good health. Poor nutrition and unawareness utilisation of health facilities can cause various issues regarding health. Goa is known to have one of the most extensive health care systems in India and is often rated one of the better states in India with regard to General Health Indicators. The present study mainly focuses on the general health indicators in Goa and its present scenario of health condition. A primary survey was conducted to gather information about resident's health status. In order to know health facilities secondary information from Directorate of Health Services (Goa) is taken. Overall results show the good health condition among people of **Calangute** and adjacent areas with several health facilities that also can give encouragement to other states of the country.

Keywords: *Community health centre, vaccination, maternal health, intoxicants.*

Former Post graduate student, Department of Geography & Applied Geography, University of North Bengal, District: Darjeeling. Email: basak.bikram1999@gmail.com

2.1 Introduction

Goa is a state in western India. It is located with coastlines stretching along the Arabian sea. This state has long history of Portuguese colony in the earlier times. Old churches of 17th century are preserved there. Goa is also known for its beaches as Arabian Sea forms its western coast. This state has scenic charms and it is settled beautifully amidst seas and lush greeneries. So, it is a dream destination for millions of travellers across the globe. The sparkling sand, exotic beaches, the architectural splendour of its temples, churches, old houses and rich culture has become a popular leisure destination which attracts domestic and foreign tourists from all over India as well as across the globe. For these reasons Goa is also popularly known as- '**The pearl of the east**'.

One of the most important features of a state is health status of people. Because without health care and health facilities no state can develop in a good manner. Goa has one of the best qualified professionals in Hospitality. Some of the well-equipped hospitals of Goa are, Apollo Victor Hospital, Vrundavan Hospital Research Centre, Manipal Hospital, Goa Medical College & Hospital Bambolim, Bhandare Hospital etc.

2.2 Area of study

The geographical location of Goa is between Latitude 15°48'00" North to 14°53'54" North and Longitude 74°20'13" East to 73°40'33" East. Our study area is **Calangute**, a small town under Mapusa municipality in Bardez taluk of North Goa District. **Calangute** is a Town: place category with the GPS coordinates of 15° 32' 0.2904" N and 73° 45' 53.8344" E.

2.3 Objectives

The major objectives of the study are mentioned below:

a. To state the condition of health of North Goa, especially in Calangute area, Mapusa.
b. To know about regular diseases people are suffered from and their daily health care routine.

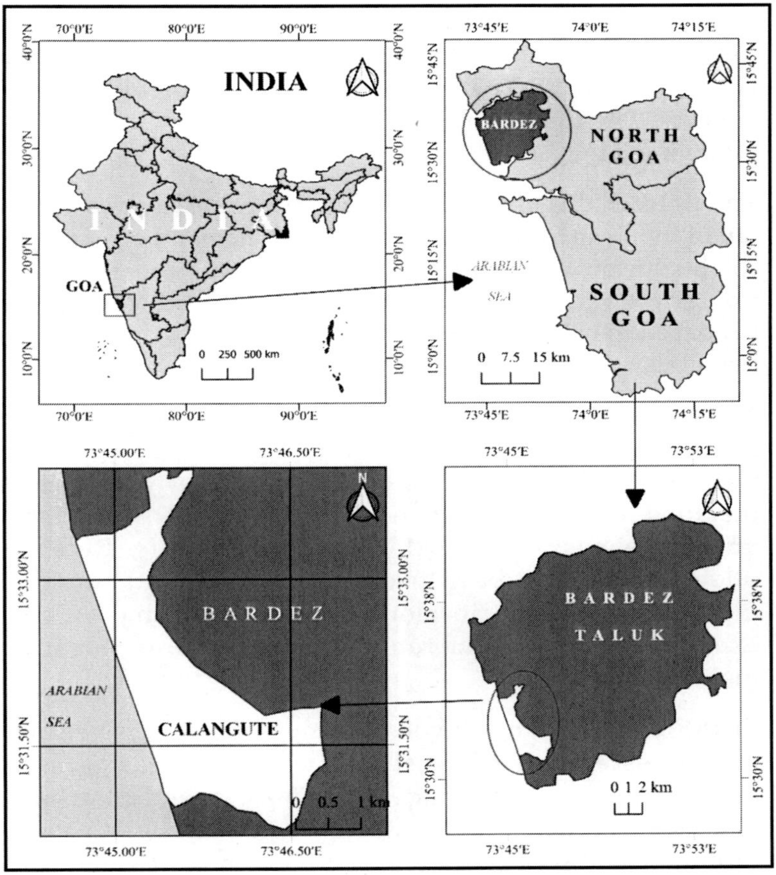

Fig. 1: Location Map of the Study Area

Source: Department of Tourism, Government of India.

c. To know the fact about alcohol and drug addiction of people in that area.
d. To point out the facility given by Govt. For people of that area basically on health purposes.

2.4 Data Base and Methodology

This research work is based on primary and secondary data. Primary data has been collected through pre-designed questionnaire survey based on 50 household samples and some hospital survey. The information about registered hospitals, community health centres and primary health centres are collected from Directorate of health service website. The methodology adopted can be divided into the following parts.

Pre-field: In this phase, general literature survey was carried out of the health condition, status of women and child health, the health programs was done from various government or non-government sources. A structured questionnaire is prepared to collect the data from respondents and from the hospitals.

Field: To collect data from different respondents stratified sampling was done on random basis. Specifically, in Calangute area, Bardez the household survey was done. At that time survey was also done in some hospitals of Calangute and some hospitals in Mapusa municipality. Relevant photographs have been taken during the field survey to illustrate the scenario more specifically. Some officers, experts, executive in different organizations were personally met and interviewed.

Post-Field: This stage involves computation of master table from questionnaire, Statistical application, cartographic representation, drawing map, analysis of data and information obtained in order to understand the present health status, hospital facilities, women and child health etc. Finally, some strategies and initiatives are suggested for future development of health facilities and conditions in Bardez, Goa.

2.5 Scenario of Health Profile in Goa

To know about the present scenario of health condition of a place some indicators or factors have to be analysed. Because health condition of a certain areas depends upon its population characteristics and some other factors associated with population.

2.5.1 Demographic Information

As per 2011 census, the population of Goa is 14,58,545 as against the country's total population of 1,210,569,573 constituting around 0.12% of the country's population. The average density of the population of the state is 394 persons per square kilometres which is higher than the national average 382.

It is shown in fig. 2, that during the first six censuses i.e. from 1900 to 1960, the population of the State increased from 4.75 lakhs to 5.90 lakhs thereby indicating an overall growth rate of 24% during that period. During the period from 1960-1971, the population increased from 5.89 lakhs to 7.95 lakhs

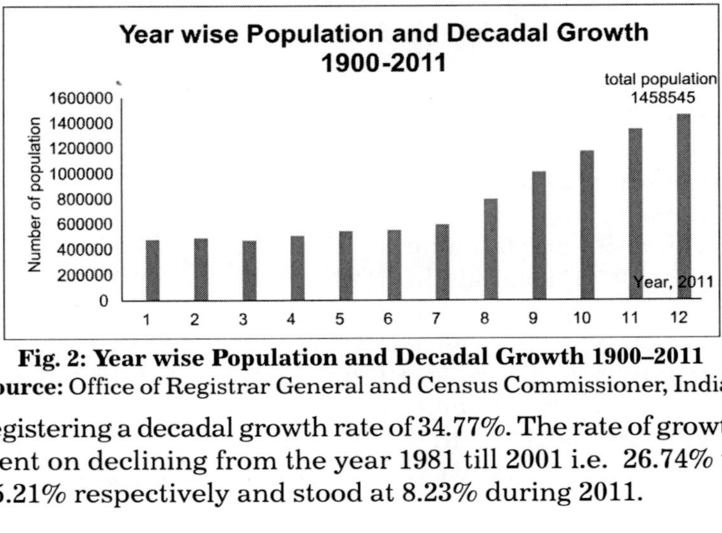

Fig. 2: Year wise Population and Decadal Growth 1900–2011
Source: Office of Registrar General and Census Commissioner, India.

registering a decadal growth rate of 34.77%. The rate of growth went on declining from the year 1981 till 2001 i.e. 26.74% to 15.21% respectively and stood at 8.23% during 2011.

2.5.2 Literacy

Another important factor is literacy which has very important role in maintaining health status. As per 2011 Census, the number of literates in Goa is reported to be 1165487 of which 615823 are males and 549664 are females. More than 88% Goan people are literate. Out of them 92.65% males and 84.66% females are literate.

Table – 1
Literacy of the population of Goa

Classification	Total	% of total literate person	Rural	% of rural literacy	Urban	% of urban literacy
Literate person	11,65,487	88.70	4,31,271	86.65	7,34,216	89.95
Males	6,15,823	92.65	2,27,143	91.71	3,88,680	93.21
Females	5,49,664	84.66	2,04,128	81.63	3,45,536	86.56

Source: Statistical handbook Goa 2016-17.

2.5.3 Health Status and Health Consciousness

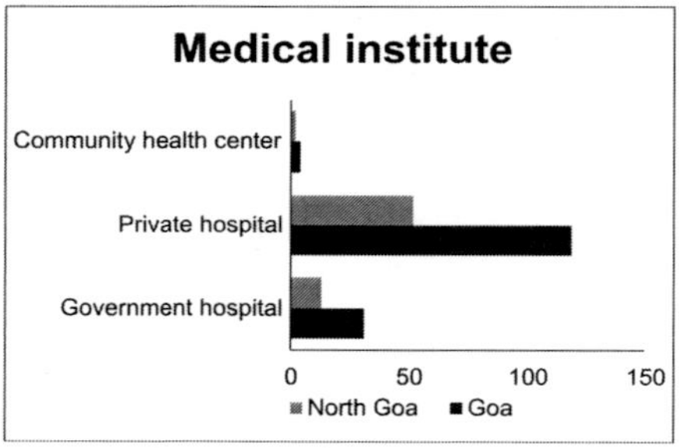

Fig. 3: Medical Institute
Source: Statistical handbook Goa 2016-17.

In entire Goa state there are 31 government hospital and 119 private hospitals. Out of them North Goa District occupies 13 government hospitals and 52 private hospitals. Obviously, the number of private hospitals is more than the government hospitals in the state. Total number of community health centre is 4 and North Goa District has 2 community health centres. From the above-mentioned data, it can be said that people are getting good health service as there is sufficient number of health centres.

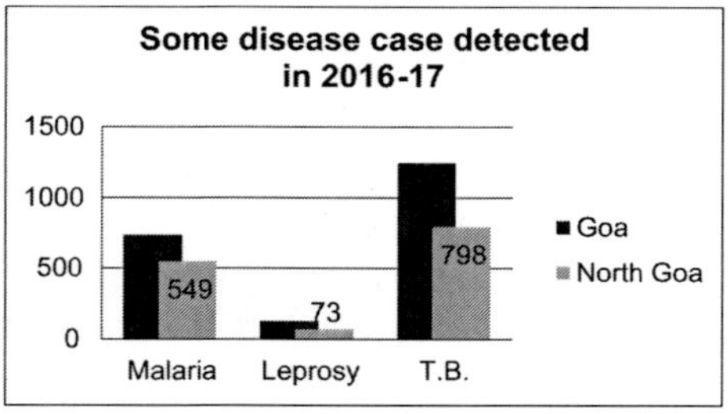

Fig. 4: Some Disease Case detected in 2016-17
Source: Directorate of health, Goa.

From the fig. 4 some diseases detected in the year 2016-17 can be found. Here malaria, leprosy and T.B. have been taken into consideration. In 2016-17 total malaria detected cases in the state are 739. Out of which 549 malaria cases are in the north Goa District. As Goa is located in coastal areas, mosquito effected diseases are common for these areas.

Not only physical problems are causing various issues in our health, but there are some mental illnesses which affect our activities and stability of our health. In 2016-17 there are 1472 psychiatric patients treated indoor, out of which 1000 are male and 472 are female patients. 52131 people were treated out door at the institution of psychiatry in the year of 2016-17.

2.5.4 Drugs Addiction to the People

It is one of the most common facts that there is a trend of increasing drug addicted persons throughout Goa state.

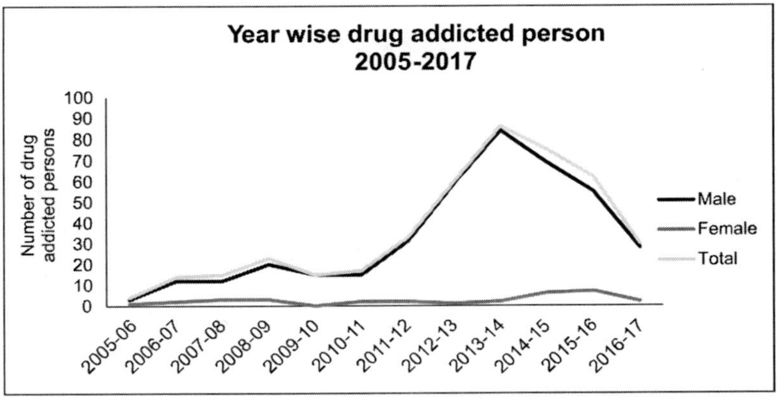

Fig. 5: Year wise Drug Addicted Person 2005-2017

Source: Institute of Psychiatry &Human Behaviour, Bambolim Goa.

If we see the increasing trend of drug addiction from 2005 to 2017, there is continuous rising in drug addiction among the people. In the year 2013-14 there was height number of drug addiction in the state. 84 males and 2 females were recorded as drug victim in that year. However, after 2013-14 there is seen decreasing trend in the state. It can be assumed that the reason behind decrease are public awareness and government policy.

2.6 Type of Disease and Medicines:

The Fig. 6 represents that 40% people are taking homoeopathy medicine for treatment whereas percentage of taking allopathic and others medicine are 36 and 24 respectively. It is stated that people are conscious about taking medicine. Most of respondent take homoeopathy medicine due to its good cure capacity.

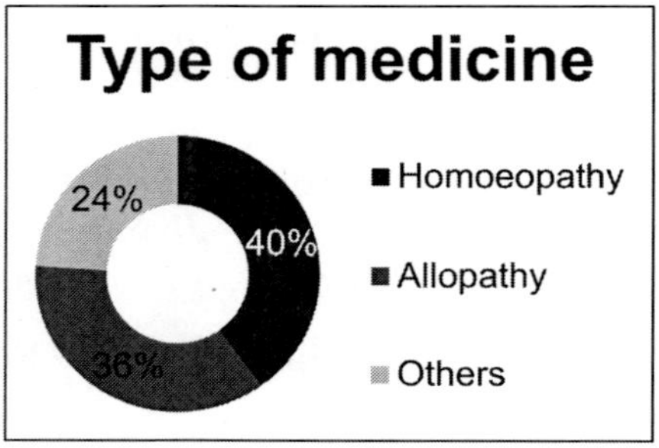

Fig. 6: Type of Medicine
Source: Primary Survey, 2020.

From the primary survey study, it is found that 42% family are suffering from different disease where as 58% respondent said that they are free from disease. The Fig. 7 gives percentage of disease where 19% person are affected from normal fever, almost 24% from skin disease, 9.5% from respiratory problems, 4.7% from heart problems and approximately 43% from other diseases respectively. Here it is found that some people are affected from AIDS and some deficiency disease which are categorized as other diseases. There is other diseases also like diabetes, heart trouble 8%, high blood pressure etc.

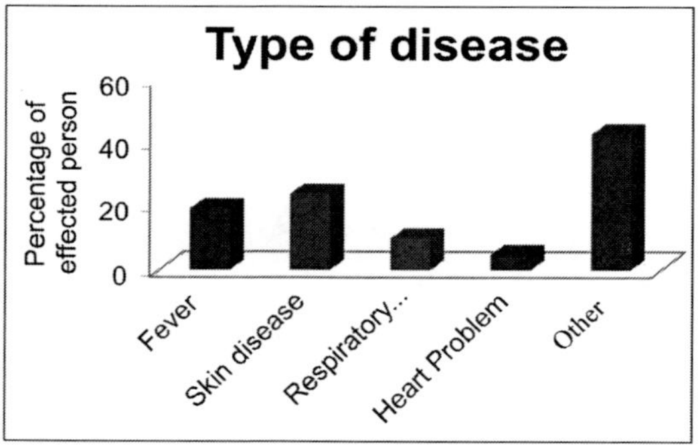

Fig. 7: Type of Medicine

2.6.1 Major Health Issues:

Almost 20% respondents said that they have faced big problem on his/her health. Not only that many people also died earlier due to this issue. The figure shows about the statistics of such health issues where 20% respondents have faced to stroke, 10% have faced heart disease, 30% asthma and 40% other problems respectively.

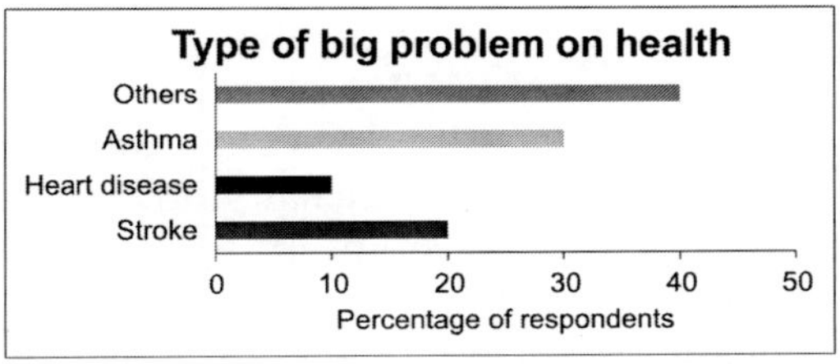

Fig. 8: Type of Big Problem on Health

Source: Primary Survey, 2020.

2.6.2 Child Health Condition:

The Fig. 9 represents that 16% out of total children have diseases and rest 84% children have no disease. Various types of diseases found in children of Calangute area. Here percentage of fever and diarrhoea effected children both is 16.6%, 25% children have skin diseases, 8.3% are suffering from whooping cough and more than 33% out of total diseases effected children have some other diseases like malaria, dengue etc. It is stated that though overall health status is good but children are suffering from some diseases.

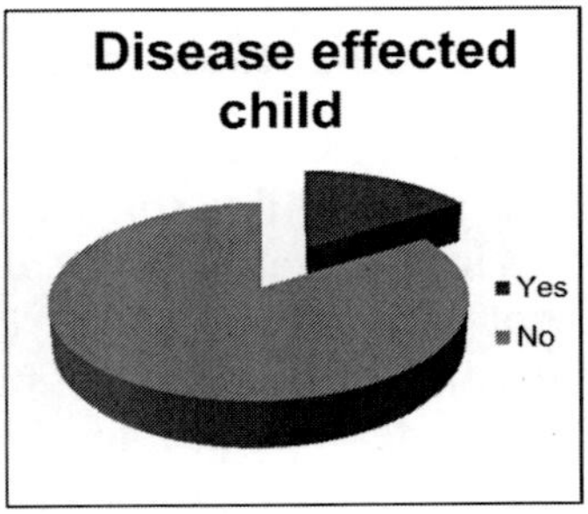

Fig. 9: Disease Effected Child

Source: Primary Survey, 2020.

2.6.3 Child and Maternal Health Care

All children in Calangute area are getting vaccine timely

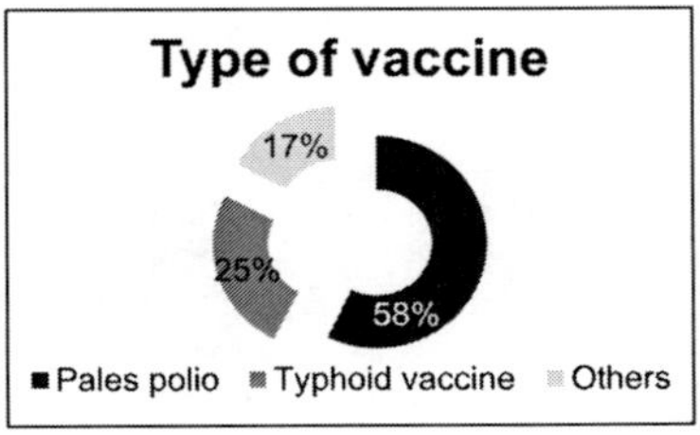

Fig. 10: Type of Vaccine

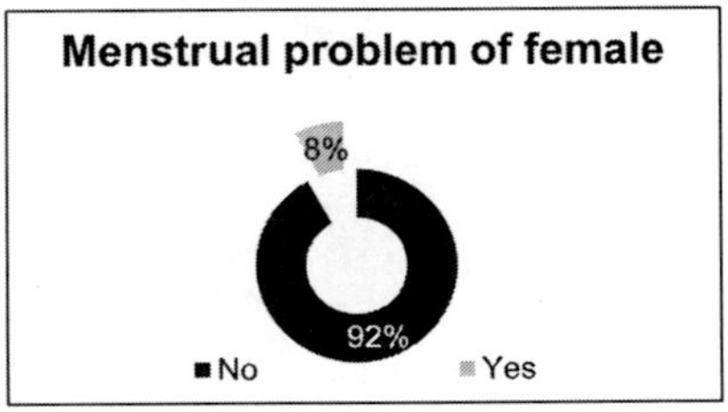

Fig. 11: Menstural Problem of Female

Source: Primary Survey, 2020.

from health centres. In the figure 15 it is informed that out of total children 57% have received Pales polio vaccine, 25% children get typhoid vaccine and 17% children get others vaccine. Here it can be said that the people as well as health workers are aware about the vaccination program to their children. On the other hand, 92% out of total female have not suffering from any menstrual problem whereas only 8% women are facing such problems. The female members of the respondent family use proper menstrual hygiene. They very much conscious about that fact and it reflects the good maternal health care also.

2.6.4 Some Habits of Local Residents

The Fig. 12 shows some habits of the local people. Here it is represented that 52% people are eating fruit regularly to maintain their good health, where as 48% of respondent are not taking fruits regularly. Only 22% out of total respondents control their diet for maintaining good health but rest of them don't aware about diet. They think that they have no need to control diet. 64% of total respondents sleep 8 hours regularly and 36% respondent don't sleep 8 hours regularly. Out of total 42% respondents exercise regularly for good health, but rest 58% don't go for exercise to maintain good health.

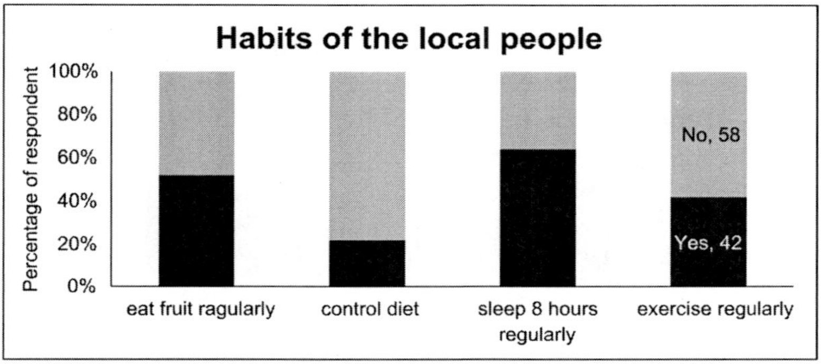

Fig. 12: Habits of the Local People

Source: Primary Survey, 2020.

2.6.5 Other Diseases

The Fig. 13 represents the presence the diseases caused by mosquito. Some family members of respondent have such diseases. Out of total Effected people more than 42% are suffering from dengue, 14.29% of malaria, 14% of encephalitis

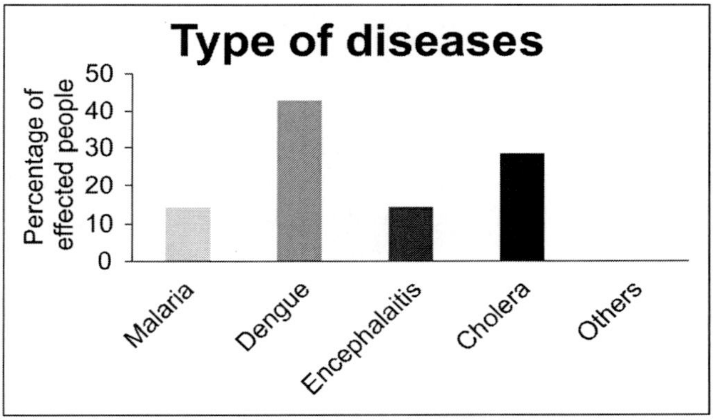

Fig. 13: Type of Diseases

Source: Primary Survey, 2020.

and 28% of cholera respectively. Here it is stated that being a coastal area and some other environmental conditions there may be the presence of such diseases.

2.7. Findings of the Study

- 34% people are found suffering from disease. 40% people are taking homoeopathy medicine for treatment whereas percentage of taking allopathic and others medicine are 36 and 24 respectively.
- Different types of diseases have been found there were 19% person are affected from normal fever, almost 24% from skin disease, 9.5% from respiratory problems, 4.7% from heart problems and approximately 43% from other diseases respectively.
- Here percentage of fever and diarrhoea effected children both is 16.6%, 25% children have skin diseases, 8.3% are suffering from whooping cough and more than 33% out

of total diseases effected children have some other diseases like malaria, dengue etc.

- People go to hospitals for avail any treatment. And rest of them either go to the nearby health centres or others places (private nursing home). Government hospital facilities are good also. People go government hospital for good services of doctors and supply of medicine.
- People are easily getting medicine from dispensaries within their affordable cost.
- 58% respondents go for health check-up, more than 62% of respondent go to government hospital for health check-up, almost 4% respondents go to health centres, 10% go to Nursing home and more than 24% respondents go to others places like private hospital for check-up.
- Only 36% respondents drink mineral water where as 64% of total respondents drink normal water all time. As people are educated, they avoid junk food in the study area. More than 66% respondents do exercise regularly in their own home where as rest of them 33% go to the Gym for exercise.
- 64% of total respondents are taking alcohol. Here it is stated that drugs addicted people are more in Calangute locality and it has also affected on society.
- As the hospitals have good amount of medicine to provide the patient and ambulance also available there in well condition, so it can be concluded that Hospital authority and government also much aware about the health status of that place.

2.8 Problems of the Study Area

Though overall health system is very good in North Goa. But some problems are also present there.

- Our study area is located in coastal areas. So, some misquote effected diseases like malaria, dengue, influenza etc. are normal disease for that place.
- Day by Day number of motor vehicles is increasing in the

roads of Goa. This causes air pollution and some diseases like allergy; lung cancer and asthma are being found now.

- Not only pollution, intoxication habits of youth are also the major reason behind the growth of many diseases.
- Abnormal changes in lifestyle of local people, specifically the youth make some time bad situation is social environment.
- Specifically in private hospital few numbers of doctors and less amount of bed available there. Most of the private hospitals have no blood bank or no ambulance services.
- Most of the people do not habituate with dieting or exercising for betterment of their health.

2.9 Government Policy in the Study Area

There are many governments policy and government help in the issue of health. Some of them are mentioned below.

- National leprosy eradication program in the state.
- National T.B control program.
- Maternal Death Audit initiated in the State.
- Aadhar enabled payments for Janani Suraksha Yojana beneficiaries.
- Janani Shishu Suraksha Karyakaram. Is fully implemented in the State.
- Drop back home facility and bringing the pregnant mothers and sick neonates to the hospitals is implemented with the support of EMRI 108 Ambulance services and Ambulances of the Health Centre / Hospitals.
- Complete immunization coverage is 88.9 % which is the best in the country.
- Goa has implemented the activities of National Rural Health Mission efficiently and effectively for attaining the goals and objectives of National Population Policy and Millennium Development Goals.

2.10 Suggestions and recommendations

- Physical environment, specifically water and air condition should be checked.

- Good initiatives should be taken for some epidemiological diseases like malaria, dengue, leprosy.
- Habits of taking alcohol and drug should be checked.
- Some hospitals should have increased their bed capacity and have more facilities to bring patients in hospital.
- Specifically private hospitals should have more treatment ward than one or two wards only. They need a greater number of doctors and workers with modern equipment for treatment.
- People should take a proper healthy meal. Not only that exercising, dieting & sleeping well are needed for betterment of their health.

2.11 Concluding Observations

After the above discussions it can be said that overall health condition of Bardez is very good. There are also some problems in health issues where government need to work. Particular status of health is very good for North Goa, specifically for people of Bardez. But in some cases, it needs to improve. Government should take good initiatives to solve all these problems related to various health issues and people also need to be more conscious about their health.

References

An overview of health status of Goa, State of Goa's health Report, Sangath, 2000.

District Census Handbook North Goa, Directorate of Census operations Goa.

Economic survey 2017 - 18, Directorate of Planning, Statistics & Evaluation Porvorim - Goa.

Manual on health statistics, idea, Central Statistical Office Ministry of Statistics and Programme Implementation, Government of India.

Mr. Frazer Taylor, Dr. Sanjay P. Sawant Dessai: Conceptual Framework of Public healthcare in Goa.

National Family Health Survey, State Fact Sheet Goa 4, 2015-16.

National Health Profile 2018, 13th Issue: Directorate general of Health Services Ministry of Health & Family Welfare, Government of India.

Prof. A. Balasubramanium: Goa at a Glance

Ranjit Kumar Dehury, Janmejaya Samal, Nafisa Vaze Desouza, Parthsarthi Dehury; Status of Women's health in Goa and Sikkim: A Comparative Analysis of State Fact Sheets of National Family Health Survey (NFHS) - 3 and 4.

Statistical Hand Book of Goa (2016-17); Publiction Division, Directorate of Planning, Statistics and Evaluation, Porvorim-Goa.

Websites

Directorate of health service, Panaji, Goa.

http://www.dhsgoa.gov.in/

https://en.m.wikipedia.org/wiki/Bardez

3

Study on Health Status in Vishakhapatnam City of Andhra Pradesh: Challenges and Prospects

Bandana Sarkar

Abstract: Health, as defined by the WHO, is "a state of complete physical, mental and social well-being and not merely the absence of disease or infirmity. The meaning of health has evolved over time. In the case of Vizag city health means overall fitness of a person. In the Vizag city they are highly educated and they are very conscious about their health. In the case of female health they are also very conscious. Here, mainly vector and water borne diseases found in high number. People are suffering mostly different kinds of fever. Here dengue, malaria, hypertension, diarrhea, typhoid, chikungunya are mainly dominated diseases. But in all of them hypertension are found in highest number in last 4 years till 2019 January. As a result this city not frequently face any kind of huge health related problems but they face lot of water and vector borne diseases. So, this study is mainly focusing to know about the health status of the Vizag city.

Keywords: *educated, aware, water and vector borne, health status*

Research Scholar, Department of Geography & Applied Geography, University of North Bengal, District: Darjeeling. Email: bandanasarkargeo96@gmail.com

3.1 Introduction

In the developing world, poverty not only excludes people from the benefits of health-care systems but also restricts them from participating in decisions that affect their health. The resulting health inequalities are well documented, and the search for greater equity attracts many concerned players and initiatives. India, as a developing country it is also facing lots of health issues. In health sector, India has made enormous strides over the past decades. The life expectancy has crossed 67 years, infant and under five mortality rates are declining as the rate of disease incidence. The main motivation of this paper is to analyze the health status of Vizag City. In India, Vizag as a smart city it has also a good rate of life expectancy as almost 68 years. As Vizag is a highly educated, the people are conscious about their health issues. They are mainly suffered from water or vector born diseases. So, the paper is nothing but a useful effort to identify the health status about the Vizag City.

3.2 Objective of the Study

The major objectives of this research work are enumerated below:

- To state the condition of health of the Vizag People.
- To analyse about their recent health status.
- To point out the facility given by Govt. for the people of the city on health purpose.
- To find out the overall healthcare treatment facility of the city.

3.3 Data Base

This research work is based on both primary and secondary data, collected from different sources.

3.3.1 Primary data

Primary data has been collected through pre designed questioner survey based on 100 sample, based on the respondent, hospital survey.

3.3.2 Secondary data

The information about the registered hospital and the health centers collected from the GVMC office. Some other information like the different health programs arranged from Health department of Andrapradesh websites, "Andrapradesh, Reproductive and Child Health, District Level Survey (DLHS-2), "City development plan-GVMC", published paper by office of the state Medical Commissioner ESI Corporation, Regional office. More over some relevant data, map were collected from the library of Vizag city, newspapers also from the journal.

3.4 Study Area

Visakhapatnam District is one of the North Eastern Coastal districts of Andhra Pradesh and it lies between 17°-15' and 18°-32' Northern latitude and 18°-54' and 83°-30' in Eastern longitude. It is bounded on the North partly by the Orissa State and partly by Vizianagaram District, on the South by East Godavari District, on the West by Orissa State and on the East by Bay of Bengal.

3.5 Methodology

The methodology adopted can be divided into the following parts:

3.5.1 Pre-Field: General literature survey was done on the health condition, status of women and child health. A structured questionnaire prepared to collect the data from the respondents and from the hospitals.

3.5.2 Filed: Relevant photographs have been taken during the field survey to illustrate the scenario more specifically. Some officers, experts, executive in different organization were personally met and interviewed.

3.5.3 Post field: This stage involves computation of master table from the questionnaire, statistical application, cartographic representation, analysis of data and information obtained in order to understand the present status, finally

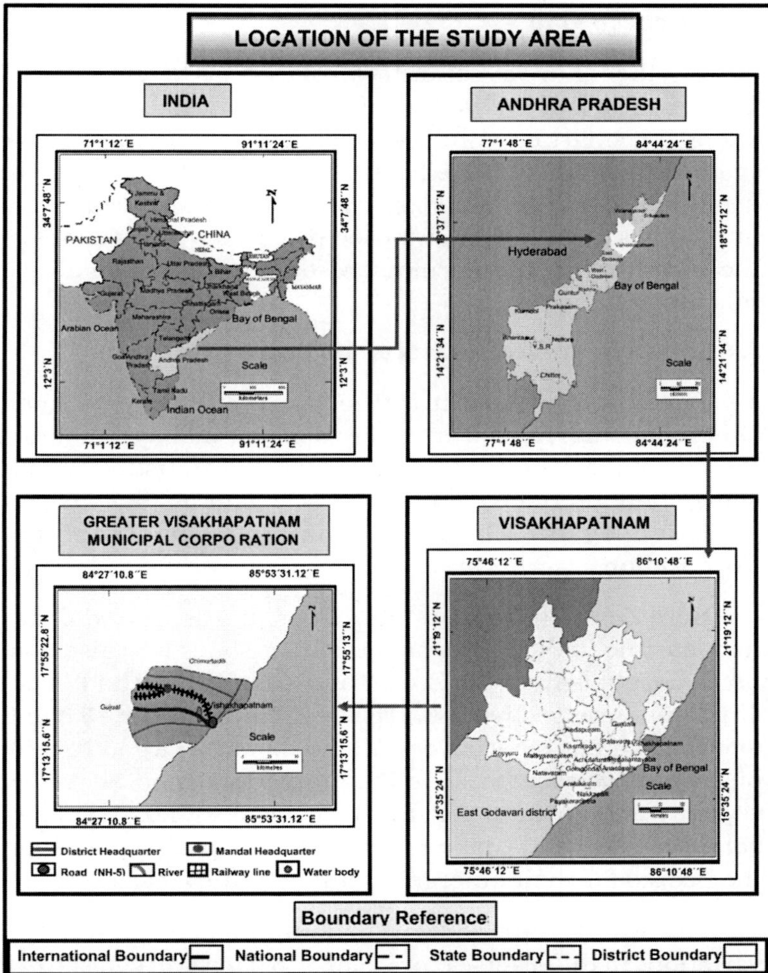

Fig. 1: Location of the Study Area

Source: Oxford school of ATLAS, Vishakhapatnam Urban Development Authority, GVMC

some strategies and initiatives are suggested for future development of health facility and condition in Vizag. 21st century GIS, professionals, Global Mapper, QGIS, Map info, have been used for digitization of maps.

3.6 Research Gap

Yes, there have a research gap of that has been identified. There are lack of availability of articles, journals and books. Vizag is a smart city but there are less number of work on the health status of the city. As a smart city the health care facilities are also good here so it should also be a focus point, but there is not relevant proposed research work available in the websites, so an enormous research gap is available in this topic.

3.7 Scenario of Health Status in Vizag City

The status of health in the Vizag city is quite good. Different health related issues are done by mainly depending on secondary data. Many hospital related statistics are also shown here on the basis of secondary data. As per the Map provided by the Greater Visakhapatnam Municipal Corporation.

Here Zone 3 has highest no. of hospital as, 49 and Zone 1 had least no. of hospitals as, 11. Other Zones had also good no. of hospitals specially Zone 2 and Zone 4. They had 41 and 45 hospitals respectively. And lastly Zone 5 and Zone 6 had 15 and 15 hospitals respectively. All the zones had a good quality of hospital service because they provide a good no. of bed capacity and good doctor facility. If the least no. of hospital zones can increase their no. of hospitals it also help more the people for their emergency and in critical case.

The Fig. 2 represents the Component wise monthly variations in different sectors of health. Here we can see that Op has the highest no. in Different Months. It is Continuously

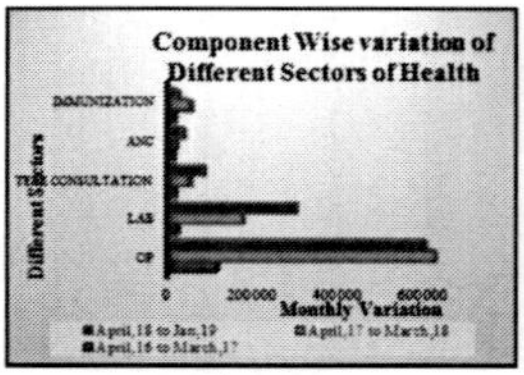

Fig. 2

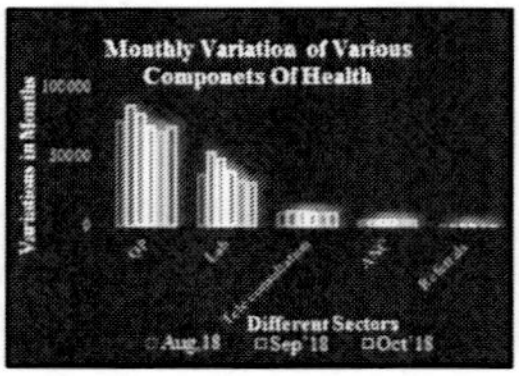

Fig. 3

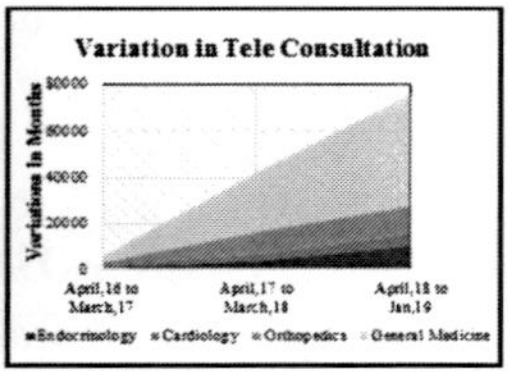

Fig. 4

Source: GVMC

increasing year after year. In the other cases like Lab facility, Immunization, ANC, Tele Consultation process also increasing year after year. It showed that development is taking place year after year with the development if technology. In the Diagram (Fig. 3) tells about the Last Six months variation in different sectors in health. Here we can see lots of variation in every sector from August, 2018 to January, 2019. In this last six months Referrals is continuously decreasing and other sectors except ANC, all of them are decreasing from Aug, 2018 to Jan, 2019. It shows there are may be some problem associated with this sectors. In the Data (Fig. 4) stated the variation of Tele Consultation in Different Year. Here we can see that tele consultation process is Increasing year after year. All the sectors of tele consultation from April 16th to Jan 19th. We can conclude that this sectors are gaining more development due to modern technology and highly trained workers. This shows the high level of development in Vizag City.

In the Diagram (Fig. 5) represents about the Variations

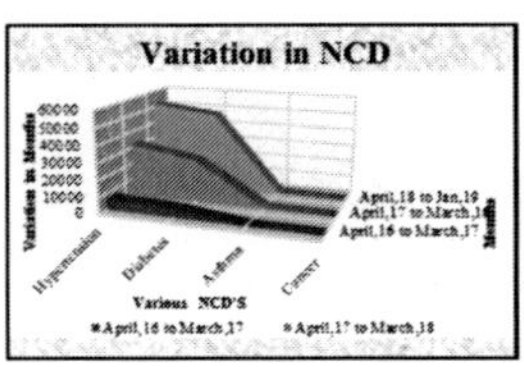

Fig. 5

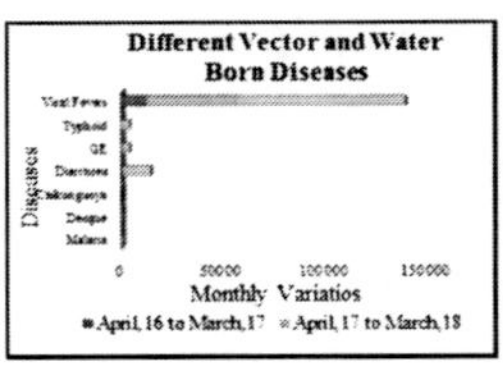

Fig. 6

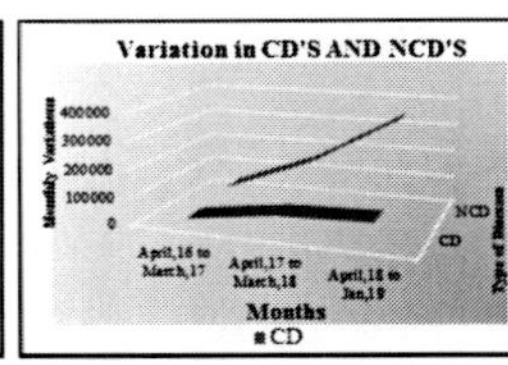

Fig. 7

Source: GVMC

of Non Communicable Diseases from April 16th to Jan 19th. Here We can also see that NCD's are increasing day by day. It shows that Although Vizag is a Smart City, but due to their busy lifestyle and Different types of Bad habits NCD's are increasing. In the Fig. 6 showed about the Different types of Vector and Water Born diseases. This are mainly Communicable Diseases. Among all the diseases viral fever is happened highest times and after that Diarrhoea is in No. second. It shows that Viral fever is a communicable disease and it spreads most. In the Diagram (Fig. 7) represents about the variation in communicable disease and Non Communicable Disease. This picture showed that CD's are less happened than NCD's. It reflects that Vizag is mainly very hygienic and very clean so, communicable disease is not mostly happened but due to their lifestyle and different habits Non Communicable Diseases are mainly happened.

In the Data (Fig. 8) tells about the OPD facility of Vizag City. Here we can see that OPD has the highest no. in 2018 and we have the data till Jan 19, as we see the trend we can assume that it will increase throughout the year. This means here OPD doctor facility is good and patients are also increasing due to many problems. In the diagram (Fig. 9) tells about the no. of Anti Natal Check-ups and Post Natal Check-ups. Here we can see ANC patients are more and in

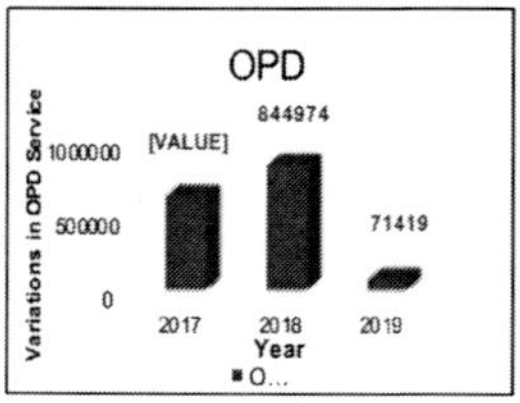

Fig. 8

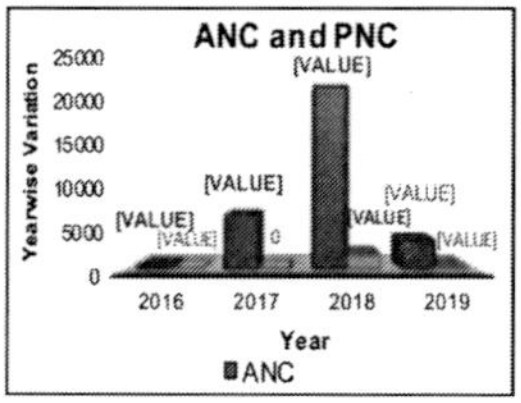

Fig. 9

Source: GVMC

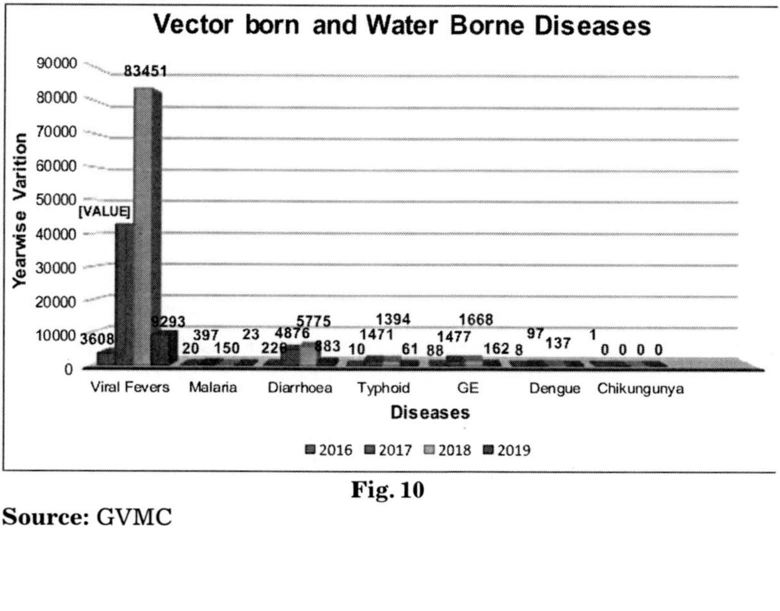

Fig. 10

Source: GVMC

2018 ANC patient is high in number. It means people of Vizag is highly concerned about ANC check-up but in the case of PNC check-up they are not much concern compare to ANC check-up. People need to more aware about PNC check-up.

In the data (Fig. 10) represents about the year wise Vector and Water borne disease variation. Here we can see that among all the diseases viral fever is happening high in number specially in 2018. It shows that it mainly happens due to change of weather or their lifestyle. People need to more concern about this communicable diseases because it spread by interaction.

3.8 Perception Study on Health Condition

Research paper is mainly based on perception study. As Vizag city is very developed city in India and one of the smart city so, it is identified as a one of the good health status region of India. This study mainly depend upon the people opinion about their health status in the city. So, questionnaire has

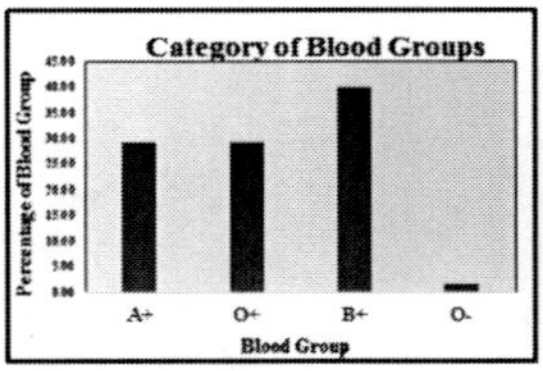

Fig. 11

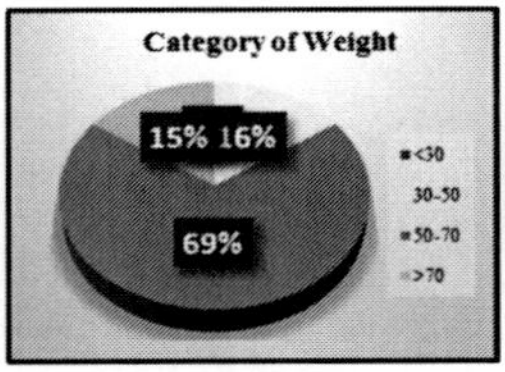

Fig. 12

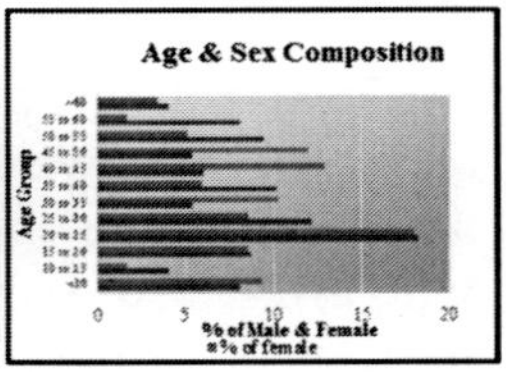

Fig. 13

Source: Primary Survey, 2019.

been selected for the survey work.

This diagram (Fig. 11) represents that 29.23% respondents belong to A+ and O+ where as 40% are B+ and 1.54% are O-. Therefore most of the respondents are categorized under B+. In the Fig. 12 informed that 16% of the people have their weight in between 30 to 50 kg and 15% have their weight >70kg but Almost 69% of the people have their weight in between 50-60 kg. So, as a concluded part it can be said that everyone is pretty maintained about their health in Vizag. In the Fig. 13 stated the age & sex composition of Vizag city. In this fig in between 20 to 30 years population are mainly in high number and less than 15 years and more than 50 years population in comparatively less. It means in this city working population is very high means independent population is high in number.

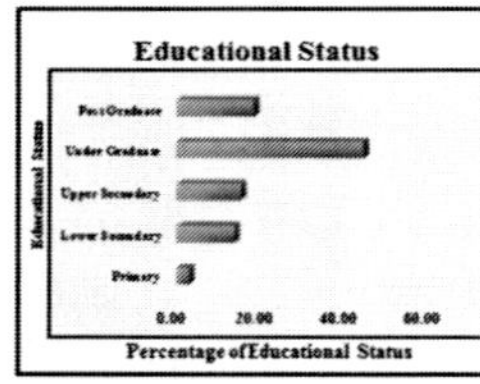

Fig. 14

Source: Primary Survey, 2019.

In this Information (Fig. 14) stated about the educational status of Vizag city. Here, primary, lower secondary and upper secondary studied people are very less in number. 45% and 15% people are under graduate and post graduate respectively. Therefore most of the respondents are highly educated here.

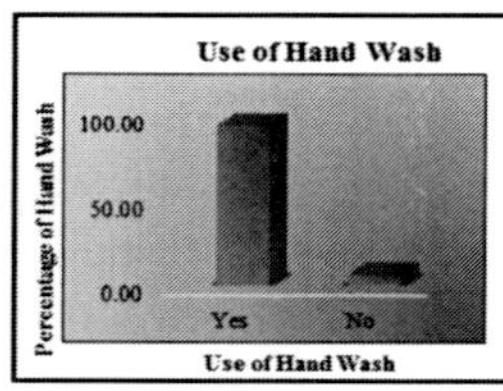

Fig. 15

Source: Primary Survey, 2019.

In the Fig. 15 showed about the use of hand wash habit of the people of Vizag city. Here, 93% of the people uses hand wash before taking food. It means they are very careful about their hygiene and health.

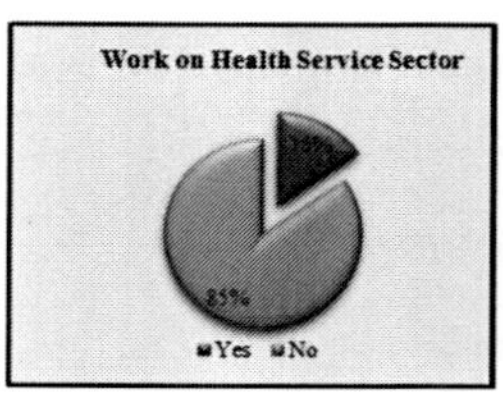

Fig. 16

Fig. 17

Source: Primary Survey, 2019.

In the diagram (Fig. 16) showed about the people who are worked on health service sector. Here 15% of the respondents are only worked in health service sector and rest of 85% of the people are not engaged with any kind of health service work. This represents that they are mainly interested in tertiary or secondary activity. In Fig. 17 tells about the smoking habit of the Vizag people. 24% of the respondents only have the habit of smoking and rest 75% do not have the smoking habit. It shows about

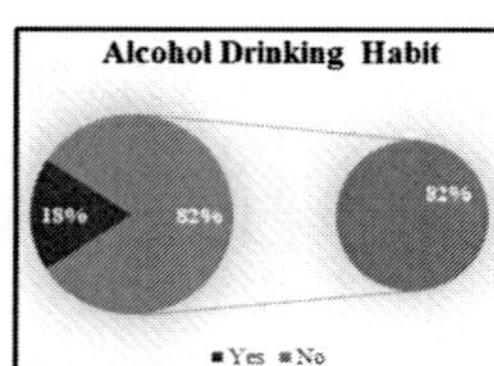

Fig. 18

Source: Primary Survey, 2019.

the awareness of the people about their health.

In the diagram (Fig. 18) stated about the alcohol drinking habit of the respondents.18.46% of the respondents intake alcohol and rest of 81.54% of the respondents does not intake alcohol. It means they are very conscious about their health. They are not addicted with any kind of intoxication.

In the Fig. 19 represents the medicine taking habit of the respondents. Here 46.15% of the people take medicine regularly and rest of 53.85% of the respondent take medicine occasionally. therefore it shows about their good health status.

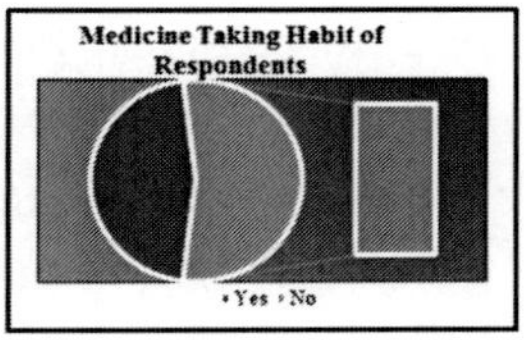

Fig. 19

Source: Primary Survey, 2019.

In the diagram (Fig. 20) informed about the regular check-ups status of the respondents. 87.69% of people does not go for regular check-ups and rest of them go for check-ups. As a overall outcome it can be said that they are very conscious and they are very heathy as they do not eat junk food and do not check-up their health regularly. But they also do not get any major problem regarding their health.

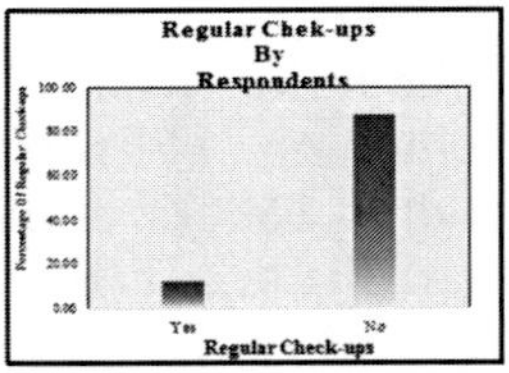

Fig. 20

Source: Primary Survey, 2019.

In the Information (Fig. 21) showed the problem in menstrual cycle. Only few of females have the problem on this particular topic as 6.15% and rest of 93.85% does not have any type of problem regarding this. It shows that they are

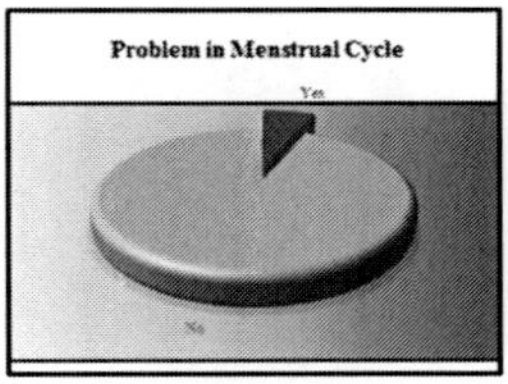

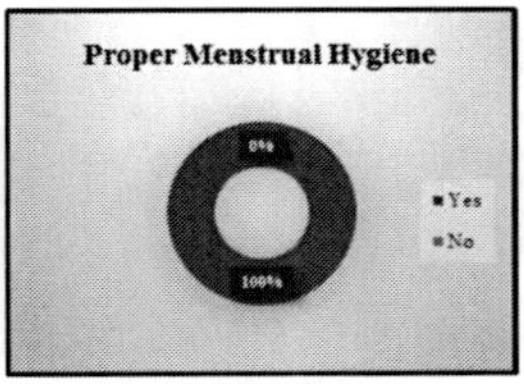

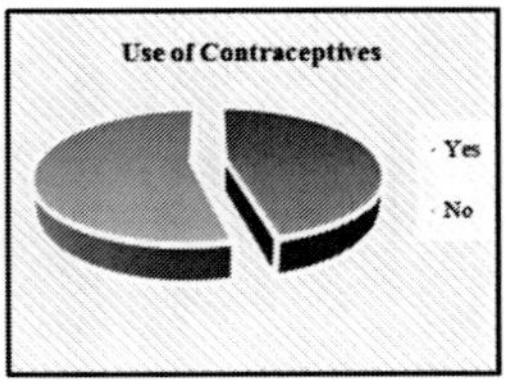

Fig. 21 **Fig. 22** **Fig. 23**

Source: Primary Survey, 2019.

very hygienic and there are very less problem regarding this cycle. It means they take proper food and care their health with proper manner. In the Fig. 22 tells about the menstrual hygiene of the female. 100% of the people they take proper menstrual hygiene. Therefore they are very concerned about it. In the diagram (Fig. 23) tells about the use of contraceptives by the respondents of Vizag city. Here 46.15% of the people use contraceptives for birth control and rest of them mostly don't know about that or does not use.

In the Data (Fig. 24) informed about the mental disable person of the Vizag city. 96.92% of the people are not mentally disabled here and rest of them are disabled mainly they are mental patient. In the Fig. 25 tells about the physically challenged respondents. 95.38% of the respondents does not have this type of problem and rest of 4.62% of the respondents have this problem specially in backbone and leg disability. It shows that there are very less percentage of people who are mainly mentally and physically challenged. It means that health condition of the people of Vizag is very good.

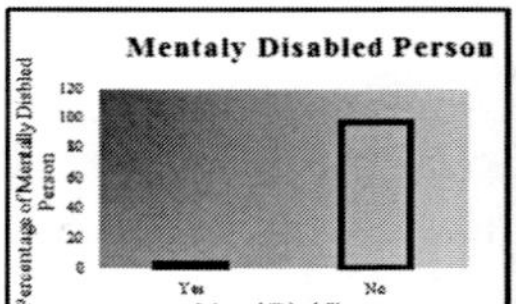

Fig. 24

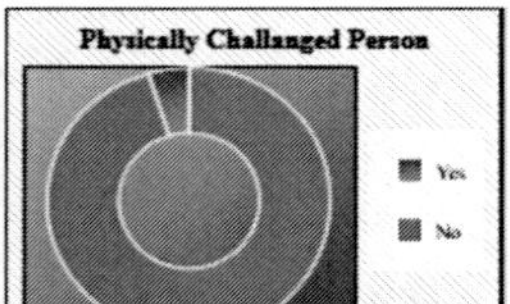

Fig. 25

Source: Primary Survey, 2019.

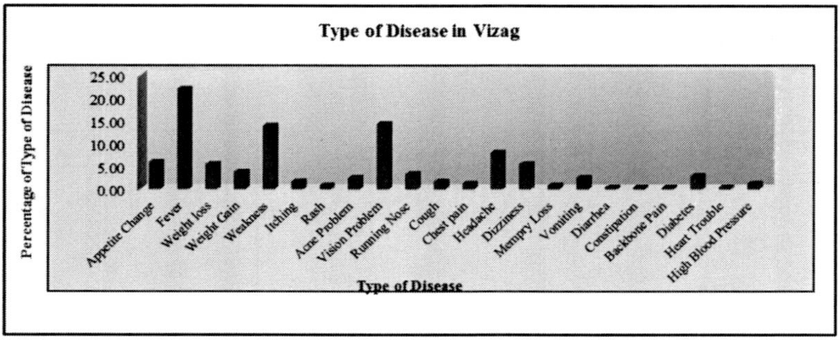

Fig. 26

Source: Primary Survey, 2019.

In the Fig. 26 represents about the diseases of Vizag city. Here we can found different kinds of disease variety. Here fever takes place mostly as about 22.03% and vison problem are also found in high number as 14. 4.11% and also weakness problem is about 13.98%. These three are the major disease as found and except that many disease can also be found as weight less and gain, skin problems, dizziness and headache, heart problem, diabetes etc. Here mainly minor diseases are found in great number. It shows that the people are Vizag not fall ill in any king of critical diseases.

In the Fig. 27 represents about the doctors facility of the Vizag city. According to the respondents 100% of the people get good doctor facility. In the diagram (Fig. 28) shows about the quality of health acre infrastructure of Vizag city. According to the respondents 92.31% is the good quality of health infrastructure and 7.69% said they have excellent kind of health infrastructure. None of one said that they have bad health infrastructure.

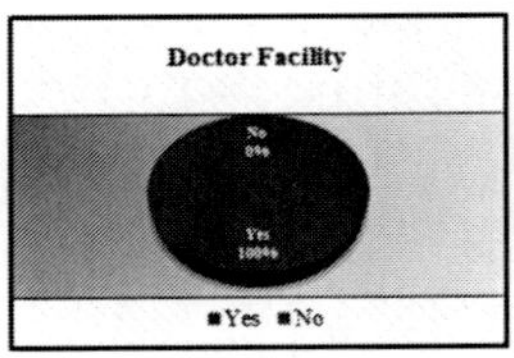

Fig. 27

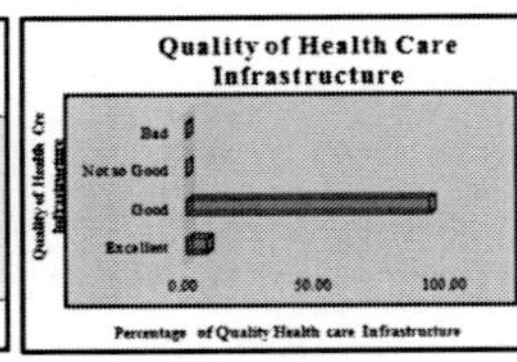

Fig. 28

Source: Primary Survey, 2019.

The Fig. 29 represent that there are all hospital have Test Lab Facility. So we can say that all the hospitals are developing and give the patient all facilities.

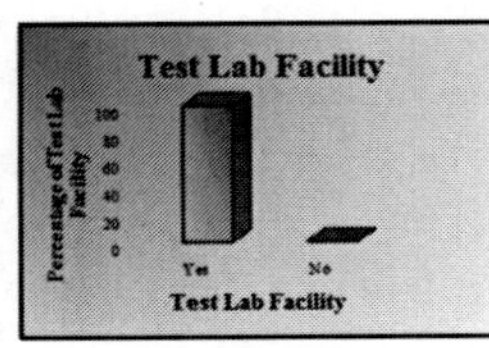

Fig. 29

Source: Primary Survey, 2019.

This Fig. 30 informed that 50% of hospitals have facility of emergency department where as 50% have not facility of emergency department. The diagram (Fig. 31) stated that in the

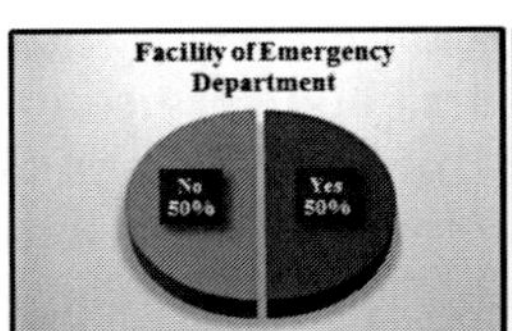

Fig. 30

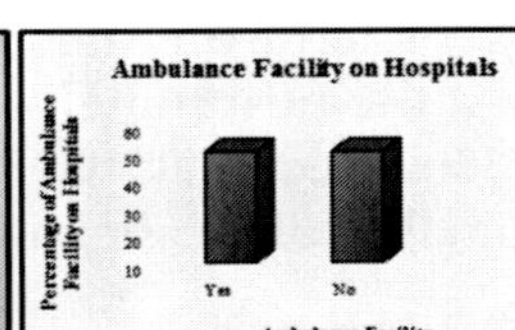

Fig. 31

Source: Primary Survey, 2019.

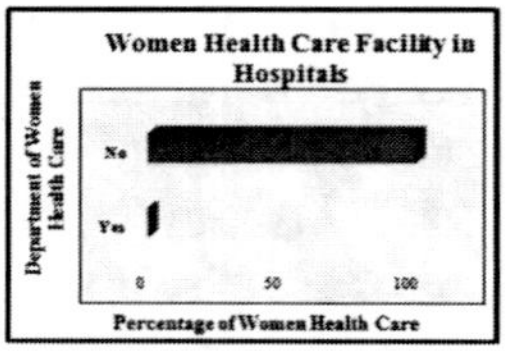

Fig. 32

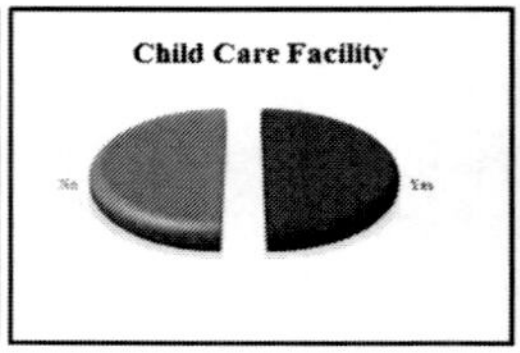

Fig. 33

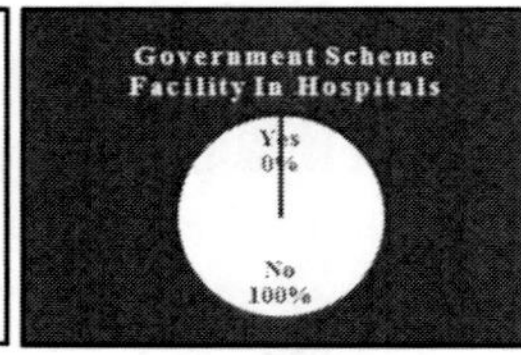

Fig. 34

Source: Primary Survey, 2019.

total number of hospitals 50% hospitals have ambulance facility where as other 50% hospitals have no ambulance facility which conclude that there are some hospitals are under develop.

In the diagram (Fig. 32) we can see all the hospital have no women health care facility . From those diagrams we can conclude that the child health care department is more develop than the women health care department. Women health departments needs more concentration to improve their quality of treatment and facility. The diagram (Fig. 33) inform that 50% of hospitals have the child care facility, where as other 50% hospital have no child care facility. The information (Fig. 34) stated that in all the 100% hospital no government scheme facility is given.

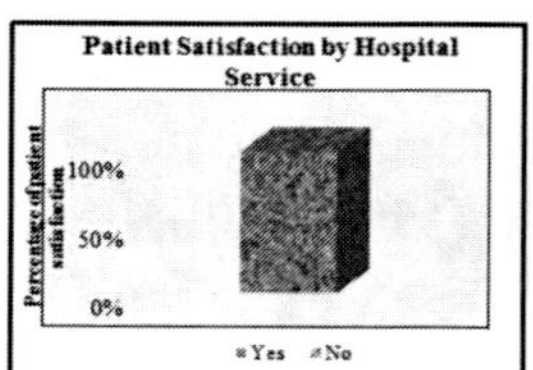

Fig. 35

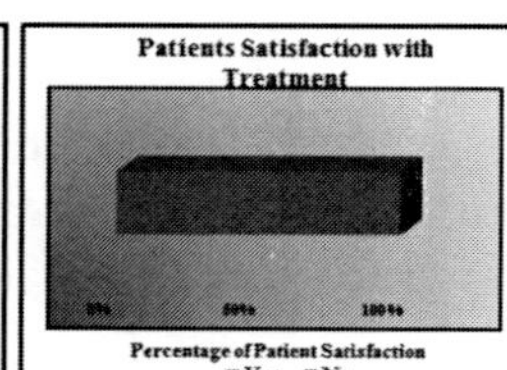

Fig. 36

Source: Primary Survey, 2019.

The diagram (Fig. 35) informs that 100% of patient satisfied from the hospital service. So we can conclude that all the hospital gives a good service to the patient. The Fig. 36 stated that 100% of patients satisfied by the treatment facility of the hospital which make a good scenario.

3.9 Findings

- The people of Vizag mostly concerned about their health.

- Here, Independent population (20 to 30 years) are comparatively high. It is showing a good population structure.
- People of Vizag are very hygienic. They properly maintain their regular hygiene and everyone have toilet facility on their home.
- In the case of intoxication habit they are very aware. Very less amount of the people supposed to take intoxicated things like smoking, alcohol etc.
- In Vizag mainly water borne diseases are found. Mosquito is a a big problem of all of the diseases. Here mainly Dengue, Malaria, Swine flu, Typhoid are found in high number. Other than vision problem is also seen in a high amount of number.
- Doctors facility and quality of health infrastructure is very good in Vizag. People of Vizag are very satisfied by them.
- As the Vizag people are highly qualified they know how to take care of their health. They take proper diet and do their physical exercise regularly. Most of them avoided junk food.
- In Vizag female heath and female education both are in a good situation but male population are dominant in every case.

3.10 Problems

- Diseases are on the rise in Vizag city due to increasing pollution level and due to the abnormal changes in the lifestyle of youth.
- Increase in motor vehicle is also one of the major problem in Vizag city. It increases the air pollution which also increase the number of patients in allergy, asthma, lung cancer.
- The industrial areas situated in Vizag are also affected the health of people.
- The city is generating so much of bio-medical waste that GVMC is unable to handle it.
- If we see our respondent hospital then the women and child health care facility needs more attention to develop their facility.

- Females are comparatively less in the any kind of field than males.
- Few of the hospitals don't have proper bed capacity and many modernized facility.

3.11 Suggestions

- Females should more motivated to do any kind of activity in any field.
- Air pollution should be cheeked properly.
- Sewerage system needs more attention for proper management.
- Private vehicles should be use in less number and public vehicle should use in a higher number.
- Hospitals should increase their bed capacity and more modernized facility to attract the people.

3.12 Conclusion

Health is defined as a state of complete mental and physical wellbeing. Living a healthy lifestyle can prevent long term illnesses. After the above discussion it can be said that overall Vizag has a good health status. They almost maintain a healthy lifestyle. There are also some bad affected areas where govt. need to work. Govt. should take good initiatives to cater all the problems related to health and people also need to more conscious about their health.

References

Print media:

City Development Plan–Greater Visakhapatnam, Visakhapatnam City Development Strategy and Slum Upgrading Action Plan.

Climate Resilient Infrastructure Services, Case Study Brief: Visakhapatnam.

Districts At a Glance Andhra Pradesh 2017, Directorate of Economics & Statistics Government of Andhra Pradesh, Vijayawada.

Kumari, T. Anitha, "Health Status of Fisher Women–A Case

Study of Visakhapatnam District", The International Journal Research Publication's.

Nayak, M. Siva Durga Prasad and Sreegiri, Sunita (2016), "A Study on Nutritional Status of Tribal Women in Visakhapatnam district, Andhra Pradesh, India" International Journal of Community Medicine and Public Health, Vol 3.

Naidu, S. Appala and Nayak, S.D.P. Mudavath and Sadi, Narasinga Rao (2016), "Prevalence of Hypertension among Reproductive Age Group Tribal Women in Visakhapatnam District" Andhra Pradesh, India, International Journal of Research in Medical Sciences, Vol 4.

Patrudu, M. Srinivasa and Naidu, G. ChantiBabu and Rao, D. Pulla (2013), "Health and Educational Status of Scheduled Tribes In Visakhapatnam District of Andhra Pradesh", the International Journal of innovative Research and Development, Vol 2, Issue 13.

Rao. Prashad. M. et.al. (2002-04), Reproduction and child health district level household survey 2002-04.

Sample Registration System SRS Bulletin Volume 50 No.1, July, 2016 and No.2, December, 2016 of the Office of the Registrar General of India, Ministry of Home Affairs, Govt. Of India, New Delhi.

Statistical Abstract Andhra Pradesh 2016, Directorate of Economics and Statistics Government of Andhra Pradesh Gollapudi, Vijayawada.

The Urban Primary Health Centre (UPHC) under NUHM; Roles, Responsibilities and Management.

Webliography:

censusindia.gov.in/2011-Common/CensusData2011.htm (Date of accession–5.3.18).

en.climate-data.org>india (Date of accession–6.3.18).

en.wikipedia.org/wiki/Visakhapatnam (Date of accession-8.3.18) https://www.mapsofindia.com (Date of accession–8.3.18)

http://visakhapatnam.nic.in/ (Date of accession–12.3.18)

http://www.internationaljournalcorner.com/index.phpijird_ojs/article/view/134362 (Date of accession–20.3.18)

http://www.theinternationaljournal.orgojsindex.php?journal=rjebs&page=article&op=view&path%5B%5D=3252 (Date of accession–22.3.18)

www.tandfonline.com/doi/abs/10.1080/09709274.1998.11907357 (Date of accession–30.3.18)

www.ijcmph.com/index.php/ijcmph/article/view/353 (Date of accession–1.4.18)

www.msjonline.org/index.php/ijrms/article/view/681 (Date of accession–5.4.18)

4

A Geo-critical Narrative on the Monumental Makeover in the Panorama of Transit within the Cultural Capital of India

Dr. Ayan Das Gupta

Abstract: In order to facilitate development inside and outside the city-limit and effectively to improvise or upgrade the land resource within the city, the Government is trying to prioritize recently (after 2005) the development of proper infrastructure such as roads, drainage and public transport systems. The Metro-railways and flyover projects are getting prioritized with mammoth thrust. Kolkata Metropolitan Development Authority has now realized that all the developed countries over the globe such as Singapore, China and Malaysia have laid gigantic thrust on infrastructural development and that is their primary cause of phenomenal growth and prosperity. The urban infrastructure of Kolkata city is getting changed rapidly and effectively in a time-bound manner through Public-Private-Partnership module. The inaugurated Gitanjali Stadium at Rashbehari Connector in record time is such a burning example in this premise.

Keywords: *Transport Renewal Projects, New looks in Flyovers, Missions of Renovation, Transit-development, Urban Infrastructure and Governance.*

WBES, Assistant Professor, Post-graduate Department of Geography, Chander nagar Government College, Hooghly, West Bengal.
Email: dasguptaayan11111@gmail.com

4.1 Introduction

The Government is trying to encourage township development through transport renewal in the city of Kolkata significantly and here the entire development is planned and pretty sustainable. Future areas of growth in Kolkata are supposed to be planned in such a way that a person can live and work within commutable distance and all urban amenities such as markets, hospitals, shopping malls, beauty-parlors, cyber-cafe etc. are found in the same vicinity. For that, some amendments are done in township-laws and land-reform acts, so that the issues associated with land-acquisition and land conversion can be ideally addressed, The Government is also planning to establish some modified land-banks for long-lasting development in transport and communicational sectors. The mission has been quite successful and appreciated amongst the global planners conspicuously.

4.2 Overall Transport-Development in Kolkata

Transport is, in true sense, the lifeline of a city's economy (Mitchel, 1954) and Kolkata is not also an exception. The transport system of Kolkata is a mixture of modern mass rapid transport and the old transport modalities like the hand-pulled rickshaws and others. Since the economic liberalization of the 1990s, development of transport network within the country has progressed at a rapid pace and the A1 cities of India including Kolkata are experiencing massive growth in the transport sector currently. Today there is a wide variety of modes of transport found in the city-core and urban-periphery. Despite ongoing improvements in this very sector within the city, several aspects of the transport are still riddled here with problems due to outdated nodes and linkages and lack of investment in proper places. The demand for transport services has been rising in Kolkata by around 10% to 12% per year. In order to cope-up with this situation, JnNURM has taken bunch of projects to develop the transport scenario of this city. These projects included: a) Construction of flyover between E.M. Bypass and Kazi Nazrul Islam Sarani,

b) Vivekananda Road Flyover (Ph.-I) from Howrah Bridge to Chittaranjan Avenue, c) Construction of Flyover at Nager Bazar on Jessore Road connecting Kolkata city, d) Flyover from Parama to Park Circus, e) Construction of Eastern Metropolitan Bye-pass connector from Padmapukur to Kamalgazi in Garia, f) Construction of left-turning Northbound off-Ramp at Beckbagan connecting Acharya Jagdish Chandra Bose Road Flyover, g) Construction of Interchange at Dunlop Junction bridging Kolkata, h) BRTS (Bus Rapid Transit System) from Ultadanga to Garia in Kolkata Metropolitan Area, i) Elevated Corridor from Keshtopur to Jora Mandir on Kazi Nazrul Islam Avenue, j) Four lane flyover at Kamalgazi intersection on Eastern Metropolitan (EM) Bypass connector near the starting point of Adi Ganga (Mathur, 2010).

Table – 1
Renowned Transport-Renewal Projects Undertaken in KMC from JnNURM

S. No.	Names of Newly initiated transport-renewal projects in KMC	Location-Code of the Projects
1	Fly-over between E.M Bypass and Kazi Nazrul Islam Sarani	Kolkata-006
2	Vivekananda Road Flyover From Howrah Bridge to Chittaranjan Avenue	Kolkata-015
3	Flyover at Nager Bazar on Jessore Road connecting Kolkata	Kolkata-027
4	Flyover from Parama to Park Circus	Kolkata-016
5	E.M Bypass connector from Padmapukur to Kamalgazi	Kolkata-007
6	Left-turning North-bound Off-ramp at Beckbagan connecting Acharya Jagdish Chandra Bose Road Flyover	Kolkata-014

7	Interchange at Dunlop Junction, connecting Kolkata	Kolkata-011
8	Bus Rapid Transport System from Ultadanga to Garia in KMC	Kolkata-049
9	Elevated Corridor from Keshtopur to Jora-Mandir on Kazi Nazrul Islam Sarani	Kolkata-054
10	Four-lane Flyover at Kamalgazi Intersection on Eastern Metropolitan Bypass connector near starting point of Adi Ganga	Kolkata-007

Source: KMDA

4.3 Recent Development in Railways

Kolkata is connected to the rest of India by the National Highways and the extensive network of the Indian Railways. Most traffic to North-East India routes through via Kolkata (Chaudhuri, 1995). Two major divisions of the Indian railways– the Eastern Railway (ER) and the South Eastern Railway (SER) are headquartered in the Kolkata city. The two major railway stations of the city are at Howrah and Sealdah. A third terminal called Kolkata station at Chitpore near Shyambazar has been constructed. This station is located in North Kolkata and can be reached by a road opposite to the Radha Gobinda Kar Medical College just beyond the Shyambazar 5-points crossing. The Electrified Suburban Rail Network of the South Eastern Railway and the Eastern Railway is extensive and stretches far into the neighboring districts of North 24 Parganas, South 24 Parganas, Nadia, Howrah, Hooghly etc. Some massive constructional changes have taken place by the direct initiative of Kolkata Metropolitan Development Authority in this sector to facilitate better accessibility and connectivity of other Metropolis within this city. The stations of Kolkata are frequented by a sophisticated type of train popularly known as Duronto Express ('Rebel' or 'Rebellious' or 'Restless' in a positive way) and this is a category of long distance train run by the Indian Railways. The special feature of these trains is that they run non-stop from source to destination, barring technical halts. All Duronto Express trains can be easily recognised by the characteristic yellow-green livery of their passenger coaches. Several Duronto Express services connect the metro cities and major state capitals of India. The Duronto Express trains are projected to be the fastest trains between the particular pair of cities they serve, although this is not necessarily commensurate for all types of services. The circular rail encircles the entire city of Kolkata and has been extended to some new dimensions. It is supposed to be well-connected with Netaji Subhash Chandra Bose International Airport and one of its new branches is linking-up Kolkata directly with Barasat. A new railway line off-shoot is also constructed that to connect the airport to the lines going to Sealdah.

4.4 Some New Transformations in Kolkata-Metro

Kolkata was the first city in South Asia to have an underground railway system that started operating from 1984. It is considered to have the status of a zonal railway. It is run by the Indian Railways. The Metro is a very well maintained and clean system. The line begins at Dum Dum in the north and continues south through Park Street, Esplanade in the heart of the city till the southern end in New Garia or the Kavi Subhash Metro Station.

There are new metro lines being built to serve other parts of Kolkata as well, including an east-west corridor linking Howrah to Salt Lake Sector 5. Trains run every 6-10 minutes from 7 am to 10:30 pm. from Monday to Saturday and from 2 pm to 10:00 pm usually on Sundays. Fares vary upto 22-25 rupee. In 2010-2015, the Railway Ministry announced four new metro link projects for the expansion of Kolkata Metro, which had one operational line (North-South Metro) and a second line under East-West Metro. These new projects are:- a) Joka to B.B.D. Bag, b) Dumdum Junction to Barrackpore via Sodepore, c) Noapara to Barasat via Kolkata Airport, d) New Garia to Kolkata Airport and e) Baranagar-Dakshineshwar-Barrackpore metro linkage .

As of 2011, all the projects are reportedly under construction and trials. After the extension of the metro-railway route upto New Garia from Dum Dum, the residents of south Kolkata have embraced the Metro wholeheartedly and the passenger-traffic has been increased by almost sixty percent to 65 percent. Several new infrastructure projects are in pipeline and will further improve this region. The six-line new link that has been proposed, especially from New Garia to Netaji Subhash Chandra Bose International Airport, has got attention of transport economists and planners abroad as well. This 32 km route via Eastern Metropolitan Bypass, Salt-lake and Rajarhat will comprise of 24 stations with an underground terminus at the Airport.

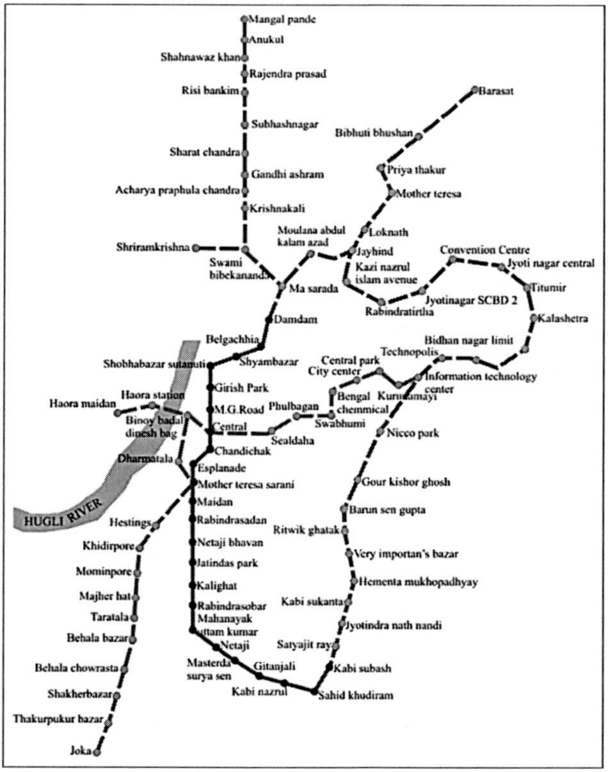

Proposed Network of Metro Rail in Kolkata

Source: KMDA

4.5 Renewal in Bus Services at Kolkata

Kolkata has an extensive network of Government-run and privately run buses. Also there are multiple organizations running buses, a private Organisation and multiple government services like CSTC (Calcutta State Transport Corporation), CTC (Calcutta Tramways Company), WBSTC (West Bengal Surface Transport Corporation) etc. There are also various types of privately run buses. The privately owned buses are quite typical of Kolkata. The private-owned buses are of two types, the regular ones and the mini-buses. The regular buses are coloured light-blue and yellow. The mini-buses are of brown and yellow colour and contain lesser number of seats. The mini-buses were started in the late seventies as a relief for the office commuters from the overloaded buses by being a sitting-only service, but this has given way to severely overloaded and crowded mini buses (and other buses too), largely due to the massive population-hike of Kolkata. The Government buses are run by several authorities like Calcutta State Transport Corporation (CSTC), South Bengal State Transport Corporation (SBSTC), North Bengal State Transport Corporation (NBSTC), West Bengal Surface Transport Corporation (WBSTC) and the Calcutta Tramways Company (CTC). Government buses have no colour code and can be identified only by the appropriate symbols (CSTC or CTC or WBSTC) on their body. Both the name of the place where the bus is going to, as well as the name of the place where its route originated is mentioned on the bus and that makes it easy to identify the source and destination of the bus. On the Route Board of the Private and Mini Buses that ply through (via) stoppages, clear route-lists are kept mentioned. Recently air-conditioned buses have been introduced by the WBSTC. These buses connect places like the Airport, Santragachchi (a station on the Howrah-Kharagpur railway line) and Tollygunge. The road network in Kolkata is vast. Long distance buses starting from Kolkata to various places like Bakkhali, Digha, Siliguri and other cities originate from the central bus depot at Dharmatala (popularly known as

Esplanade) and sophisticated Volvo buses are also found there but their fare is pretty high. Under Jawaharlal Nehru National Urban Renewal Mission, air conditioned buses have been included as a part of travel comfort to commuters. Air-conditioned buses are operated by WBSTC through outsourcing. These buses are served by Tata Marcopolo Buses and Volvo Low Floor Buses. A Bus Rapid Transit System (BRTS) corridor that's under construction from Ultadanga to Baishnabghata-Patuli is having a dedicated two-lane corridor for buses and the existing six-lane road will be widened more in future to eight to ten lanes in order to accommodate passengers from this huge urban corridor. Big-budget flyovers are being constructed over the major intersections. Some of the works are already completed.

4.6 Renovations in Trams

Kolkata is the one and only city in whole India to have a tram network (Marlok, 1978). Trams are under the administration of the Company, a Government of West Bengal Undertaking, popularly called CTC. The trams are claimed to slow down other traffic, leading to groups who currently voice abolishing the trams. But the eco-friendliness and the old charm of the trams attract many people still today. The tram lines laid in some major roads are being renovated to a great extent in order to maintain the tram lines on the same level plane as the rest of the road, thereby smoothening the road. In places, the original central boulevards reserved only for the trams have been removed totally; the tram-lines are thus brought in the same plane as that of the road. The usable space of the road for vehicular movement has thereby been considerably increased. With embedding of tram tracks in the road surface, the overall surface has become smoother, easing the traffic to some extent. With the tracks now running in the centre of the heavy traffic roads, commuters are encountering difficulties in getting to the trams' stops through the traffic and as a result, less number of people is able to use the tram easily. Government of West Bengal has promised to look after the matter by issuing some strict orders for the track-drivers so that they obey the traffic rule properly but no concrete step has been taken yet legally. Mostly trams are found to be running with many seats vacant even during rush hours. This has also caused reduction of revenue for Calcutta Tram Company. One possible remedy towards difficulty of approachability to the trams could be to relay the tracks on outside left and the right sides of the road, adjacent to the footpaths. However, relaying the tracks as a whole is not possible right now and it will take some times as the modification will need enormous expenditure. Very recently the CTC has structured some new trams which look like elongated glass-tubes. Currently, some trams have been completely renovated to world-class standards with front and back glasses, fluorescent lights, Frequency-Modulations radio, digital display boards, slanted seats and a fiberglass ceiling. More renovated trams are planned from 2015 onward and the Nonapukur workshop has manufactured 19 brand new-look trams, of which four are finalized for regular movement on road. The rooftop is of clear polycarbonate sheeting with a wide window space, comfortable seating and better visibility from inside and out. An air-conditioned tram is popular, which will use more sophisticatedly an M-and-G system. These innovative plans through different Medias have already attracted commuters and foreign tourists in Kolkata. Nonapukur Workshop is now manufacturing new tram cars and renovating existing steel-body tram cars. Currently-manufactured tram cars in the CTC workshop are now comparable favorably with those of other developed countries. In addition to passenger cars, there are also rail-scrubber cars (which polish the tracks using jets of water), flat cars for goods transportation (some of which are modified from obsolete single-coach Howrah-trams) and a tower-inspection car for checking wires.

4.7 New looks in Taxis The Popular Para-transit Mode

The metered-cabs in Kolkata city are mostly of the brand 'Ambassador' manufactured by Hindustan Motors. Once in a while, one or two Maruti Omnies and Tata Indigo can be seen painted in yellow on the roadway of the city. Recently, air-conditioned cabs (known as 'Blue-Arrow') and maroon cabs (running on compressed natural gas or CNG) have been introduced. The meters - though digital - are generally out-of-date and there is a conversion chart to refer to while converting the meter-reading to the actual fare. But recently ORIX Auto Infrastructure Services Ltd. has introduced an air-conditioned Radio Taxi service in Kolkata with the name 'Kolkata Cab' with fleets consisting of Indigo Marina only, which has gained popularity among the city dwellers because it has comfortable seats, Global Positioning System monitoring, digital tamper-proof meters, receipt printers and lost-and-found facilities. Mega Cabs are also there with the same facilities. Some other Radio Taxis to ply into the city are Easy Cabs and Meru Cabs. For last a few years, the Ola and Uber Cab services have become widely popular amongst the urbanites of Kolkata and with the app downloaded from Google Play-store they are booking large number of cabs in Kolkata at different points of time in a day. These services are more or less reliable and not that much pocket-pinching.

4.8 Light Rail Transit System (LRTS) in Kolkata

The proposal for a light rail transit system on elevated tracks for Kolkata is being pursued by the Government of West Bengal, but it is still on drawing board mostly. Kolkata Light Rail Transit System (LRTS) is again a mass rapid transit system proposed for the city of Kolkata in India. The West Bengal Government and SREI Infrastructure Finance have signed a memorandum of understanding (MoU) to set up the light rail transit (LRT) system. A special purpose vehicle, Kolkata Mass Rapid Transit Pvt. Ltd. has been formed to execute this 6000/- crore project. In February 2009, The LRTS project was listed under JnNURM. It is now to be jointly executed by SREI and the Czech-based AMEX Corporation on a Build-Operate-Transfer (BOT) basis. It is also decided to make the LRTS station at Barrackpore- a terminal point connecting it with the main line station. Mr.

Hemant Kanoria, Chairman and Managing Director of SREI Infrastructure Limited have signed very recently a MoU with the Government of West Bengal to execute this project in an urgent basis along with their consortium partners.

4.9 Some new alterations in Rickshaws and Auto-rickshaws

Rickshaws pulled by men and auto rickshaws are common place At Kolkata. Many migrants from Bihar and rural Bengal are involved in Rickshaw pulling. Rickshaws are also on the list of probable abolishment in Kolkata on humanitarian grounds. In southern Kolkata, the rickshaws pulled by men have been replaced remarkably by cycle rickshaws. Fares are usually set by the rickshaw unions and are quite reasonable. These rickshaws usually operate over short and semi-long distances due to the manual effort involved, and mainly run on narrow lanes where buses and auto-rickshaws don't ply. Auto-rickshaws have become a very common para-transit mode for short distances. They are usually not metered, and are usually shared in Kolkata. There are several routes and the auto-rickshaws of a particular route ply between two distinct places of that route only. Auto rickshaws can accommodate 3 people in the backseat, and one passenger in front beside the driver legally. The fares are usually quite low in comparison with other metro cities like Delhi and Mumbai. In the year of 2009, CNG auto-rickshaws were supposed to be introduced in the city of Kolkata but a Division Bench of the Calcutta High Court ordered in August-2009 that only four-stroke auto-rickshaws running on liquid petroleum gas (LPG) will be allowed to ply on Kolkata's roads. So the old-fashioned two and three-stroke auto-rickshaws had to be withdrawn from the city-road.

4.10 Some Changes in Air and Water Transport

Kolkata airport (previously known as Dum Dum airport and now famous as the Netaji Subhash Chandra Bose International Airport or CCU) has undergone a period of modernization, resulting in the commercial operation of a

233,000 m2 (2,510,000 sq. ft.) integrated terminal in March 2013. Commercial operations were intended to start on 23rd January 2013, the 116th birth anniversary of Netaji Subhash Chandra Bose. However, the shift to the new terminal was supposed to be completed on recent 16th of March but still slight tasks are pending. The Netaji Subhash Chandra Bose International Airport (CCU) at Dum Dum is the only airport in the city, operating both domestic and international flights. It is a gateway to North-East India, Bangkok and Bangladesh. The number of people using the airport has consistently increased over the last few years. There is a flying club in the city venued at Behala. After several years of inactivity, it has recently been restored from 2012. Kolkata is also a major port and is standing together with the Haldia dock systems. The Kolkata Port Trust has been amongst top performers in the country. Kolkata Port has regular passenger services to Port Blair from the Netaji Subhash Docks. Also the twin cities or better known as Sister towns namely Kolkata and Howrah are connected by local water ferries through the extensive ghats like Fairly Ghat, Howrah Ghat, Shibpore Ghat, Princep Ghat, Cossipore Ghat etc. Small boats are used here for recreational purposes. There are plans in the pipeline to begin utilizing the canals running through the city as water-transport network. The first service has been started from September 2006 - and will cover fully the Belgachhiya-Lake Town stretch of Keshtopur Canal.

4.11 Make-over of Flyovers in Kolkata

Flyovers are easily the most visible symbol of development, often considered to be the new temples of modern India. Kolkata, despite a slow start, is in the grip of feverish activity as a host of new flyovers are being built, aimed at reducing congestion and ensuring smoother flow of traffic. In a city like Kolkata, where road space has dwindled to only six percent and traffic volume is increasing with every passing day, flyovers are considered to be the panacea for all traffic problems. A flyover is an elevated road at a junction with different streams of traffic creating congestion, signals and traffic round abouts. Initially, Kolkata had very few flyovers compared to Delhi or Hyderabad, one of the earliest being the flyover at Sealdah, followed by Brabourne Road and Jadavpur. However, then came a long lull primarily due to lack of funds. But the Japanese came to our rescue and the Japan Bank for International Cooperation funded the flyovers at Gariahat, Park Street and AJC Bose Road. All three came under fire since none of them had arms at the beginning and were practically road over-bridges, thereby offering only a partial solution to traffic ills. In recent years, the city has witnessed a flurry of construction and thanks go to central funds made available through the Jawaharlal Nehru National Urban Renewal Mission.

A large number of flyovers are being built for improving traffic flow in the city. Work has been completed for a couple of flyovers like the one at Parama Island on EM Bypass or at the Main Arterial Road (MAR) in Rajarhat connecting Kolkata city while regular maintenance is going on in full swing for the flyover linking Nazrul Islam Sarani (VIP Road) and EM Bypass. The other flyovers of Kolkata that have been renovated after 2006 include canal south road flyover, Barabazar Flyover, Park Street flyover, Taratala Flyover, Khiderpoor flyover and Race-course interchange.

4.12 Burning Problems of Transport in Kolkata

Before implementation of Transport-renewal plan under JnNURM, the Kolkata Metropolitan Development Authority has chalked out the most alarming transport-issues in Kolkata. According to KMDA, Transport planning and transport investment in all the cases, must contain some purposes which must be clearly identified and reflected through the view points of different nodal agencies and Non-Government Organizations. KMDA has started adopting some fruitful measures to fight against the current transport-malaises in the city. These maladies incorporate a) high rate of air pollution, b) raising noise-level by indiscriminate use of vehicular horns, c) shortage of further space for future development, problems of safety and security, d) discomfort for pedestrians and cyclists; e) occupancies of payements by hawkers, f) preponderance of cars and lorries on the roads and these are hindering the journeys accomplished by walking and cycling; g) non-preference of those modes of transport that are of zero pollution on the streets (e.g. the tram); h) tremendous traffic-congestion on routes to schools, hospitals, workplaces etc. i) frequent occurrence of road-accidents, j) high amount of total energy consumption through fossil-fuel combustion, k) insufficient amount of green space in urban arena of the city (Mitra,1996). Targets have already been set as well as quantified in terms of extrapolation of the progress-rate which is expected to become prominent over a pre-defined time period. For example it is possible and desirable to plan to reduce particulate pollution (black smoke) in Kolkata by 10% (or more) each year for the next 6-7 years until a minimum level is achieved.

4.13 Recent Initiatives to Solve Some These Problems

Recently in Kolkata, some positive measures have been taken into consideration to alleviate the menace of traffic congestion and frequent road-accidents and these steps include– a) Marking the roadsides with yellow colour, where no vehicle are permitted to park or load and unload people or goods and these are near all crossings. In those marked areas, any parking will be spot-fined; b) Right hand turn at major and high flow crossings should not be allowed and such turns preferably will be at T crossings and must not be at four road crossings; c) All major traffic flow roads will be devoid of any legal space for big and small vehicular parking and only on roads connecting to main road, there will be provision of single row parking only; d) All big Market areas or shopping malls must have parking space created compulsorily and preferably at their basements, otherwise they are asked to follow the design of new market; e) All goods' movement should be at night strictly from 10:30 pm to 7:30 am (Kundu,1999).

1.14 Urban Infrastructure and Governance (UIG) under JnNURM

The Asian Green City Index (AGCI) was a study conducted by Siemens in the year of 2005-2010 and performed by the Independent Economist Intelligence Unit (EIU). According to that Index, Kolkata is one of the 22 major cities of Asia having been studied based on some specific transport-indicators for framing some development strategies in transport sector. Despite having the third longest transport system among the cities selected in Asia, Kolkata is well below the average level in the transport category. Kolkata is all set to receive benefit from the green initiative as the Jawaharlal Nehru National Urban Renewable Mission is undertaking ten projects under Urban Infrastructure and Governance Scheme that are aimed at reducing traffic congestion in the city. This US$194 million project will incorporate construction of new flyovers, bypasses and interchanges throughout the city's urban panorama. India's first underground railway, the Kolkata metro, was said to be extended upto Howrah as a green transport initiative under transport-renewal. This construction is funded by the Kolkata metro rail corporation and was due to be completed by October, 2014. Another praiseworthy initiative is the Kolkata monorail that has been designed to ease traffic congestion. The completion of this project is not yet confirmed. Under Sub-Mission for Urban Infrastructure and Governance of JnNURM in Kolkata, till date about 227 DPR have been received and 79 have been approved after examination. Projects valued at approximately 4,430/- crore are under various stages of implementation. Content and quality of DPRs received vary considerably and the cases of inadequately or hastily prepared submissions have resulted in rework, delay, and wastage of time. To address this situation, the Mission Directorate has put together a DPR Preparation Toolkit. This document provides reference guidelines for preparing good quality project report. Since specific details required in any DPR would vary by sector and specific project conditions; it is re-emphasized that the Toolkit may be regarded as a reference document that advocates minimum information requirements. Project planning team/ urban local bodies/parasternal need to ensure that all additional information deemed important to make the project report complete in all financial and technical aspects and those are included in the DPRs forwarded. This will facilitate early appraisal, approval, and movement towards project implementation. Total 53 projects of UIG have been sanctioned for KMA whereas the share of KMC in it is fifteen only.

4.15 Major Transport-renewal Projects of Urban Infrastructure and Governance in Kolkata

Total ten projects for transport renewal, four projects for sanitation and sewerage renewal and one project for heritage renewal have been sanctioned in Kolkata under UIG Scheme of JnNURM. All the transport projects have been mentioned in a tabular format already and herein the vivid description and analyses of those projects are given

4.16 Flyover between EM Bypass and Kazi Nazrul Islam Sarani

In fringe areas of Kolkata, flyovers are being constructed to ease traffic problems. For instance, one major flyover has been constructed on VIP Road (Nazrul Islam Sarani). This EM Bypass-VIP Road Flyover which saw a number of deadlines being overshot resulting in cost escalation, is finally inching towards completion to the fullest fruition along with proper as well as continuous maintenance. The Eastern Metropolitan Bypass, or simply E.M. Bypass, is a major road on the east side of Kolkata that connects Bidhannagar on the northeast to southern parts (Kamalgazi) of Kolkata.

It was designed like a bypass or beltway on the eastern side of Kolkata to lessen the perennial traffic congestion on the entire stretch of Gariahat Road. Subsequent to the construction of this road, several connectors have been built to connect Gariahat Road to the EM Bypass to deviate traffic away from the Gariahat Road. This, along with moving significant parts of public and private offices to Bidhannagar is deemed necessary to maintain the future growth of Kolkata. Starting from the northern hub of Ultadanga to Kamalgazi in the south, the road runs a distance of 21 km along the eastern rim of the city and is one of the most important roads of the metropolis, and can be described as one of its economic lifelines. Plans are currently underway to extend the road up to the Falta Export Processing Zone (FEPZ) on the Hooghly River.

The Falta Export Processing Zone is of paramount significance from economic value as well as revenue earning of the State of entire West Bengal and that's why profound thrust has been given regarding the ideal execution of this particular Transport Renewal Project. A greenfield SEZ is also proposed to be developed at Kulpi (next to the proposed port). The Falta SEZ has been in operations since 1985, with a developed area of 233 acres. Any goods and services exported out of, or imported into, or procured from the Domestic Tariff Area by, a Unit in the Special Economic Zone or a Developer will subject to certain terms, conditions and limitations as prescribed in Rule 22, Chapter IV of SEZ Rules,

EM Bypass–Kazi Nazrul Islam Sarani Flyover

be exempted the targets from the payment of taxes, duties or cess.

FUND-SHARING IN RUPEES CRORES FOR FLY-OVER-CONSTRUCTION BETWEEN E.M BYPASS AND KAZI NAZRUL ISLAM SARANI

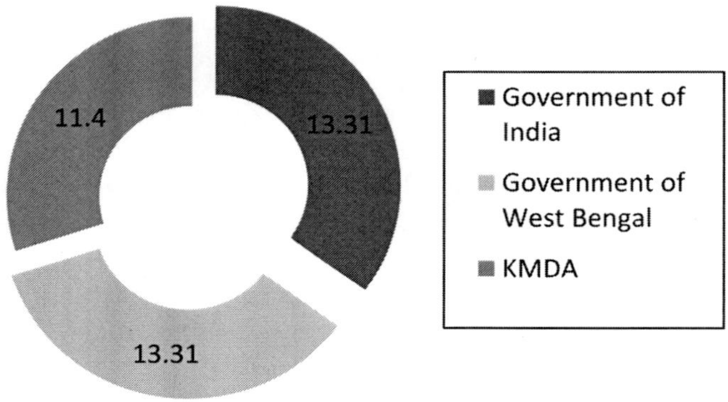

The main proposed impacts of the construction of this flyover includes removal of congestion at Ultadanga crossing and smooth flow of traffic between EM Bypass and Kazi Nazrul Islam Sarani, better flow of traffic between the central business district and North Eastern part of KMA as part of futuristic traffic master plan of area. Traffic route along North Eastern part of KMA is planned to be served by this project and entire population of KMA will be extremely benefitted after the finishing of this project. Here the major components of the scheme include construction of a four-lane Flyover including approaches with flexible pavements involving a) Bored Cast in situ piles, b) M-35 and higher grade reinforced concrete substructures and superstructures, c) Fabrication and erection of structural steel, d) Wet mix Macadam over granular sub base, e) Bituminous work, Mastic Asphalt, f) Illumination arrangement and other allied works etc. Here the approved project cost is 38.02/- crore that is shared by different bodies and the pattern of sharing is also very interesting. Here the maximum fund has been shared equally by Government of India and Government of West Bengal whereas KMDA has taken the remainder.

4.17 Vivekananda Road Flyover (Phase-I) from Howrah Bridge to Chitta Ranjan Avenue

The 2.2km long Vivekananda Road Flyover will connect Howrah Station with Girish Park at a cost of 153.60/- crore which is proposed to be completed in 18 months' time. Its work is in progress at a remarkably faster pace. The likely impacts of this project encompass removal of the traffic congestion at Posta Bazar and Girish Park from Rabindra Setu (Howrah Bridge). Posta Bazar, Nimtala Street and Girish Park areas are being served by this project and all the vehicular traffic in the region are extremely benefitted after execution of the project. Its major components are a) Construction of RCC Columns, b) Construction of Steel Girder and RCC Beams with Deck Slabs, c) Electrification and installation of Road furniture etc. Here the mammoth share of the fund has been shouldered equally by Government of India and West Bengal whereas the remainder is carried forward by KMDA. In the satellite image-view collected from the platform of goggle-earth, the total extension of the Vivekananda road flyover has been shown.

Proposed Vivekananda Road Flyover

4.18 Flyover at Nager Bazar on Jessore Road

In another fringe area of the city, a big-budget flyover has been constructed to ease traffic problems. Here the flyover is built-up at Nager Bazar-Jessore Road intersection. The major impacts of the construction of this flyover include a) Removal of traffic congestion at Nager Bazar with better traffic flow towards and away from airport, b) improvement of traffic flow from NH 34 to Barrackpore Trunk Road and Dum Dum railway station. The area near crossing of NH 34

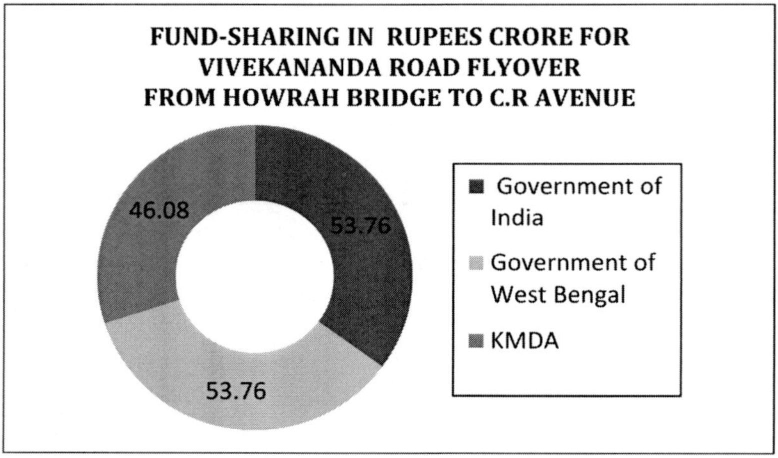

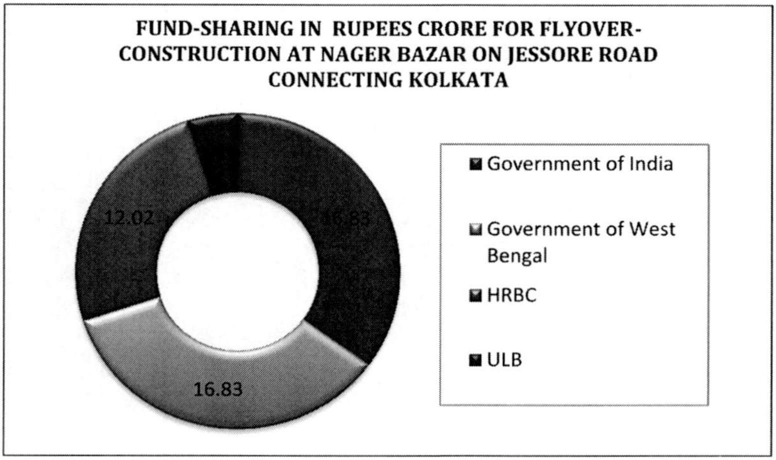

and Dum Dum Road has become congestion-free after the project and the entire vehicular traffic at this important junction is served by the flyover. Here the major components of flyover-construction encompass a) Construction of RCC Columns, b) building of Steel Girders, RCC beams and deck slabs and c) electrification and installation of Road furniture. Here the fund-sharing bodies are four and the mammoth share is divided by the Central and the State Government whereas HRBC (Hooghly River-bridge Commissioners) is sharing 12.02 crores rupees and urban local body's share is 2.41 crore rupees.

4.19 Flyover from Parama to Park-Circus

Among the proposed flyovers, the most significant is the one at Parama Island connecting Park Circus with EM Bypass. It is the new link between the Central Business District and the northern part of the Kolkata Metropolitan Area aimed at accommodating the high growth of traffic of one lakh vehicles per day. It is easily the longest flyover in the city stretching over 4.32 km. Initially, the cost was estimated to be 291.66 crore rupees but was revised ultimately to 317.93 crore rupees in view of price escalation. The flyover is of two tiers at Parama Intersection off Science City, one in the

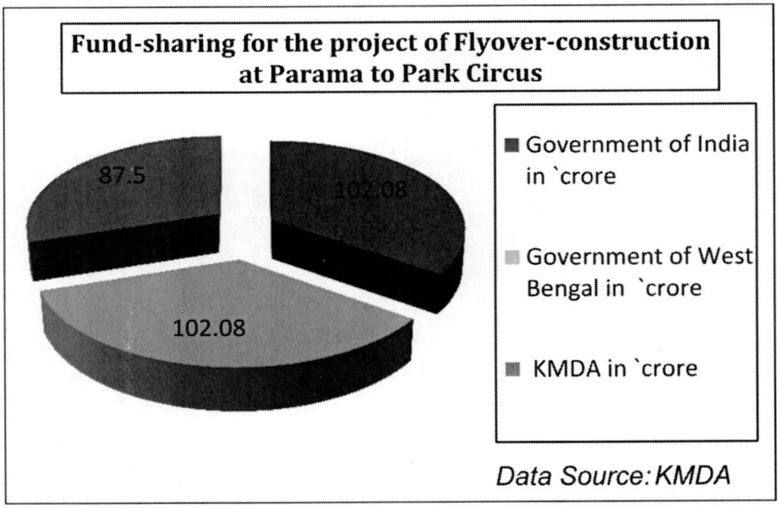

north to south direction with ramps towards Salt Lake and Garia while the other in east-west direction, ending at Park Circus rotary, only a few metres away from the AJC Bose Road Flyover. The flyover is of a four lane one with a median in between. The flyover is a component of a bigger design to ensure smooth traffic flow for airport bound vehicles from south. The EM Bypass has also been widened to six-lane for the same purpose. Pre-construction work for the flyover has just begun. Here the proposed elevated corridor acts as a new city link between the central business district of Kolkata and the Northern part of KMA. It accommodates very high growth of traffic, estimated at one lakh vehicles per day. EM Bypass, Park Circus connector and Park Circus seven point crossing-these areas is being covered by the project. All the vehicular traffic in the region are benefitted a lot .The major components include here construction of RCC Columns, Construction of Steel Girders, RCC Beams and Deck Slabs and Electrification and installation of Road furniture. Here the major fund-sharing load is on the Central and the State Government. The rest is taken by KMDA.

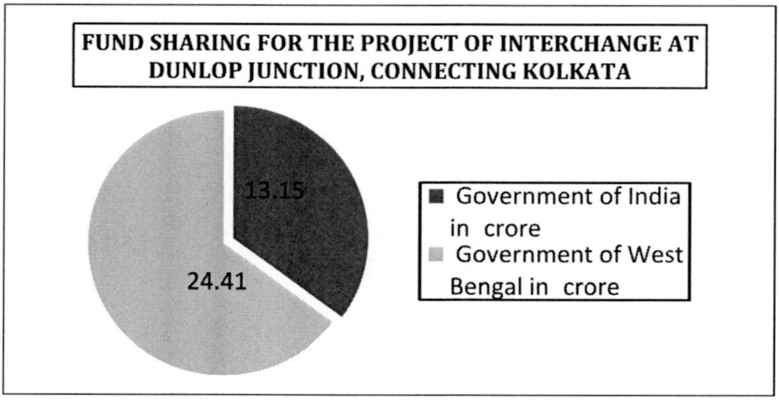

4.20 EM Bypass Connector from Padmapukur to Kamalgazi

One gigantic EM Bypass connector is constructed from Padmapukur to Kamalgazi. The likely impact is to improve connectivity to NH 117 through Baruipur Amtala Road providing better access to Diamond Harbour and proposed

Kulpi port. Area from Kamalgazi to Baruipur is being covered here and South 24 Parganas bound traffic from Kolkata along the EM Bypass is greatly benefitted by this project. For this project, the major components are road work upto stone metal consolidation, fixing precast concrete boundary pillar, bank protective work and allied works, desiltation and lining work, afforestation etc. Here the approved cost is 53.10 and it is shared amongst the Central and State Government along with KMDA. The highest share is for the Central and State Government.

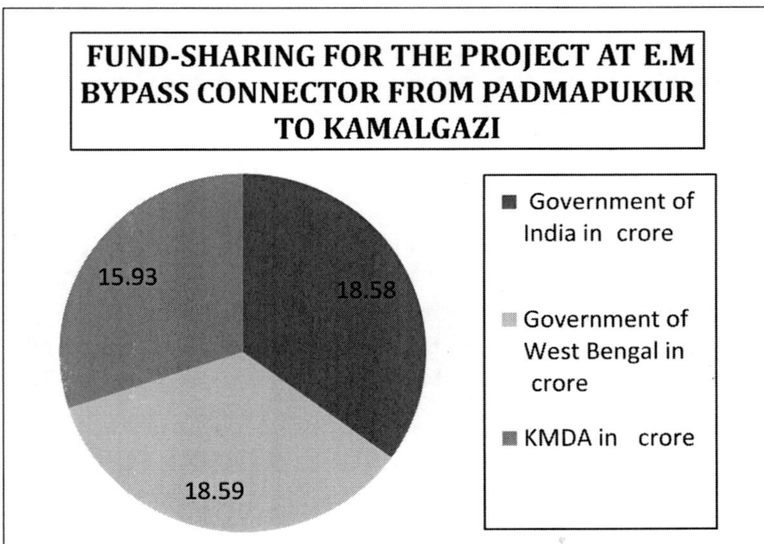

4.21 Construction of Left Turning North Bound Off-ramp at Beckbagan Connecting AJC Bose Road Flyover

In a typical example of short sightedness of the town-planners, there was no provision for north bound vehicles to access the AJC Bose Road Flyover to reach Beckbagan. Now, a left turning north bound ramp is being added to the AJC Bose Road Flyover, seven years after it was built. The construction throws traffic haywire causing immense hardships to commuters since there are a number of schools and office buildings on the stretch. The estimated cost is about 18.06 crore rupees while it has taken 15 months to be ready. The ramp will ease congestion at Shakespeare Sarani -Mallick Bazar crossing and facilitate Beck Bagan bound traffic to use the flyover as well, in future also. Its main goal is the Removal of traffic congestion at the junction of Shakespeare Sarani and Mallick Bazar with AJC Bose Road Flyover. AJC Bose Road, Shakespeare Sarani and Beck Bagan area are benefitted by this project. All the vehicular traffic in the region stand blessed after the construction of the entire project. Major components for this work include foundation (RCC Pile), steel Column, steel Girder installation for supportive Deck slab and construction of RCC Deck slab. Here the mammoth share is taken by the State Government whereas the least share is shouldered by the GoI.

4.22 Construction of Interchange at Dunlop Junction of Kolkata

It will provide traffic dispersal facilities a lot in future also to meet the need of the increased volume of traffic due to development of 6 lane Barrackpore Trunk Road and Nivedita Setu as also the Belgharia Expressway. The Barrackpore Trunk Road and the approach to Nivedita Setu

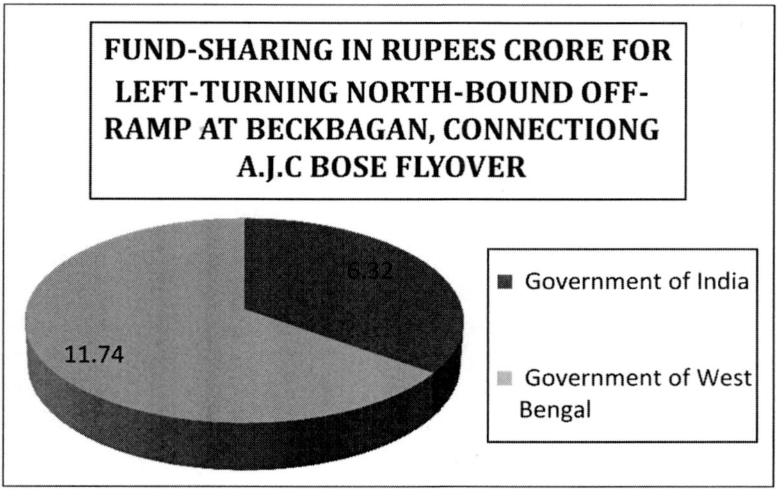

Data Source: KMDA

crossing with the connector to Belgharia Expressway are fully covered by this project. About 1.10 Lakh passenger car units are served per day by this project. Major Components here are bored cast-in-situ piles, RCC Column, Steel Girder and RCC Beams and RCC Deck Slabs. Here the total project cost is 37.56 crore rupees and the highest share is for the GoWB. And the GoI is shouldering the financial load just less than half of the share of West Bengal Government.

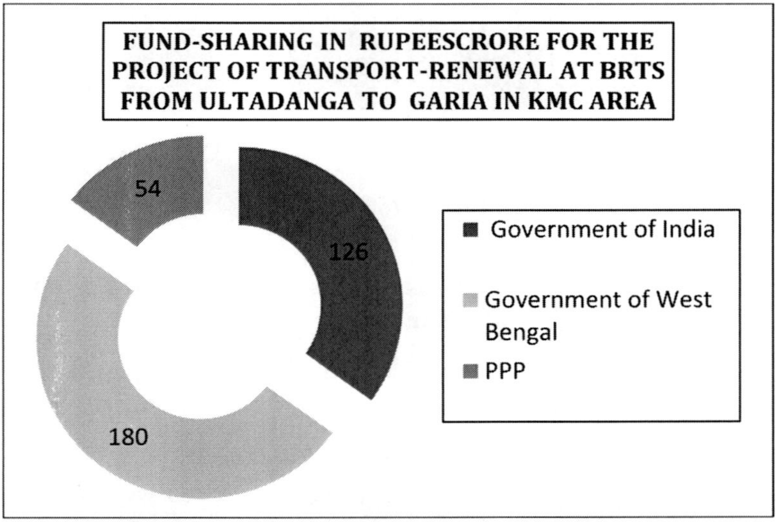

4.23 BRTS from Ultadanga to Garia in Kolkata Metropolitan Area

This bus rapid transit system bestows immense benefit to all the commuters of the city and the entire city-area of KMC with special reference to South Kolkata gets covered by this very project. The likely impacts include easing of Road transport facilities in the city with higher comfort level and setting of new standard in modern transport of the city. Major Components of the project encompass procurement of buses as per specification, route planning, leasing out to operators and starting bus operations in a systematized manner. This is actually a sister-project of the construction of recent Ultadanga Flyover.

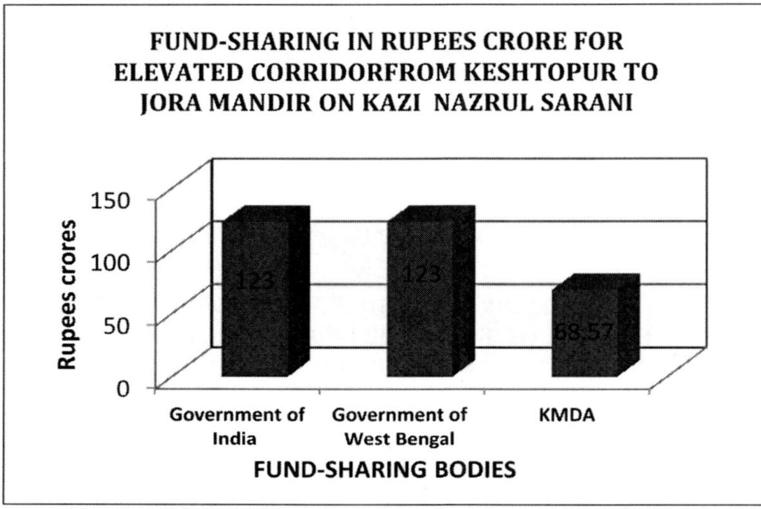

4.24 Elevated Corridor from Keshtopur to Jora Mandir on Kazi Nazrul Islam Sarani

This project is a very big-budget project and after completion to the fullest fruition of this work, the huge

Ultadanga Flyover

Source: KMC

population of the entire city will be benefitted a lot and more than one lakh passenger car units will be served per day. Here from the point of view of entire fund-sharing, it can be said that the main fund-load has been shared equally by the Central and the State Government whereas the remainder is paid by KMDA and the amount payable for this nodal agency is 68.57 crore rupees.

4.25 Four-lane Flyover at Kamalgazi Intersection on E.M Bypass connector near starting point of Adi Ganga

This project is a big-shot project for South Kolkata and after completion to the fullest fruition of this project, the real estate value of South Kolkata will be escalated a lot. Here the highest share has com from the Central Government and the second-highest fund-sharing has been accomplished by the Government of West Bengal. 19.16 crore rupees have been paid by KMDA.

4.26 Conclusion

In a nutshell, the overall spectrum of makeover the domain of Transport-sector at Kolkata city has explained above. There will be another ramp in near future that will be connecting the Nimtala Ghat Street totally as well. The flyover aims to help faster movement of Howrah bound traffic from north Kolkata. The flyover near Jadavpur Police Station on Raja SC Mallick Road has helped a lot to the commuters to get rid of traffic congestion due to the grim traffic situation on the stretch, especially after the opening of South City Mall and residential complexes (Oak, Maple, Cedar and Pine of South City) in the area. Kolkata Metropolitan Development Authority (KMDA) has initially prepared five alternative proposals. Under the current plan, the four lane flyover has begun at a distance of about 400 metres from Dhakuria Bridge near Jodhpur Park and continues to south along the Raja S.C. Mallick Road up to Sukanta Setu. The cost of the flyover is around 120 crore rupees and the Centre is supposed to provide around 35 per cent of the entire fund under JnNURM scheme while the private developers of the Mall are asked to chip in 20 per cent of the cost and the rest stands shared equally by KMDA, Kolkata Municipal Corporation (KMC) and the State Government.

Reference

Chaudhuri, S (1995), Calcutta: The Living City-Vol-II, Oxford University Press, USA.

Harvey, J.(1996): Urban Land Economics, Hounds mills Macmillan, USA.

Izard, W. (1956): Location and Space Economy, Cambridge, UK.

Ken worthy, J. and Felix, L. (2002): Urban Transport Patterns in a Global Sample of Cities and Their Linkages to their Infrastructure, Landuse, Economics and Environment, World Transport Policy and Practices, Oxford University Press, USA.

Kolkata Municipal Corporation (2005): Urban Renewal in the Kolkata Metropolitan Centre, Report No.l, Public Relations Section of KMPO, Kolkata.

Ibid (2008):Urban Renewal Programme in the Kolkata Metropolitan Centre, Report No.3, Public Relations Section of KMPO, Kolkata.

5

Geo-Cultural Study on Beach Tourism and its Prospects in Calangute Town, North Goa, India

Suity Ghosh

Abstract: The green paradise of India is Goa state a holiday maker's destination. Beautiful blue beaches, golden sands, flora and fauna, a lively nightlife and rich cultural heritage make Goa a premier universal tourist destination. The number of visitors to Goa between 2008-2012 nearly doubled, signifying the increasing appeal of the state. Annual air Traffic in Goa is predicted to reach a high of 2.4 million by 2014 and 4.6 million by 2024, almost a 50% increase. Foreign travellers very essential for Goan tourism. The number of foreigners arriving in Goa during the ongoing tourism season has come down by around 30% compared to 2018 due to reduction in frequency of chartered flights. Child sex tourism is threatening to become the darker side of life in Goa's tropical paradise and there is evidence that the Indian authorities are turning their back on the problem. Goa is in danger of replacing Bangkok as Asia's prime sex resort. The coasts have become the location of tourism that actually covers up things such as money laundering, drugs, prostitution, and trafficking of women, children, and workers. Behind the smiles of local people, a sense of uneasiness is creeping in as the state becomes more corrupt.

Former Post graduate student, Department of Geography & Applied Geography, Rammohunpur, Darjeeling. Email: ghoshsweety.slg@gmail.com

Keywords: *scenario of tourism, estimation of tourist arrivals, tourist accommodation units, analytical approach.*

5.1 Introduction

Goa is a tiny emerald land on the west coast of India. It is an all year round tropical paradise with the natural scenic beauty swaying palms, miles of golden sands, lush greenery, an incredible cultural heritage, magnificent churches, temples and monuments a unique cultural synthesis of East and West Goa, an erstwhile Portuguese colony, since its advancement from 1960's, has experienced a change in its social and economic sector. This has subsequently increased tourism activities in the State. Today, the State provides a variety of tourist activities but the most popular is beach tourism .There is more than 40 odd beaches spread over 110 kms. Coastline and more than 95% of the tourist prefer beach tourism. Today it is one of the most important sectors for employment and SDP. Tourism undoubtedly helps in economic enhancement but there is social and economic costing. Since the research is on socio- cultural impact due to tourism it is essential to focus on the same.

Goa is often referred to as the 'Perl of Orient' and is a 'Tourist Paradise'. Legends have it that Lord Parshwrama an incarnation of lord Vishnu has created Goa. On December 1961, Goa was liberated from the Portuguese clutches by Indian Army and made an Indian Union Territory. It attained statehood in 1987. (http://www.goatourism.gov.in)

5.2 Area of Study

Calangute

Goa is called as 'Place of Sand and Sea' and it is the paradise where Monsoon sky meets river, Lake and Sea. Goa is bounded on the north by the Terekhol river, surrounded on the south and east by Karnataka while on the west is the Arabian sea.

North Goa is one of the two districts that make up the state of Goa in India. The district has an area of 1736 km^2.

North Goa is mainly famous for beaches which include Anjuna Beach, Candolim Beach, Mandrem Beach, Calangute Beach, Morjim Beach, Arambol Beach and a few others.

Calangute is a town in North Goa, famous for its beach. The beach is the largest in North Goa and visited by thousands of domestic and international tourists alike. The

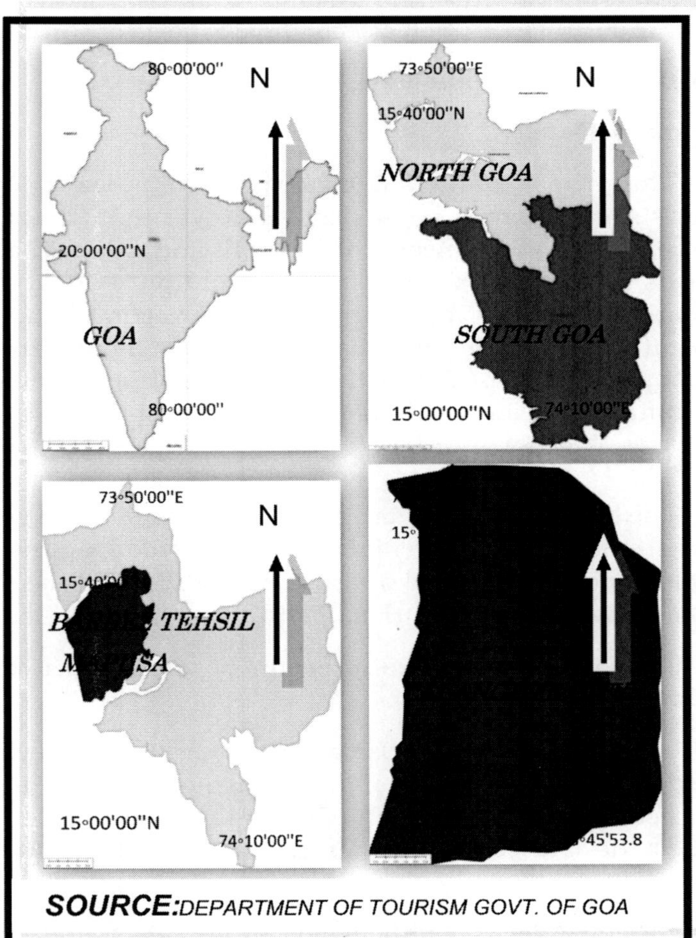

Fig. 1: Location of the Study Area

peak tourist season is during Christmas and New Year, (https://en.wikipedia.org/wiki/Calangute)

5.3 Objective of The Study

The major objectives of this research work are enumerated below:

1. To know hospitality of locals provided to visitors.
2. To identify the crimes related to coastal tourism of Goa.
3. To determine the relationship of tourism with other various social as well as economic aspects of Goa.

5.4 Database & Methodology

Primary Data

The primary data was generated from local people, tourists and through hotel visits. However the data based on perception about income of the locals and tourists, health status, age and sex structure, occupation, educational qualification, length of stay, types of accommodation, hospitality of locals, purpose of visit, ratings of hotels, recommendation of Goa, cab drivers, local officials, quality of traffic, connectivity of roads, life quality of Goa etc.

Secondary Data

The secondary data's are collected through office visits. The tourist map, various information about Goa, tourism leaflets and tourist arrival statistics from 2019-2020 I collected from Department of Tourism, Patto, Panajji, Goa.

The methodology adopted an be divided into the following parts:

5.4.1 Pre-field: In this phase general literature survey was carried out and collection of maps and questions for survey has been prepared. A structure questioner was prepared to collect the data from respondents, tourists and hotel owners or staff.

5.4.2 Field: As it is a difficult job to take each and every person as a respondent for primary survey so, simple random sampling was done to cope that problem. Some offices, departments were personally visited.

5.4.3 Post field: This stage involves computation of master table from the questioner, statistical applications, cartograms, drawing maps from secondary collections, digitization of maps, analyzing the data and information of the problems. Finally some strategies and initiatives are suggested for future of Goan tourism.

5.5 Tourism of Goa

Tourism

For almost three decades now GTDC (Goa Tourism Development Corporation) has been at the wheel of the tourism industry in Goa. GTDC reasonably literally has been the helmsman on board inviting and guiding tourists from the country and from abroad on an attractive and enlightening journey across the beautiful land of Goa. The North Goa is the main attraction centre of tourism industry which has a deep impact in lives of locals.

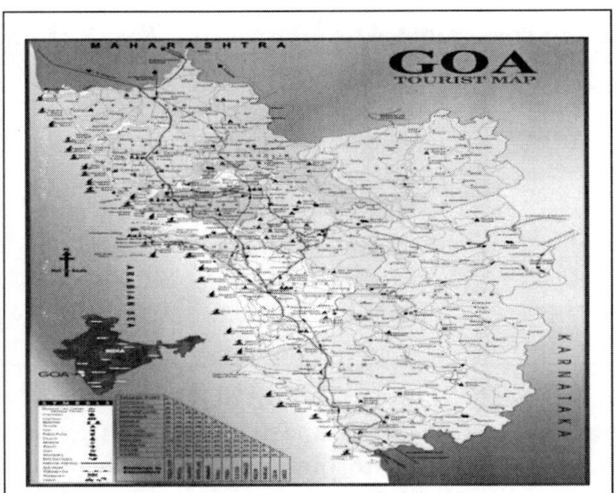

Fig. 2: Tourist Map of Goa

Source: Department of Tourism Govt. of India, Panaji

The emphasis on domestic tourism as a major driver of tourism growth is focused in the national tourism policy and also in the policy of the state of Goa. Goa is the only state after Kerala where beaches are the focal points of the tourism industry. It is for this reason that Goa is known as the beach country of India. The pearl of the east," Most of the tourism in Goa is concentrated in the coastal stretches of Bardez, Salcete, Tiswadi and Marmagao. Over 90 percent of domestic tourists and over 99 percent of the international tourists frequent these areas. (Collection of domestic tourism statistics for the state of Goa, 2005-2006)

5.5.1 Estimation of Tourist Arrivals

Two types of tourists visit Goa; the first is the domestic tourists, who comprise 80 percent of all tourists. The second is the international tourists who visit Goa purely for the natural environment of tropical climate. Within the category of international tourists there are two sub-categories: backpackers and charter tourists.

Table – 1

Domestic and Foreign Tourist Arrival Statistics

Calendar year	Domestic	Foreign	Total	Percentage
2012	2337499	450530	2788029	4.38
2013	2629151	492322	3121473	11.96
2014	3544634	513592	4058226	30.01
2015	4756422	541480	5297902	30.55
2016	5650061	680683	6330744	19.5
2017	6895234	890459	7785693	22.98
2018	7081559	933841	8015400	2.95
2019 (P) upto Aug	3706614	493820	4200434	100

Fig. 3 reveals that the amount of foreign tourists are far more less than domestic tourists, In 2018 it is 7081559 for domestic and 933841 for foreigners. There is a gap of 6147718 visitors. Foreign tourists are crucial for Goa as they spent 10-15 nights as compare to domestic tourists who spent only

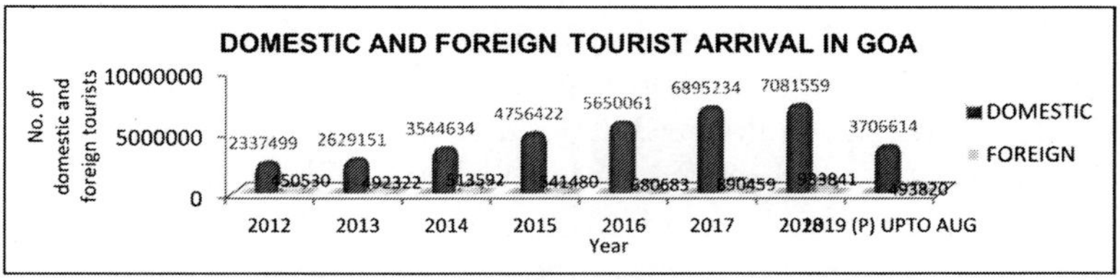

Fig. 3: Domestic and Foreign Tourist Arrival in Goa

Source: tourist arrival statistics, Department of tourism, Goa 2020

3-4 nights in Goa.

5.6 Analytical Approach on Tourism Activities in Calangute and Adjacent Area, Mapusa Municipality, Goa

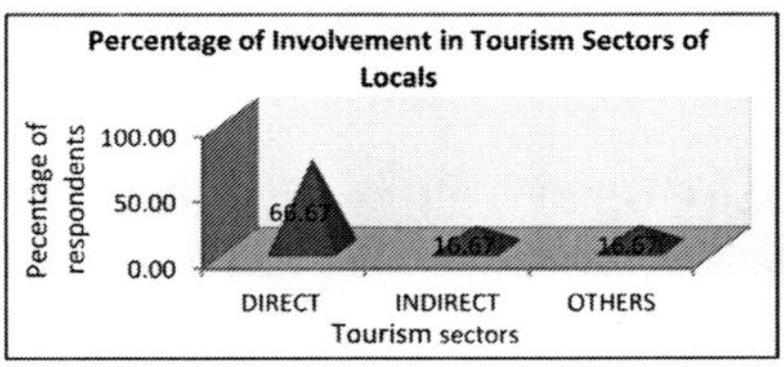

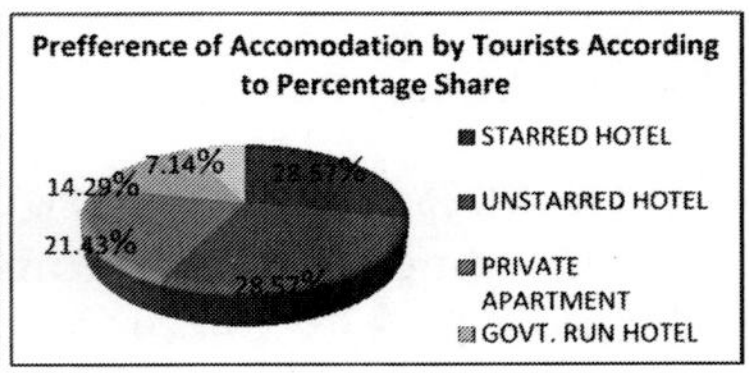

Fig. 4 **Fig. 5**

Source: Primary Data, 2020.

Fig. 4 shows Involvement in direct sector is highest among the respondents which are 66.67% and others are followed by it which is 16.67% only which makes the tourism sector stronger. Fig. 5 reveals equal numbers of visitors prefers starred and un-starred hotels which are 28.57%. Others recommend private apartment (21.43%), Govt. run hotel (14.29%), others (7.14%). So, the hotel industry is flourishing day by day in Goa.

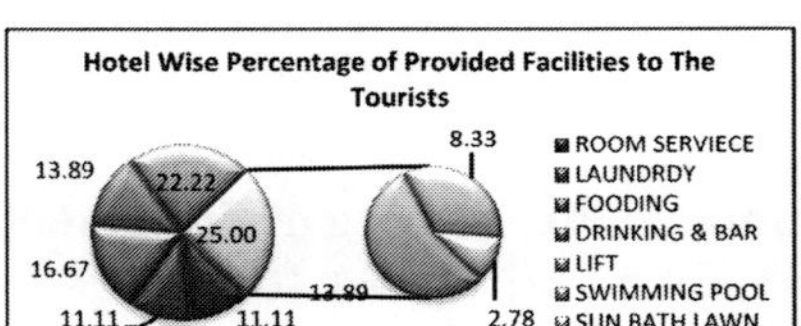

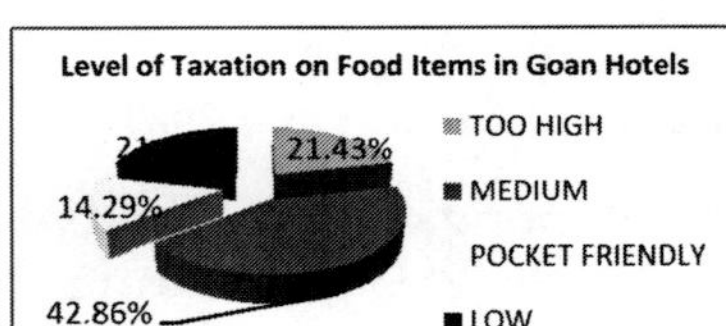

Fig. 6 **Fig. 7**

Source: Primary Data, 2020.

The fact lies in the wheel diagram of Fig. 6 lift is available in 22.22% hotels followed by food (16.67%), drinking and bar (13.89%), laundry and room service (11.11%), swimming pool (8.33%), sun bath lawn (2.78%) and others. In 42.86% hotels the taxation on food items is medium. Whereas in 21.43% hotels it is too high, in 14.43 % hotels it is low and in 14.29% hotels pocket friendly. That means 21.43% belongs to the royal class where the charges are higher than other hotels.

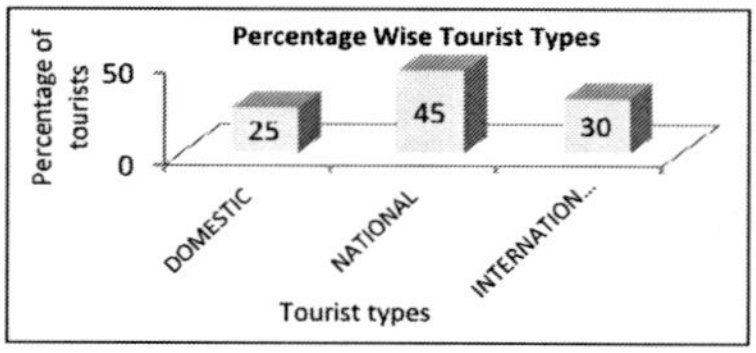

Fig. 8

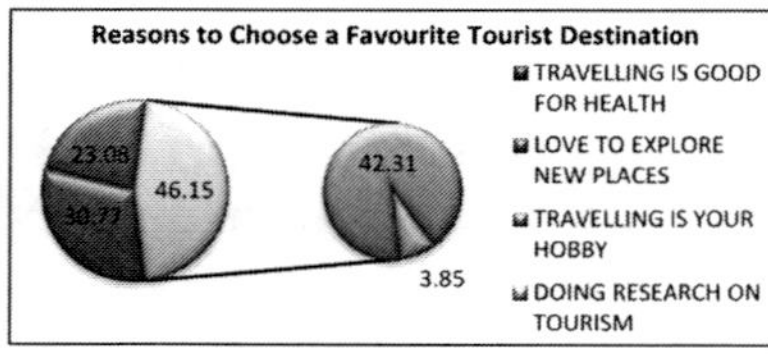

Fig. 9

Source: Primary Data, 2020.

In 50% tourists are national (Fig. 8), 30% are international, 20% are domestic. So, the tourism business of Goa is hugely depends upon national tourists, if due to any reason national tourist inflow decreases then the economy will collapsed. Tourists love to travel at their favorite destination as because travelling is health friendly, they want to explore new new places, some people have a hobby to travel etc. (Fig. 9)

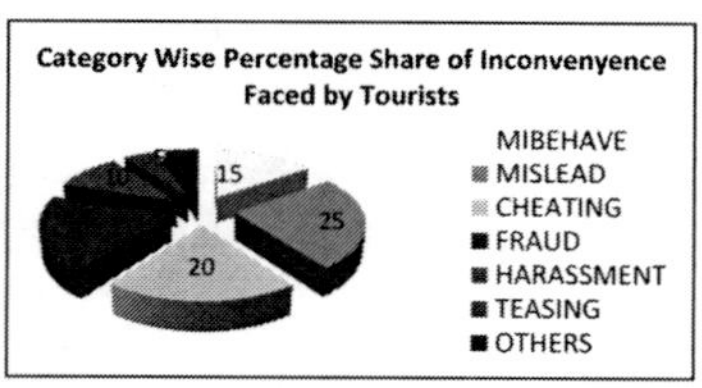

Fig. 10

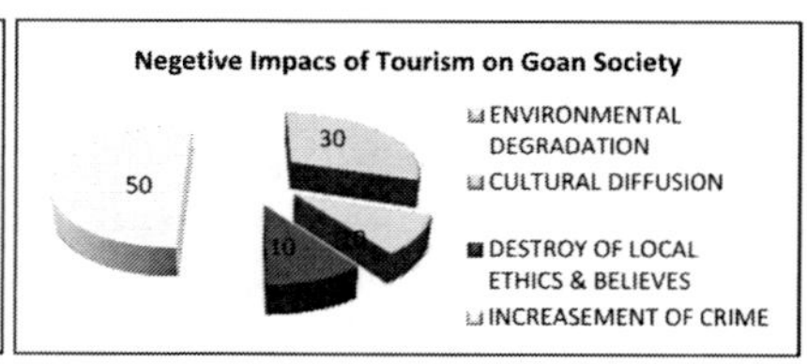

Fig. 11

Source: Primary Data, 2020.

Among various inconveniences the visitors mainly faced mislead (25%), cheating (20%), fraud (20%) followed by misbehave (15%), harassment (10%), others (5%). It is also noticeable that they rarely faced teasing (50%). So, Goan govt. should take actions against these things and also should look after the tourists and should assure them proper justice. So, from Fig. 11 that is observed among various negative impacts of tourism the severe problem is increasing of crime by 50% followed by environmental degradation by 30%, destroy local ethics and beliefs by 10%, cultural diffusion by 10%. It may be said that the govt. of Goa should take care the sector of crime as because due to incensement of this the popular is distorted among tourists.

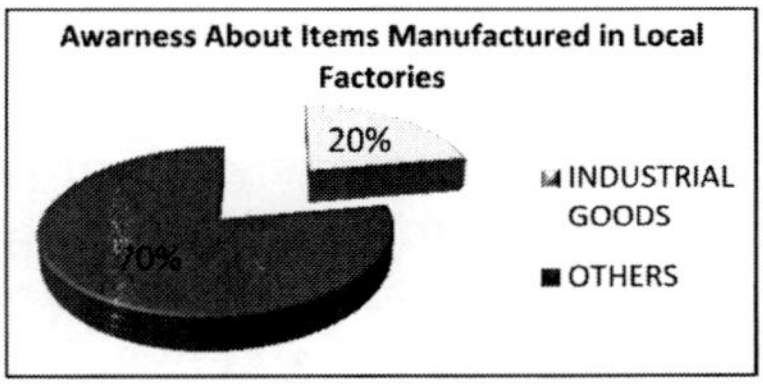

Fig. 12

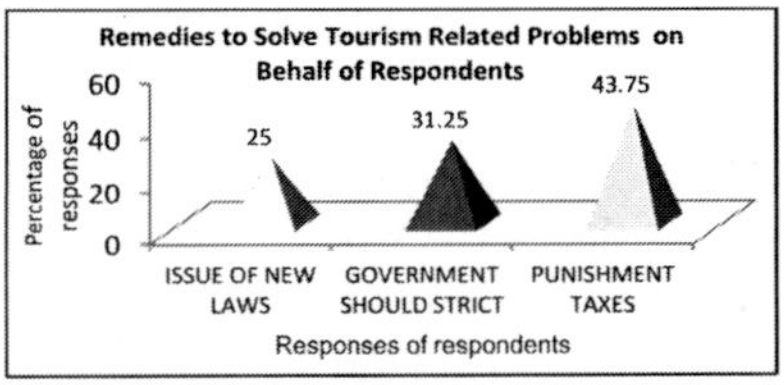

Fig. 13

Source: Primary Data, 2020.

The data reveals that (Fig. 12) only 20% industrial materials and 70% other items are manufactured in the local markets. The kaju is the most produced product of these factories. From Fig. 13 it is observed that 50% of inhabitants demands punishment laws to stop negativity of tourism upon their lives. 40% demands government should strict and rest of respondents demand issue of new laws only can change this. So, the government of Goa should take decisions on these demands on behalf of locals, at least they should hear the suggestions for remedies.

5.7 Findings of the Study

An observer had this to say as his narrative about tourism in Goa: '*Goa was a hippy paradise; the locals were friendly, the dope was cheap and the beaches were beautiful. Apart from bewildering the locals with their strange looks and behaviour, the hippies*' impact in Goa was minimal.

The study on Beach Tourism of Goa reveals various conclusions and findings which are discussed below:

- Condition of hotels where it is found that 42.86% of hotels are in too good condition, 35.71% are in average and 21.43% are in poor condition. Most of the visitors prefer the hotels which are between 1000-2000 Rs./day.

- In 25% cases tourists have to face misbehave. It creates bad image among the tourists. 45% tourist harassed by fraud and cheat but for them 57.14% hotels have complained forum and the hotel takes initiative within few hours. Top demanded dishes are sea food, king fish and Goan cuisine, approx 38% do not want to visit in near future may be the suffered from different inconveniences' in Goa.
- The market economy is indicator of good economic development of Goa which mainly runs upon younger people. 50% male, 20% female and 30% others are involved in market. Besides all business rental business is another type of popular source of earning money to the local community.
- Life style of Goan people is very smooth running except a little. Most of the money earning from tourism and other sectors government expenses on social development. The crime rate is decreased; development of hotel industry, nourishment of local economy is in progress. These are the major socio economic changes which are mainly observed besides connectivity development, heritage conservation, school and college development.
- Manufacturing industry is not increasing at a high rate. Cause of slower development of industries is urbanization, local employment, advancement and potentiality of tourism.

5.8 Problems of the Study

- Child trafficking is an organized racket, about which there is little concern. Stricter laws and implementation/ monitoring mechanisms are required to counter the growing problem before it reaches epidemic proportions.
- Sometimes the tourists are attacked by various undesirable things like harassment, molestation, sexual abbusement and so on.
- Child sex tourism is threatening to become the darker

side of life in Goa's tropical paradise - and there is evidence that the Indian authorities are turning their back on the problem.

- Crowded streets, large numbers of street vendors, and footpath eat-outs, increased traffic in the form of cars, scooters, and tourist buses, electricity failures, water shortages, growing crime, and in-migration leading to social tensions.
- With beaches providing attractive holiday possibilities, the rich and famous from major metropolises are beginning to invest in Goa with holiday homes/second homes and coastal urbanisation occurs.
- Very little profit reached the local people. The majority of the money spent by package tourists went to foreign hotel owners or the European tour companies who arrange the holidays.
- A major concern in Goa is the effect of western culture on the youth in Goa. A growing number of young Goans are taking drugs, going to trance parties (raves) and losing interest in their own culture and society.
- In the Baga-Nerul watershed on the North Goa coast, it was found that sewage is rarely treated. In 99% of low-budget, 100% of middle-budget, 89% of high-budget and 33% of luxury hotels, the sewage is being disposed of in soak-pits or tanks. Only 11% of the high-budget and 67% of the luxury hotels are able to treat their sewage in treatment plants.

5.9 Governmental Policies in the Study Area

- The Goa, Daman and Diu Registration of Tourist Trade Act, 1982 and Rules, 1985
- The Goa Tourist Places (Protection and Maintenance) Act, 2001.
- Tourism Policy for Erection of Temporary Seasonal Structures, Beach Shacks, Huts and Others, 2013-16.
- Policy for Regulation of Water sports in Goa.

- Other Regulatory/Policy Measures Impacting Tourism in 2003.
- The New Tourism Policy (2002).
- Tourism policy for erection of temporary seasonal structures, beach shacks, huts and others 2016-19

5.10 Concluding Observations

Goa is a part of our 'Incredible India' where churches are worship and wonder together, Majority of the crowded beaches are situated in North Goa though there are various beaches spread all over the Coastal Goa. Beach tourism is the center for flourishment of various footloose tourism industries such as marine tourism, water sports activity, eco tourism, Medical tourism etc. Now beside beach tourism Goa is famous for its sex tourism and various criminal activities are increasing at tremendous rate. When everything and anyone can be turned into a commodity, there is a greater chance for exploitation of vulnerable members of poor communities including children. Approximately 22 lakh tourists visit the small state of Goa from different part of the world annually. To accommodate the infow of tourist, buildings and huts are set up on the coastal area even violating CRZ regulations. The land is also sold to outsiders in order to set up huts and shacks on the coastal area in order to cater to the needs of the tourist. Local people mostly are involved in renting vehicles to the tourist for Rs. 150-250 per day.

References

BOOKS:

Census Hand book , 2011.

Chawla, Romila, "Sex Tourism and Development"; Sonali Publications, 2004, p. 57.

District Census Handbook, South Goa, Village and Town Directory, Directorate of Census Operations Goa.

Seth, Pran Nath, "Successful Tourism Management Vol. I:

Fundamentals of Tourism"; Sterling Publishers, 1999, p. 145.

Statistical Hand Book of Goa, 2016-17, Directorate of Planning, Statistics and Evaluation, Porvorim-Goa.

PRINT MEDIA:

D'mello (D'Souza) A Carmelita (Associate Professor, Department of Commerce, ST. Xavier's college, Mapusa-Goa), "Managing Tourism Development in Goa through Sustainable Tourism", Thesis for the award of the degree of Doctor of Philosophy, 2015.

Kamat, Nandkumar M. (Asst. Professor, Department of Botany, Goa University, Taleigao, Goa) "Sustainable Eco tourism Planning for Happier and Wealthier Goa", Goa Today, Goa's largest and oldest English Magazine, 04 November 2015, P. 1-10.

Sawant N. Nandkumar (Associate Professor, Dept of Geography, Parvatibai Chowgule College, Brammer Natasha and Beech John (Coventry Business School), "Use and Abuse of Tourism: The Goan Experience", Tourism, Culture & Communication, Vol. 5 p. 23-35, Printed in the USA, DOI: 10.3727/109830404278l508.

Solomon Ranjan (NGO/ecumenical leader), "The Challenge and Prospects of Tourism in Goa Today", J&P Printers, Bengaluru, Nov. 2009.

WEBSITES:

www.goa/coastaltourismGOA1.pdf

www.goa/11%20hotel%20industry%20in%20goa.pdf

www.goa/12_chapter%205.pdf

www.goa-tourism.com

E: reservations@goa-tourism.com

www.facebook.com/officialgoatourism

6

Dynamic Nature of Urban Landscape of Selected Urban Centres in Nadia District, West Bengal, India

Iman SK

Abstract: Combining both features of physical and cultural elements, that's visible of an area of land is known as landscape. The present study is an attempt to analyze the Resolution the Dynamic Nature of Landscape of Urban Centres in a Decadal Census Period of Nadia District, West Bengal, India and also to analyze the nature of the distribution of urban centres and influenced area of the main city. Based on the urban centre wise secondary data obtained from the census 2001 and 2011 dot map is prepared for the distribution of urban centres, mean centres of urban population of the study area and also to prepare the radar diagram within Nadia district map by measuring the values of breaking point analysis distance. The results show that in a decadal census year mean centres of urban population horizontally shift almost 18 km in a north-west direction. Based on the breaking point analysis it is reflected that the influence area of Krishnanagar city increased in the northern part of the Nadia district than the southern part of the district and also the result shows that the nature of distribution of urban centres are moderately regular or uniform. However,

Assistant Teacher in Geography, Chakdignagar Tarakdas Memorial High School, Kalirhat, Krishnanagar, Nadia.
Email: imansk87@gmail.com

the normal distribution of urban centres all over the study district, the equilibrium location of mean centres of urban population and perfect regular or uniform distribution nature of urban centres are suggested for considering a demographic change of the study district.

Keywords: *Breaking point, Landscape, Mean Centres, Nearest Neighbour (Rn) and Urban centres.*

6.1 Introduction

After the urban revolution in 1990 urban population continuously increased all over the world as a consequence of global urbanisation. Urbanisation is not a recent phenomena, it is a continuous process from the ancient periods of human civilisation. The fast-paced urbanisation in many developing countries seems to have been escorted by irrationally high levels of concentration of urban population in metro cities (Tiwari. et al, 2018). By the various patterns, process, causes and their consequences urbanisation are delineated in a dynamic landscape. Before the development process started the whole civilisation was in rural settlements (Baker, W.L. 1989). Due to the socio-economic changes and transformations of the society rural settlements started acquiring urban character, later slowly they are transformed into suburban or census towns and then urban settlements or towns. In a same way town transformed into city, then city into metro city, metro city into metropolitan city, super metropolitan city, the changes and transformations are more, than in a metropolitan city and other urban centres. Most of the rural settlements have already changed and merged into urban areas with changed characteristics in terms of pucca houses, pucca roads, availability of infrastructure, etc. Such changed villages are called urban villages while the others remained the rural villages (Lopez, et al., 2001). In 2001census period in Nadia district the rural urban population share was 78.7 % and 21.3 % and growth rate was 21.6 % and 12.4 %. In 2011 the share of rural population decreased in 72.2 % from 78.7 %, urban population increased 27.8 % from 21.3 % and similarly rural growth rate decreased in 02.9 % from 21.6 %

and also urban population increased in 46.9 % from 12.4 %. The study attempts to study the delineation of functional region of Krishnanagar city in Nadia district, to understand the dynamic nature of functional region of Krishnanagar city from 2001 to 2011 census and to analysis the nature of distribution of urban centres of Nadia district and also to study the shifting mode of mean centre of population from 2001 to 2011.

6.2 Material and Methods

6.2.1 Study Area

Nadia is a district in the state of West Bengal along India Bangladesh border in eastern India. The latitudinal and longitudinal extension of Nadia district is 22°53' N to 24°11' N latitude and 88°09' E and 88°48' E longitude. The shape of Nadia district is irregular linear with North-South orientation. The altitude of the district from mean sea level is Approximately 46 feets or 14 metres above. The geographical boundary of Nadia district comprises Bangladesh in East, Bardhaman and Hooghly district in West, Murshidabad district in North and North West and North 24 Parganas towards South and South East. The district has 17 blocks and covered an area about 3927 sq. km or 1,516 sq. mile.

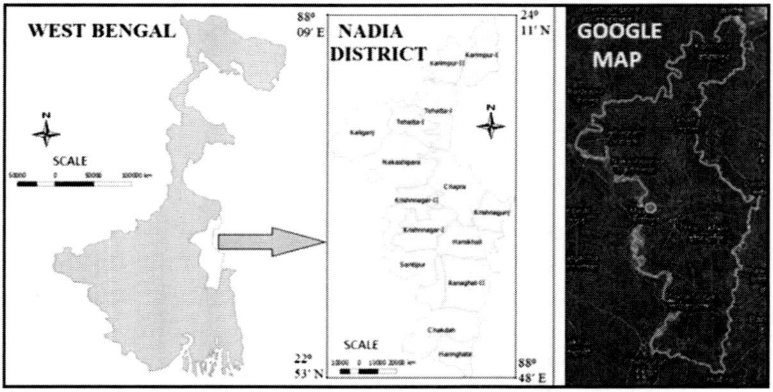

Map 1: Location of Study Area: Left Nadia District in West Bengal Map, Middle Nadia District Map, Right Google Map of Nadia District.

6.2.2 Data Analysis

The study is based on the secondary data obtained from Government of India Report of Census and District Census Handbook. Urban centre is taken as a unit of study for analysis and mapping purpose. Data thus collected, interpreted and represented cartographically by using mean centre, braking point analysis and nearest neighbour analysis technique. To calculate the mean centres of study area, an arbitrary coordinate system has been superimposed on the map of Nadia district, with its origin at the bottom left-hand corner. For simplicity the horizontal axis measuring easting's has been labeled as X, and the vertical axis measuring northing's has been labelled as Y. This convention for labeling coordinate axis will be followed throughout the study. Thus, rows for Y-axis and columns for X-axis are utilized for measurement.

The mean centre can now be found simply by calculating the mean of the X co-ordinates and the mean of the Y coordinates. These two mean coordinates mark the location of the mean centre. The equation for the mean centre is following:

$$MX = \frac{\sum PX}{\sum P} \text{ and } MY = \frac{\sum PY}{\sum P}$$

Where MX and MY are the mean centre of X and Y coordinates, P represent the population of distinct urban centre in definite year, ΣP is the total population of urban centres in definite year, X and Y are the measurement values of X and Y axis (Barber 1996).

The breaking point analysis by measuring the following equation:

$$Db = \frac{D}{1 + \sqrt{\frac{Pa}{Pb}}}$$

Where 'Db' is the distance from the small urban centre, 'D' is the distance between the two urban centres (large and small urban centre), 'Pa' is the population size of the large urban centre and 'Pb' is the population size of the small urban centre (Reilly, 1931).

The nearest neighbour (Rn) analysis measure by the solving the following equation

$$Rn = 2\bar{D}\sqrt{\frac{n}{A}}$$

Where '$\bar{D}$' is the observed mean neighbour distance, 'n' is the total number of point or urban centres in the study area and 'A' is the area of the study area in sq. km (Clark and Evans, 1954; Dacey, 1960; Neft, 1966; Taylor, 1977).

The main data source of this study is Government of India Report of Census 2011, Nadia District Census Handbook; 2011, Part XII-A & B, Nadia District, Series-20, West Bengal, various books, articles and Google reference etc. The data taken from Report of Census and District Census Handbook used MS Excel: 2007, IBM SPSS Statistics Version 23 to test the signification level between the associations of variables and used Quantum Geographical Information System (Version: 2.14.21) Software for analysis the cartographical representation the mean centres, delineation the dynamic economic areas and the distribution pattern of urban centres in Nadia district.

6.3 Result and Discussion

6.3.1 Mean Centre of Population and It's Shifting

The geographical point that marks the point of an entire's population of a region is refers as a mean centre of population. Mean centre of population determine and locate on Nadia district map based on urban centres wise population from 2001 to 2011 census period. It is found that this point is not fixed or static, move in different direction in different census year.

In 2001 location of mean centre of population in Nadia district was at intersection point of 3.48 cm and 4.43 cm as X and Y coordinate in the north-west corner of Badkulla taluk in the Hanskhali C.D block, but in 2011 this point found at intersection point of 3.42 cm and 5.5 cm as X and Y coordinate in the north- east corner of Jalalkhali tahasil in Krishnnagar-I block. In 10 years (2001 to 2011 census) the mean centre of population in Nadia district shifts from south-east to north-west direction (Map 2).

It indicates the emergence of new urban centres in the south-eastern part of the study district, thus setting, a change in the overall pattern of distribution. However, the process of the spatial pattern of dispersion of urbanization is not widespread.

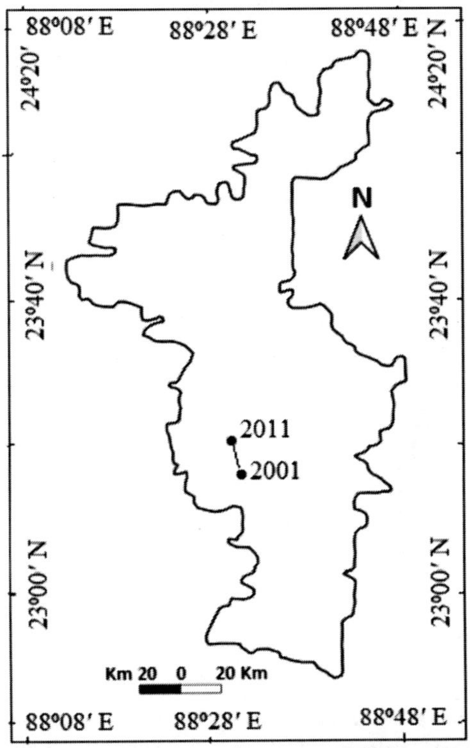

Map 2: Showing the Mean Centres of Urban Population

6.3.2 Delineation the Dynamic Economic Areas

Economic region refers to the territorial features of a country's, where different economical condition are same over a time. These regions are controlled by the different criteria likely different economic production, population, change of techniques from different point of view, standard of living and different modern fashion etc. So the features of economic regions are not static, these region's natures are dynamic. In the study area the dynamic economic regions are delineated based on urban population in 2001 and 2011 census periods and also to compare it.

From Map 3 and Map 4 it is found that the influence areas of Krishnanagar urban centre increased from 2001 to 2011census periods in the northern part of Nadia district than the southern part of the district. It indicates the new urban centres are flourished in the northern part of the study

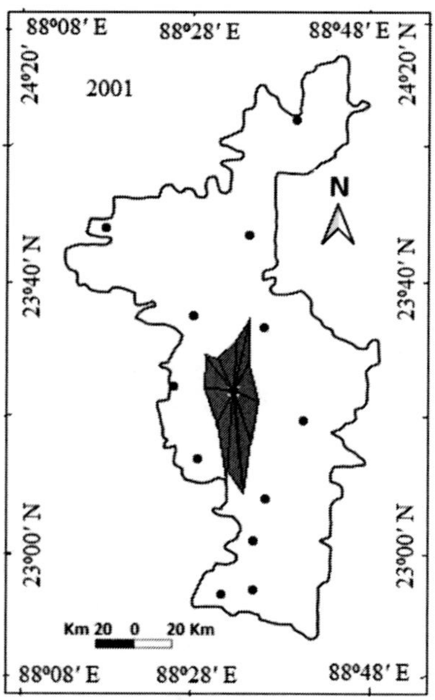

Map 3: Showing the Economic Areas of Krishnanagar City in 2001

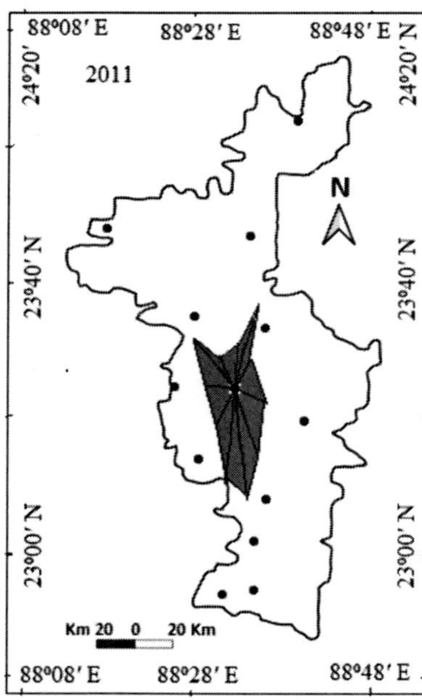

Map 4: Showing the Economic Areas of Krishnanagar City in 2011

district. Maximum influence of Krishnanagar urban centre is visualized towards Kaliganj urban centre and least towards Shantipur urban centres.

6.3.3 Distribution Pattern of Urban Centres

The urban centres distribution pattern of Nadia district is analyzed by the nearest neighbor (Rn) analysis measurment. Nearest neighbour (Rn) analysis measure the linear distance between two or more specified neighboring locations. The nearest neighbor (Rn) value determines the distribution patterns of settlement or any point location. For the determination the distribution patterns of settlement or any point location by the nearest neighbor (Rn) value, the said value will be range between 0 to 2.15 ranges. The nearest neighbor (Rn) value '0' indicates the distribution pattern is clustered, where all points are aggregated at a location, an Rn '1' value indicates the distribution is random and the nearest neighbor (Rn) value 2.15 said that the settlements distribution

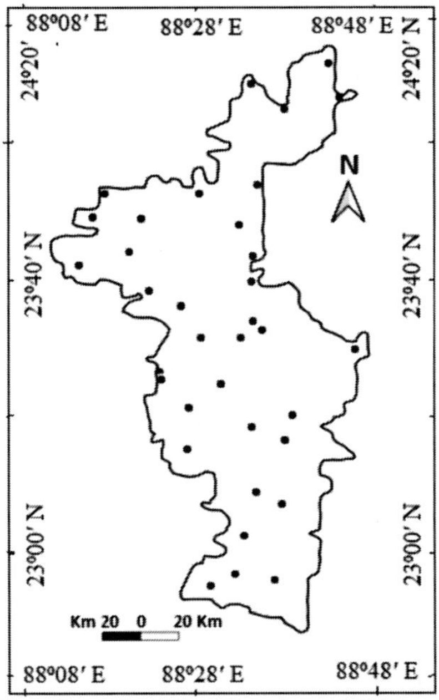

Map 5: Showing the Distribution of Urban Centres

pattern is regulated. It also said that, the distribution patterns are random if the value is perfectly '1' or near about '1' Rn value, increasing Rn values from 1 to 2.15 indicates the distribution is regulated or almost equidiatance spaced and decreasing Rn value from 1 stand for the evidence of clustered distribution pattern (Clark and Evans, 1954; Dacey, 1960; Neft, 1966; Taylor, 1977). The calculated nearest neighbor (Rn) value of the study area is 1.570, which said that the distribution patterns of urban centre are higher than least regularity and lower than high regularity, so the distributions are moderately regular or uniform.

6.3.4 Conclusion

From the study it is visualized that; all the urban centres of Nadia district are almost equally distributed except northern part of the district. The basic factors for this disparity in the northern part of Nadia district are impact of borderer impacts of India Bangladesh and climatic condition, the lack of fertility of the land, inadequate infrastructure facility, etc. Nadia district map reveals that all the maximum urban centres are located in the south and western portion of the district. The study also represents that the mean centre of population located in a southwest direction of the study district even two discuss census year. From the point of view of the distribution of urbanism, the study analysis of the urban centres of the region has provided an insight into the urban and economic problems of the region. It is also observed that if a few urban centres on the north-eastern side (i.e. Karimpur-I C.D. block), the north side (i.e. Tehatta-I, Tehatta-II and Karimpur-II C.D. block) and the northwestern side (i.e. Kaliganj C.D. block) and also the middle part in eastern side (i.e. Krishnaganj and Hanskhali C.D. block) grows up, the district can achieve a balanced distribution of urban population as well as the variation of the number of urban settlements (urbanism) and gradually may reduce the imbalances in the urbanism of the district and also the distribution of urban centres will be more and more uniform than moderately uniform.

References

Baker W. L. (1989), "A Review of Models of Landscape Change", Landscape Ecology 2(2): 111-133.

Burt J E., Barber, G M. (1996), "Elementary Statistics for Geographem", 2nd ed. New York: The Guilford Press.

Census of India. Primary Census Abstract. Registrar General and Census Commissioner, New Delhi, India, Ministry of Home Affairs.2011; Retrieved from http://www.census india.gov.in

Clark P. J. and EVANS F C. "Distance to Nearest Neighbor as a Measure of Spatial Relationships in Populations", Ecology, 35 (October, 1954), 445-453.

District Census Handbook, 2001 Part XII-A & B, Nadia District, Series-20, West Bengal http://lsi.gov.in:8081/jspui/bitstream/123456789/5381/1/39718_2001_NAD.pdf.

Dacey M F. "A Note on the Derivation of Nearest Neighbour Distances", Journal of Regional Science, 2 (Summer 1960), 81-87.

Dacey M F. and Tung T. "The Identification of Randomness in Point Patterns", Journal of Regional Science, 4 (Summer 1962), 83-96.

Lopez E., Bocco, G., & Mendoza, M. (2001), "Predicting Land-cover and Land-use Change in the Urban Fringe: A Case in Morelia City, Mexico, Landscape and Urban Planning", 55, 271-285.

Nadia District Google Map, https://www.google.com/maps/place/Nadia,+West+Bengal/@23.4598338,87.6261187,175101m/data=!3m1!1e3!4m5!3m4!1s0x39f9205cd1ce22fb:0x4469effd74c944ad!8m2!3d23.4709656!4d88.556531

Reilly WJ. (1931), The law of retail gravitation. New York: Knickerbocker Press https://en.wikipedia.org/wiki/Reilly%27s_law_of_retail_gravitation

Tiwari et al. (2018), "Urban Landscape Dynamics for Quantifying the Changing Pattern of Urbanisation in Delhi", Journal of Rural Development, NIRD & PR, Hyderabad 37(2), pp. 399-412.

7

Geographical Study on Urban Planning of Calangute Town, North Goa, India

Ruchika Saha

Abstract: A City Development Plan is both, a perspective as well as a vision document for the future development of a city. It presents the current stage of the city's development – Preparation of City Development Plan is a multi-stage exercise, involving: in-depth analysis of the existing situation, covering the demographic, economic, financial, infrastructure, physical, environmental and institutional aspects. This research paper has been based on level of development plan in Calangute and adjacent area, under Mapusa Municipality, North Goa, Goa & the paper tries to identify various development planning problems, the various measures that would have been implied to solve these problems by planning perspective. Calangute town under Mapusa Municipality has a well-developed social, physical and industrial infrastructure and virtual connectivity. However, this city is besieged with serious development issues related environmental degradation, absence of sewerage and sanitation network, lack of solid waste management, increasing life style diseases etc. By reducing these problems this city become more sustainable & liveable and can achieved high level of economic & social development.

Former Post Graduate Student, Department of Geography and Applied Geography, University of North Bengal (Jalpaiguri Campus), Jalpaiguri. Email: ruchikasahafkt@gmail.com

Keywords: *Development, Urban Planning, Sustainable, Infrastructure, City vision*

7.1 Introduction

A City Development Plan is a both perspective and a version for the future development of a city. It represents the current stage of the city's development. It provides a framework and vision within which projects need to be identified and implemented. It also establishes a logical and consistent framework for evaluation of investment decisions. City Development Plan or Urban Planning is a technical and political process concerned with the development and design of land use and the built environment, including air, water, and the infrastructure passing into and out of urban areas, such as transportation, communications, and distribution networks. The town and Country Planning Department of Goa, under the Goa Daman Diu Town and Country Planning Act.1974, prepared 'Regional Plan for Goa-2001 A.D', and the same was enacted upon since Dec.,1986. The plan should not be interpreted strictly as an instrument for development control, but should form the basis for:

- Micro-level town and country planning as well as zoning activities including the preparation of Outline Development Plans (O.D.P.s) and Comprehensive Development Plans (C.D.P.s)
- considering major proposals and taking decisions affecting land uses on a large scale.

Table – 1

Three Regional Plans of Goa

RPG 2001	First Regional Plan in India to cover entire state
RPG 2011	First Regional Plan to be Scrapped
RPG 2021	First Regional Plan to introduce Bottom Up Planning

7.2 Area of Study

Goa is a state in western India with coastlines stretching

along the Arabian Sea. It lies between the latitudes 14°53'54"N and 15°40'00"N and longitudes 73°40'33"E and 74°20'13"E. Goa is a part of the coastal country known as the Konkan which has a coastline of 160 km. Goa is divided into two part: North Goa & South Goa, north Goa is one of the two district that has an area of 1736 sq. km and is bounded by Sindhudurg district of Maharashtra state to the north and by Belagaum district of Karnataka to the east, by South Goa district to the south and the Arabian Sea to the west. Its geographical position is marked by 15°48'00"N to 14°53'54"N latitudes & 73°0'00"E to 75°0'00"E longitudes. In North Goa under Mapusa Municipal Council Calangute town and its adjacent area is our study area, which is famous for its beaches. It lies between 15°35'30"N latitude and 73°45'43"E longitude. The Calangute beach is the largest in North Goa and visited by thousands of domestic and international tourists alike.

7.3 Objectives

The major objectives of this research work are enumerated below:

- To analysis the citizen services and basic amenities.
- To identify different infrastructures and services.
- To identify housing and basic sanitation facilities.
- To measure congestion on roads, air pollution and resource depletion, local economy.
- To identify the variety of transport options–Transit Oriented Development (TOD), public transport and transport connectivity.
- To identify major environmental issue in Calangute town.
- To identify the sewerage system and waste segregation management.

7.4 Data Base and Methodology

In order to conduct the research work on city development, both primary and secondary data has been utilized, the primary data has been collected from the field on the basis of structured questionnaire & through interview survey with the local respondents. And the secondary data has been obtained from the various websites, literature, through various offices and other mobile applications.

The methodology adopted can be divided into the following parts:

7.4.1 Pre-Field: In this phase general literature survey was carried out and collection of many maps and some other secondary data was done which include overview of the area to be surveyed from many governmental and non-governmental sources (mainly from web sites). A structured questionnaire was then prepared to collect the data from the respondents from various places of the cities or towns.

7.4.2 Field: As the area surveyed is densely populated it becomes a difficult task to conduct a primary survey. To cope up with this problem stratified random sampling was done. Survey of the local respondents was finally done. Relevant photographs have been taken and some important secondary data is also collected from the North Goa Planning and Development Authority office & Mapusa Municipality office.

7.4.3 Post Field: This stage involves computation of master data table from structured questionnaire, statistical application, cartographic representation, drawing maps using QGIS techniques, analysis of data and information obtained in order to understand the present status of economic, social & environmental development of the study area. Global Mapper, Adobe Photoshop software have been used for digitization and drawing of maps.

7.5 Level of Development

Levels of development across the States has been in varies degree. States are classified under three levels of development viz Low, Medium, High. The low-level development comprises states that are economically and socially backward. The medium level indicates reasonably good economic development but relatively low social development and vice-versa. The high-level comprises states, which have achieved high level of both economic and social development. Perhaps,

Goa is the one of the states in the country to have achieved both social and economic development. The success story of Goa has been the highest priority accorded for social sector right from the beginning. Goa followed the unbalanced growth model by shifting its development focus from social sector to industrialization and tourism development thereafter. A significant achievement of Goa has been its successful attainment of replacement level in population control in 1990s. Among States; Goa is now the most urbanized State with 62.2 percent urban population, a significant increase since 2001 when urban population of Goa was 49.8%. The Town and Country Planning Department with its Headquarters at Panaji is having two District level offices, one at Mapusa having jurisdiction over North Goa District and another at Margao having jurisdiction over South Goa District. Also, there are seven Taluka level offices at Taluka Headquarters of Tiswadi, Pernem, Bicholim, Ponda, Mormugao, Quepem and Canacona.

Goa is one of the fastest growing states in the country. Goa's economic growth is driven by the strong performance of industrial sectors such as mining, tourism and pharmaceuticals. And Goa is also one of the few states in India to achieve 100 per cent rural electrification. In North Goa under Bardez Sub-district, Mapusa Municipal Council Calangute town and its adjacent area is our study area, which is famous for its beach. The beach is the largest in North Goa and visited by thousands of domestic and international tourists alike. Also known as the "Queen of Beaches", Calangute is Goa's flagship beach. Calangute offers all modern amenities like post office, banks, foreign exchange offices and medical facilities.

7.6 City Development Plan and Policy

The Planning and Development Authorities have been constituted for effective implementation of Town and Country Planning Act and preparation of Outline Development Plans. At present, six planning areas have been notified. The North Goa Planning & Development is a

Statutory Body formulated under the Town & Country Planning Board and the main functions of the Authority are as specified under the Town & Country Planning Act, 1974.

Major functions and powers of the Planning & Development Authority are to prepare the following:

(1) An existing Land Use Map;
(2) An Outline Development Plan;
(3) A Comprehensive Development Plan;
(4) Prescribe use of land within its area;
(5) Schemes of development and undertake their implementation;

- The North Goa Planning and Development Authority (NGPDA) have notified the outline development plan (ODP) 2025 for Calangute-Candolim, Goa.
- RK Pandita, Secretary, NGPDA, has shared that the development plan has been notified under Section 37 (1) of the Town and Country Planning Act. The plan shall be subject to the provisions of the Goa Land Development and Building Regulations, 2010, as amended from time to time.
- The ODP 2025 for Calangute-Candolim is available for inspection by the general public at Arpora-Nagoa, Calangute and Candolim village Panchayats and also at NGPDA office at Mala, Panaji.
- The notified development plan talks about parking spaces, rainwater harvesting, educational institutions in a comunidade land. An area for solid waste management would be properly administered. Rajesh Naik, Chief Town Planner, has notified the new land development norms.

7.7 Economic Profile of the City

Various activities are experienced in Calangute and its adjacent area under Mapusa municipality main amongst which are Trade and Commerce, tourism, hospitality, administration etc. The city houses major markets of Bardez Taluka which are frequented by the locals from the peripheral villages as by tourists visiting the coastal belt of North Goa. Although a large chunk of land is earmarked as paddy field, it is observed that the laborers engaged in the agricultural activities mainly come from neighboring villages. The major activity of the locals is however trade and commerce only. A sizeable amount of population is engaged in pottery and who are known Kumbhars of work force are the community called Kasar who are engaged in tin works.

7.8 Infrastructures, Services & Facilities

7.8.1 Educational Facilities

Calangute and adjacent area, Mapusa Municipality being one of the important towns of North Goa is having concentration of prestigious educational institutions comprising of pre-primary, primary, secondary, Higher Secondary Educational institutions and other professional colleges. Calangute has secondary schools viz. Little Flower of Jesus High School, St.Josephs High school, Don Bosco High School, Mark Memorial High School, Apart from Government Primary schools located in Umtavaddo &Naikavaddo. Some the prestigious educational institutions which are located in the Mapusa city are St.Xavier collage.

7.8.2 Health Facilities

One of the important structures of the city is Aslio Hospital which provides major health services to the populace of Mapusa City and to entire Bardez Taluka and Calangute town. The Government has constructed another new District hospital at Peddem. Beside Government hospital there are several other privte hospital, Clinic and Nursing Home which are located in different parts of the city such as Calangute town, Peddemtown, Aucchinwado town, Dattawadi etc.

Table – 2
Types of Health Facilities

Option	Frequency	Percentage of Freq.
Primary Health Centre	0	0
Govt. Hospital	10	20

Private Clinic	36	72
Other	4	8

Source: Primary Survey, 2020.

The diagram (Fig. 1) has stated that 72% respondents prefer private clinic to access health facility followed by 20% and 8% respondents prefers Govt. hospital and other for health facility respectively. Therefore, it can be concluded that most of people in study area prefers private clinic that of other health facility.

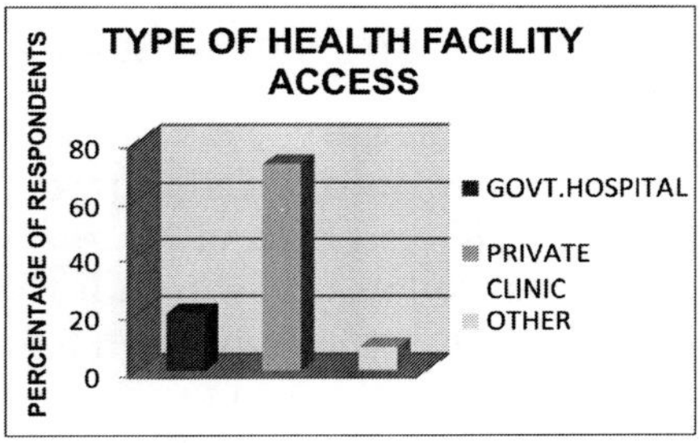

Fig. 1

7.8.3 Road Network in Municipal Boundary

The Mapusa Municipal area has two major arterial roads which are known as Colvale road having width of 30.00 mts. and Camurlim road having width of 20.00 mts. One of the important road passing through city are Bicholim road having width of 30.00mts. and Anjuna road passing through Khorlim area which is having a width of 25.00mts.The Market area of Calangute town of Bardez Taluka which is the core area is having a thick network of roads which are having designated width of 10.00 mts.

Table – 3
Types of Road in Front of House

Option	Frequency	Percentage of Freq.
Pucca	44	88
Katcha	6	12

Source: Primary Survey, 2020.

The fact (Fig. 2) has stated that type of road in front of the house. Where it can be seen that 88% respondents said that road in front their house is pucca and only 12% respondents said that type of road in front of their house is katcha. So, it is found that the condition of the road is in good condition in most of area of Calangute town and its adjacent area.

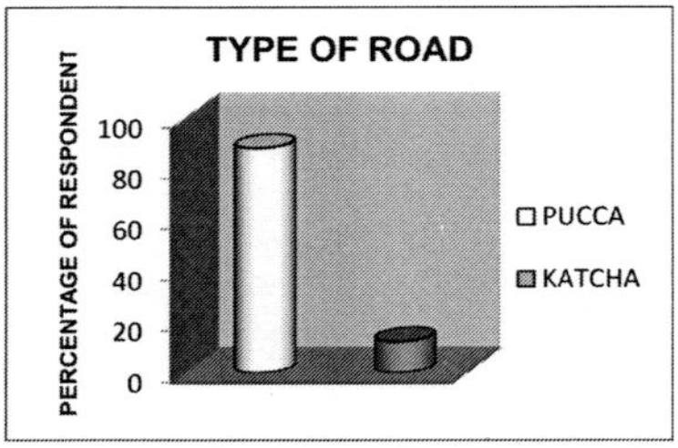

Fig. 2

7.8.4 Water Supply Facilities

As per the survey made it is seen that people of Calangute and its adjacent area of Mapusa Municipality are using well water as well as tap water for their daily usages. There is no exclusive water supply scheme for Mapusa city alone but the city has been covered under regional water supply projects. It is also seen that the water source is sufficient for providing ample water to Mapusa city and also the entire Calangute town for ultimate requirements if water conservation efforts are made in time.

Table – 4
Source of Drinking Water

Option	Frequency	Percentage of Freq.
Tap	25	40.98361
Tubewell	2	3.278689
Water Tanker	14	22.95082
Others	20	32.78689

Source: Primary Survey, 2020.

7.8.5 Traffic and Transportation

It is noticed that the Calangute town and entire Mapusa city is not fixed road patter whereby it is noticed that the city is served by two major roads running north-south which are intersected at several places by other minor roads. This thick network of road is mainly noticed in olden part of the city such as market area and Haldona Bus stand and at Anganwado. The concentration of commercial areas especially in the old areas is leading to the traffic congestion. With the increase in vehicle ownership and the increase in floating population although city roads initially appeared to be having a large width, with the development undertaken at a rapid pace, the same has started appearing narrow now. It is also noticed that the area near Bus stand is getting extremely congested during the peak hours especially during morning and afternoon times which coincides with the school starting and closing times. Authority as an attempt to ease the traffic along this road has proposed a new by-pass road and additional area is earmarked for Bus terminus which also ease the parking problems in the core of the city.

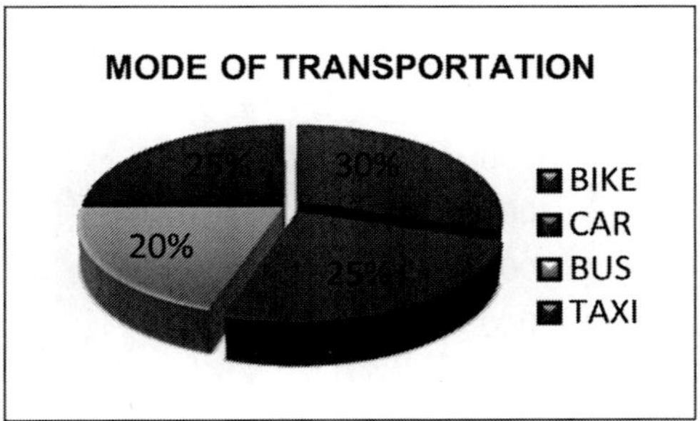

Fig. 3

Table – 5
Major Problem in Road Transport

Option	Frequency	Percentage
Traffic	2	20
Bus Schedules	1	10
Safety	0	0
Cost	1	10
Others	6	60

Source: Primary Survey, 2020.

Table – 5 discussed about the Transportation Problems of Calangute town of Goa State. Where 20% traffic problems, 10% bus scheduled 10% problems are from cost and 60% respondents not sure to say anything. So, at last we can say that the main transport problem of entire region is traffic.

7.8.6 Power and Electricity

The level of power consumption has increased from a meager 2.2 MKWH in 1965-66 to 312.4 MKWH in 1984-85. Industry is the major consumer of power(71%), followed by domestic, commercial(16%) and other purposes(13%). The

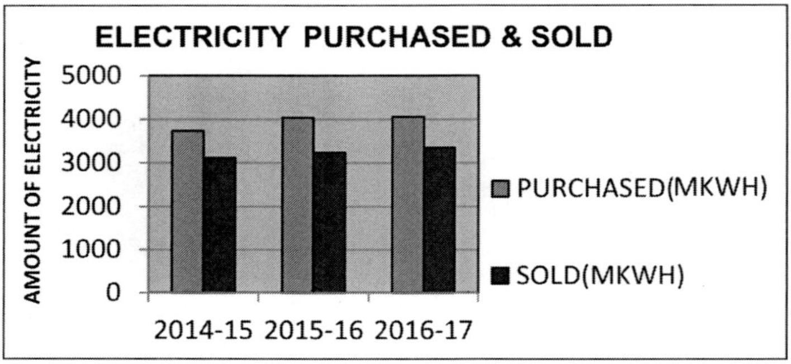

Fig. 4

Regional Plan has estimated a 2400 MKWH for the year 2000-2001. Due to limited scope of power generation, Goa has to depend on import of power from neighbouring states. The district has been assured of 200MW of power from Korba (in M.P) and Ramagundam (in A.P) Super Thermal Power Stations. Hence, The Seventh Plan envisaged the Dudhsagarhydal project with an installed capacity of 30MW. On the other hand, Regional Plan lays emphasis on these above-mentioned possibilities as well as power generation through non-conventional sources of energy.

Table – 6
Amount of Electricity Purchased & Sold

Year	Purchased (MKWH)	Sold (MKWH)
2014-15	3733	3114
2015-16	4040	3233
2016-17	4055	3351

Source: Statistical Hand Book of Goa 2016-17.

7.8.7 Solid Waste management

Goa Waste Management Corporation (GWMC), a nodal agency for executing Solid Waste Management infrastructure projects in the state of Goa. GWMC has proposed a Solid Waste Management Facility at Bainginium Village on the acquired land for the purpose, on similar lines as set up in North Goa at Saligao and Proposed Facility for South Goa at

Cacora. The main objective of the establishment of Centralized Solid Waste Management Facility (CSWMF) is for the scientific processing and disposal of the solid waste by the local bodies in compliance with the MSW Rules, 2016. The Government of Goa, is implementing this project through Goa Waste Management Corporation (GWMC), Saligao. Accordingly, GWMC has undertaken the work for establishment of the 250 tons/day (TPD) capacity Centralized Municipal Solid Waste (MSW) Processing based on Recycle & Sorting Line, Segregation, Bio-methanation and In-vessel Composting at Baingunim in North Goa District. For this proposed facility, GWMC retained CSIR-NEERI, Nagpur to carry out Environmental Impact Assessment (EIA) studies as per the ToR issued by State Expert Appraisal Committee (SEAC), Goa.

Table – 7

S.No.	Type of Waste Generator	Total Generate in a Day
1.	Households	7.00
2.	Hotel and Restaurant	14.00
3.	Hospital and medical waste	11.00
4.	Construction	0.50
5.	Horticulture	25.00
6.	Street sweeping waste	8.50
	Total	**57.00**

Source: CCP, Panaji.

In Calangute town and its adjacent area, it is recommended to earmark the place for solid waste management. The same place could very well be utilized for setting up of solid waste management plant or a composting station by Mapusa Municipal Council or any such agency to treat the waste/garbage generated in the city. Accordingly, a location at Gaunsawado is identified, which is away from any residential/ commercial area and which is having a natural Buffer Zone of its own.

7.9 Finding of the Study

- **Weak performance level:** On the time of survey it was found that the local people of this town are not convenient. They did not help in any way in the field of primary data collection.
- **Administrating Maintaining:** There were no better administrating maintaining in the adjacent area of survey.
- **Lack of Awareness:** Many people of this area are not aware about the city development. They did not try to understand its meaning.
- **Bad Performance of Authority:** There are inequalities in developing at total area because of bad performance of authority.
- **Issue:** Some political issues directly hit on the impact city development plan.

7.10 Problems of the Study

In this point of view there are different problem has been identified. Problem of the study area are as follows:

- The Municipal Corporation are not worked properly.
- There is no sufficient administrative system like police, securities, traffic police to maintain roadways and vehicles at Calangute town.
- There are large amounts of migrated people as for this they are not avail to say anything about the developing plan or projects of study area.
- North Goa development office is far away from study area, as for this there is no sufficient growth of development.
- From all types of transportation problem traffic maintaining problems are too much.

7.11 Suggestions and Recommendation

In this point of view there are different problems and many management activities are found. These both are more effect on people of this city. With the help of proper study of this area need to some remedial suggestion and recommendations, which are as follows:

- In this town there are need to more development or improving the facilities of water bodies and water availability.
- Local public of study area has to attract the attention of the authorities in the matter of transport, traffic jam and roadways.
- Corporation must to give attention on the Health and sanitation system of Calangute town the study area.
- Urban environment and Disaster management have to work properly to planning of development of the city.
- Municipal and corporation has to give attention in Housing and basic services for urban poor.

7.16 Concluding Observation

Goa is already in the 3rd stage of demographic transition characterizing high economic development. And Calangute town under Mapusa Municipality is to be developed as a city that is environmentally and economically sustainable, a city that is a mixture of heritage and modernity, a city that cares for its city citizen, a city that cares for its tourists, a city that maintains its culture, a city that provide high quality infrastructure services and facilities and a city that provides a better present and bright future to its people. However, the city is besieged with serious development issues related environmental degradation, absence of sewerage and sanitation network, lack of solid waste management, increasing life style diseases etc. Though, the city is poised for the next stage of development, it requires policy correction, and administrative and fiscal reforms.

References

D' Souza, J.A. et al. 1988. "The Regional Plan for Goa", 2001 A.D. India, Government of Goa, Department of Town and Country Planning, October, p. 108.

Government of Goa, Regional Plan Goa, 2001 and 2021, Town & Country Planning Department, Goa.

Government of Goa, "The Ancient Monuments and Archaeological Sites and Remains Act, No. 24 of 1958", Government of India.

Government of Goa, The Goa (Regulation of Land Development and Building) Act, 2008 and The Goa Land Development and Building Construction Regulation 2010, second edition November 2011.

Government of Goa, "The Goa Ancient Monuments and Archaeological Sites and Remains Act, 1978 and Rules", 1980.

Government of Goa, "The Goa Town and Country Planning Act and Rules", Government of Goa, Planning and Development Authority (Development Plan), Regulations, 1989, Panjim Planning and Development Authority, Panjim.

Joshi C., et al, "World Heritage Series–Old Goa", Archaeological Survey of India, Goa.

Report of the Tourism Master Plan: GOA- 2011 final report prepared by Consulting Engg. Services (I) Ltd. For Government of Goa, Department of Tourism.

8

Strategies of Smart City Development: A Study of Visakhapatnam City, Andhra Pradesh, India

Amlan Maitra

Abstract: Urban Planning is an important way to understand and develop the all round aspects of an urban area. It is the way of finding out the structure, morphology and functions of a given area, alongside doing analysis and giving suggestions for its betterment.

In Vizag, we can find that the overall urban development of the area is very well juxtaposed along with its socioeconomic condition. There is good literacy in the area along with good urban structure and functions. The place has good electric connections along with good awareness among people to save it. It also has a good water supply, even though it has to face a bit of crisis every now and then. The environmental condition of the area is very good because of good vegetation cover along the city coupled with of the presence of Bay of Bengal, the people get fresh air.

Everything in Vizag is in organized manner. Every office, schools, and other places are totally in well distributed format according to it's physiography and landuse. There are well organized government offices like that of GVMC office, VUDA office etc which has taken care of its sanitation, solid waste

Former Post Graduate Student, Department of Geography and Applied Geography, University of North Bengal, Siliguri. Email: amlanmaitra95@gmail.com management, sewerage, public health facility, etc. Other than that, it's a very clean city with proper transport facility as a part of urban renewal missions.

So, overall it can be said that this paper displays different problems faced by the area and recommendations done to overcome that.

Keywords: *Urban Planning, Socio-economic conditions, Vizag, Urban Development, Urban Renewal.*

8.1 Introduction

Smart City Mission, is an urban renewal and retrofitting program by the Government of India with the mission to retrofit more than 100 cities across the country making them citizen friendly and sustainable. The Union Ministry of Urban Development is responsible for executing and implementing the mission in collaboration with the state governments of the respective cities.

All the Indian states has made efforts in speeding up the industrializing process in the country. On that ground, initiatives like Jawaharlal Nehru National Urban Renewal Mission (JNNURM), and the Smart Cities Mission, including AMRUT (Atal Mission for Rejuvenation and Urban Transformation), were launched to improve the overall quality of life in cities, and developing cities with modern facilities and infrastructure.

A narrow vision approach will not be any good while planning an urban space as each aspect of a city is intimately linked with the other. If we think of developing housing, there are several aspects like water supply, electricity, garbage disposal etc. to also look at. Therefore, a holistic development needs to be adopted in order to address economic growth, employment, social change. At the same time, it needs to deal with economic deprivation, environmental degradation, waste management, and proper utilization of space.

Visakhapatnam (also known as **Vizag** and **Waltair**) is the largest city and the financial capital of the Indian state of

Andhra Pradesh. The city is the administrative headquarters of Visakhapatnam district and state headquarters of Indian Coast Guard. Its geographical location is amidst the Eastern Ghats and is situated along the coast of the Bay of Bengal. It is the most populous city in the state with a population of 2,035,922 as of 2011, making it the 14th-largest city in the country.

According to the Smart City Framework Plan, the groundwork for the development of Visakhapatnam from a 20th century port city into an integrated 21st century city-region has been made. The plan states that, each of the four major centers of Visakhapatnam Metropolitan Region (i.e., the city centre, southern industrial area, coastline, educational hub of Rushikonda and Madhurawada) will develop its own distinct urban character:

1. The city centre will raise its profile as the business and cultural centre of the region by carrying out signature development projects in the Central Business District, along the beach road and at Old Town.
2. The southern industrial area will develop of smaller, mixed-use urban sub-centres that offer jobs-housing balance and improved living conditions for the local workforce.
3. Madhurawada and Rushikonda will emerge as high-end knowledge industry clusters that offer world-class educational, recreational and tourism facilities.
4. Vizag's unique selling point - its coastline - will be developed as a set of distinct recreational, ecological and livelihood destinations.

New growth areas within all four centers will locate housing near jobs, preserve ecological assets, and minimize any risk of natural hazard binding the centers into a coherent regional whole where there will be smart transport, water and energy infrastructure that ensures smooth and timely flows of people and resources throughout the city.

8.2 Area of Study

Visakhapatnam (also known as Vizag) extended over an area of 515 sq. km is among the five major harbors in the state. The city coordinates lies between 17.7041°N and 83.2977°E. The population of Visakhapatnam Urban Agglomeration is 1,730,320 (Census 2011).

The city is located on the eastern coast of India, which is particularly vulnerable to climate change induced extreme events like cyclones and storm surges.

8.3 Research Questions

During the research, following set of questions have therefore been carefully examined and raised in the light of smart city mission programme in Vizag city.

- What is the status of sewerage and waste management in the city?
- Whether any form of urban renewal/transformation facilities present in Vizag city?
- What is the status of basic civic amenities in the city?
- Whether a good banking facilities available in the area with enough ATMs?
- What are the traffic related issues faced by general public?
- What is the most important environmental issue of the city?
- What is the status of awareness regarding sustainable living among general public?

8.4 Aims and Objectives of the Study

The main aim of the study is to assess the parameters of a smart city with respect to Vizag in the light of Urban Planning.

The major objectives of this research work are enumerated below:

1. To analyse the status of sewerage and waste management in the city.

2. To identify the form of urban renewal/transformation facilities present in Vizag city.
3. To analyse the status of basic civic amenities in the city.
4. To figure out the status of banking infrastructure within the city.
5. To identify major environmental issue in Vizag city.
6. To identify the traffic related issues faced by general public.
7. To figure out the awareness level among general public regarding sustainable living.
8. To bring out the various measures that can be implied to solve the problems.

8.5 Reasons for Selection as a Study Area

People living in Vizag city belongs to different economic strata with different occupations and activities and need convenient facilities in the city. There are number of educational institutes and also state and central government establishments (GVMC, VUDA) located in Vizag city. There are also big public sector undertakings in the city. Along with that, the city has an intricate Urban Planning which makes it a good study area.

8.6 Literature Review

Any research study is based on past research work. A literature survey will give focus to the theme, area, and serves as a background to any research study

Tong, et. Al., (2018) in their study on Optimization of Urban land development spatial allocation based on ecology, have shown how a balanced coordination of the layout of ecological spaces along with urban land development can be used to maximize the profit of developed land without affecting ecological protection.

Zubizarreta, et. Al., (2016) in their study on Smart city concept have analysed different European smart city classification standards with actual 33 smart cities distributed all around the world to see how realities aligns with the concept of smart cities.

Mir, et. Al., (2010) in their study have presented their views on space development models with special reference to India, where they have tried to incorporate the transport parameters directly into the space development (SD) model for deciding the location of economic activities in urban regions.

Raparthy (2018) in her study have assessed the role of master plans in Urban Planning policies to counter climate changes. The study highlights the use of master plans as an effective tool in mitigating climate change and producing low carbon regions through urban planning.

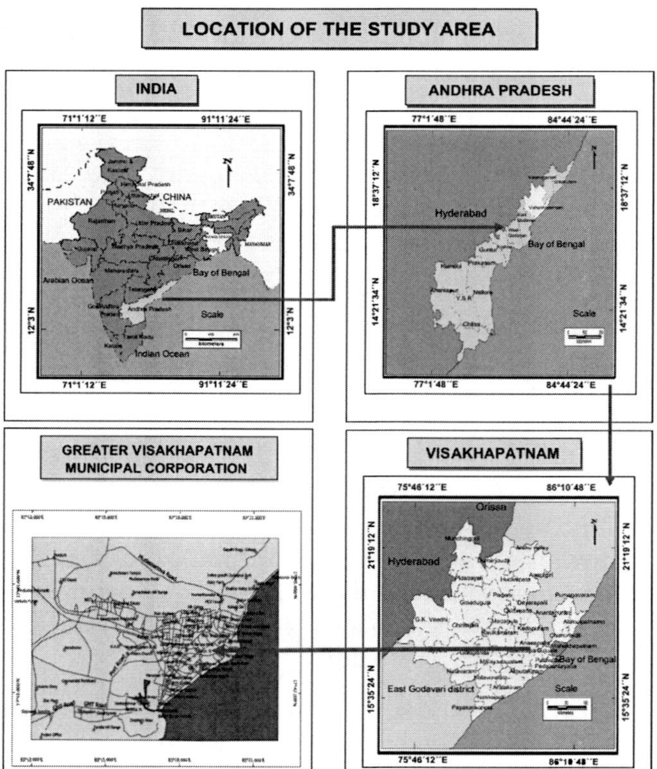

Fig 1: Location map of Visakhapatnam city

Source: Oxford school of ATLAS, Vishakhapatnam urban development authority, GVMC

8.7 Database and methodology

Based on a descriptive research design, this research work is based on various primary and secondary data, collected from various sources. Primary data were collected from the local respondents by conducting a survey upon a definite questionnaire. Questionnaires on different Geographical aspects including Urban planning were set up and asked to the people residing there. Secondary data were collected from various websites, offices and other mobile applications. After obtaining the required data and information, statistical analyses were done in M.S. Excel. After that, mapping of the required area is done based on several themes on Map info and QGIS platforms. Lastly that the problems are identified and suggestions are offered to overcome those problems.

8.8 Limitations of The Study

The main limitation of such research is the lack of reliable data. The primary data reliability sometimes suffered from the problem of suppression of facts by respondents of Vizag city. However due socio-political pressure, biased opinion and in different behaviours have been observed among the respondents while the primary survey has been done. In some cases the secondary data base was not available in government offices due to absence of proper records, legal obligation and lack of co-ordination between different departments of the government organisation. Sometime some of the officials and executive did not give time enough and relevant information due to some pressure during their service periods.

Due to irregular update of information in the respective websites, contemporary data becomes unavailable which imposed an obstacle to carry forward to present study.

8.9 Research Gap

There was no research gap as such that had been identified during the work. There are several available articles, journals, books, websites etc. related to the topic of Smart city planning of Vizag. Being a smart city, Vizag encourages researchers to work on this area.

8.10 Background of The Study Area

Based on topographical conditions, Vizag and its surroundings can be divided into four categories viz., Hilly region, Upland tracks, Rolling plains and Plains. The Kailasa and Yarada are the major hill ranges in the city. The Kailasa hill range stretches from Simhachalam to MVP Colony on the north flank of the city. The city, which appears like a small basin, is surrounded by the Yarada hill popularly known as Dolphin's nose (358 m) on the side of the Kailasgiri hills on the north, with the Bay of Bengal forming the eastern wall. The coastal line runs from north-east to south west over a distance of six kilometres. On the west there is an extensive tidal basin called Upputeru now under reclamation. Beyond Yarada there is a valley followed by another range of hills.

Visakhapatnam has a tropical wet and dry climate (Köppen Aw). The annual mean temperatures ranges between 24.7-30.6°C (76-87°F), with the maximum in the month of May and the minimum in January; the minimum temperatures ranges between 20-27°C (68-81°F). It receives rainfall from the South-west and North-east monsoons and the average annual rainfall recorded is 1,118.8 mm (44.05 in).

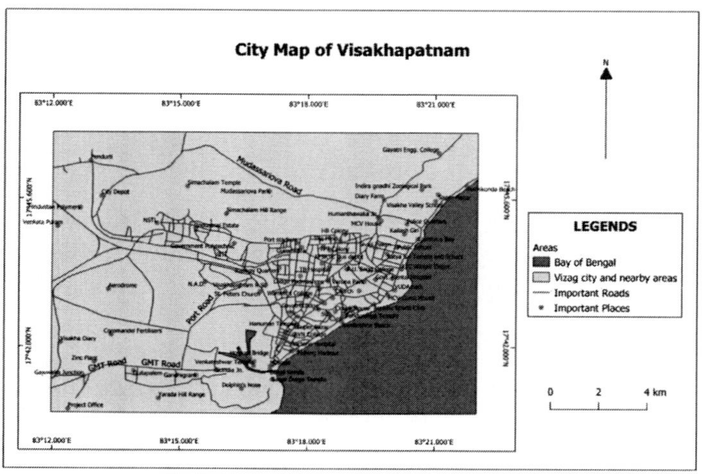

Fig 2: City Map of Vizag

Source: Digitised by the author

8.11 Perception Study on Urban Planning of Vizag

Here perception study on urban Planning of Vizag City has been done based on Primary data.

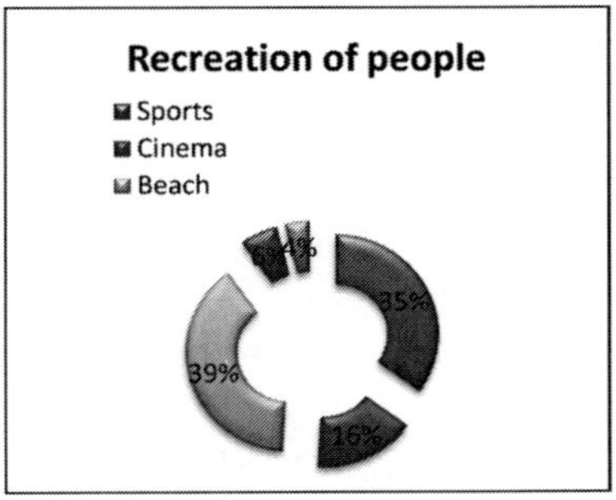

Fig. 3: Recreation for the people of Vizag

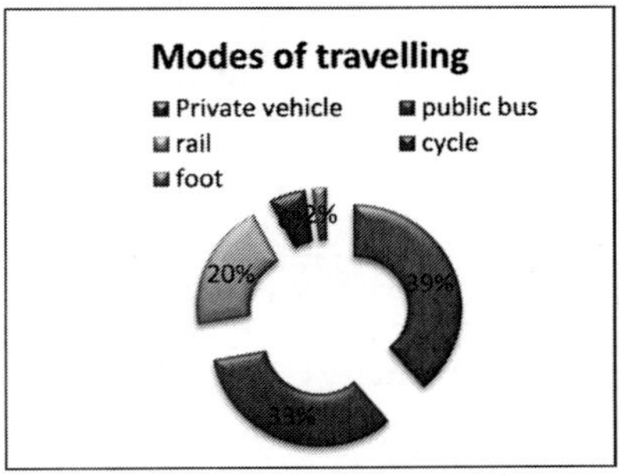

Fig. 4: Modes of Travelling of the people

Source: Primary Survey

This data (Fig. 3) discussed the recreation of people. Here a majority of the 39% of the respondents prefer beach as their main mode of recreation, followed by 35% of sports, 16% of cinema, 6% said other outdoor activities and 4% did nothing of sort respectively. Thus, it can be seen from here that maximum people goes to beach for their recreation.

This figure (Fig. 4) presents the preference of mode of travelling by the respondents. After analysis it was observed that 39% is travelling by private vehicles, 33% is by public vehicles, 20% is by rail, 6% by cycle and 2% is by foot respectively. So, a majority of the people is travelling either by private vehicles or by public vehicles.

This data (Fig. 5) describes the problems of water supply. Where 78% of the respondents says it is frequent water cuts, 12% says it is not clean, 2% says it's expensive and the remaining 14% cites other problems. So, basically there are not much problems as such related to water supply except for water cuts.

This figure (Fig. 6) presents the monthly electricity bill of the respondents. Where 3% of them says it is less than Rs. 100, 14% says it's between Rs. 100-500, 31% of them are of

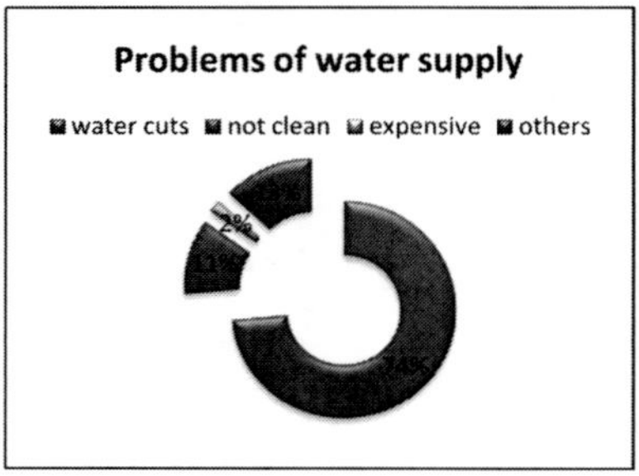

Fig. 5: Problems regarding water supply

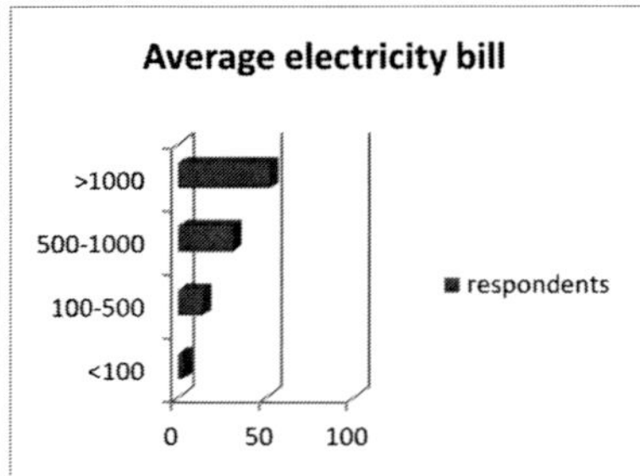

Fig. 6: Average monthly electric bill

Source: Primary Survey

the opinion that it's between Rs. 500-1000 and lastly, 52% says it is more than Rs. 1000. So basically the electricity bill of the people of Vizag exceeds 1000 bucks per month.

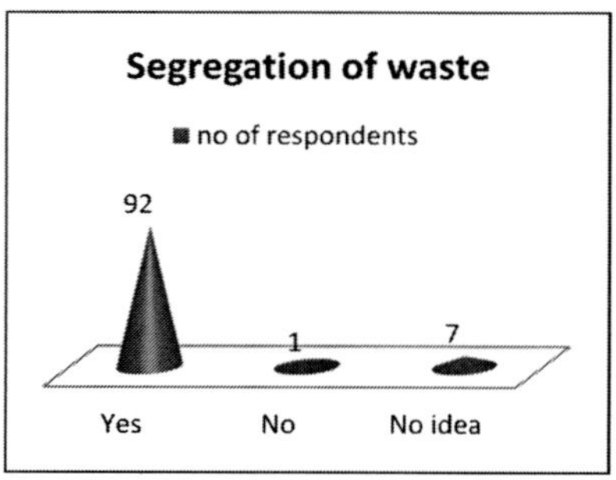

Fig. 7: Presence of Waste Segregation

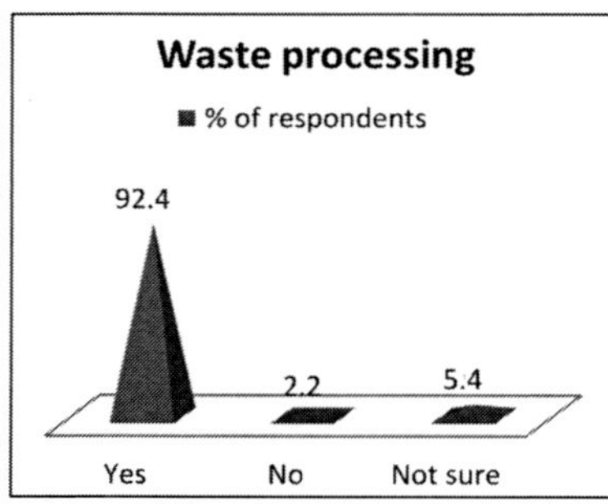

Fig 8: Presence of Waste Processing

Source: Primary Survey

This data (Fig. 7) describes the presence of waste segregation within the city. Where 92% of respondents said yes, there was proper segregation of waste which was taking place there, 1% of the respondents said no and 7% of respondents were not having any idea about the issue. So we can conclude that waste segregation properly done in Vizag city.

This figure (Fig. 8) shows the knowledge of the respondents regarding the waste processing. Here, 92.4% of the respondents was agreed about the proper processing of waste. 2.2% of respondents said no and 5.4% of respondents were not sure. So, we can conclude that waste processing is rightly done in this city.

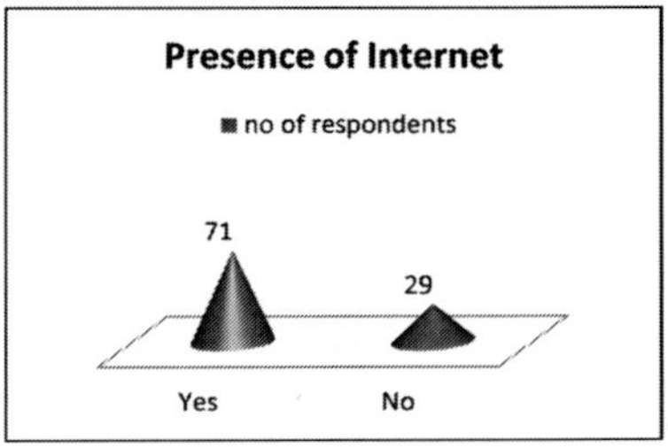

Fig. 9: Presence of Internet Connection

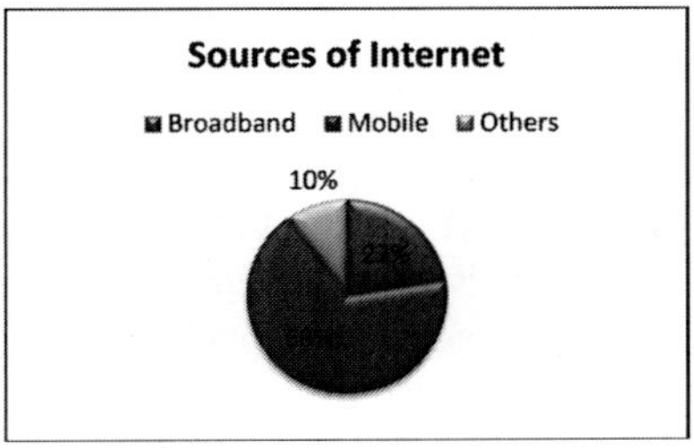

Fig. 10: Sources of Internet Services

This diagram (Fig. 9) describes the presence of internet within the city as perceived by the respondents. Where 71% of respondents said yes and 29% of respondents said no. So we can conclude that more respondents agreed with the presence of good internet connection in the area.

This figure (Fig. 10) represents the percentages for the sources of internet. Where 23% of the respondents use broadband, 68% use mobile and 10% of the respondents use other sources. Therefore, we can conclude that mobile internet users are higher percentage than the broadband and other sources of internet users.

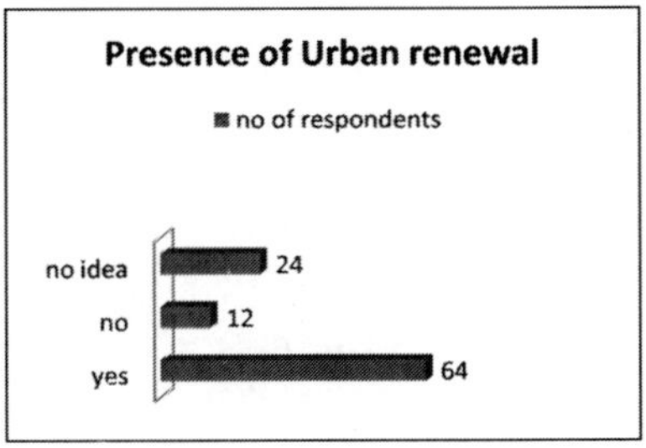

Fig. 11: Presence of Urban Renewal

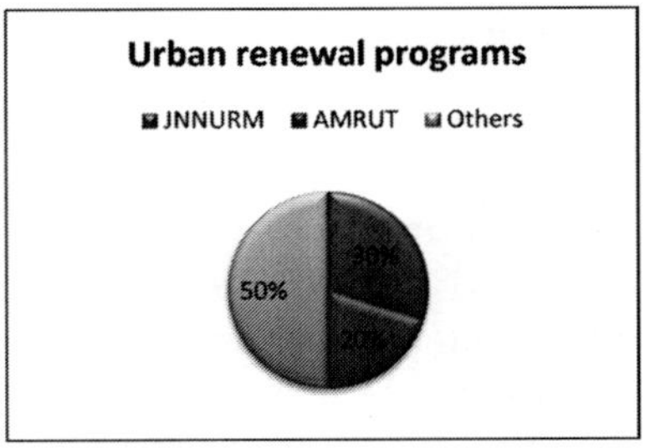

Fig. 12: Urban Renewal Programs

Source: Primary Survey

This diagram (Fig 11) discussed the presence of urban renewal programmes in the city. Here we find that 64% of the respondents agrees to the presence of urban renewal programmes, 12% said no and the rest 24% had no idea. So we can conclude that there are presence of urban renewal mission in this city.

This information (Fig. 12) stated about the percentages showing different urban renewal programs. Where 30% JNNURM, 20% AMRUT and 50% other programmes are present, which include programs like HRIDAY, BSUP, IHSDP which are much more effective in the city . So we can conclude that other governmental scheme more effective than JNNURM and AMRUT in this city.

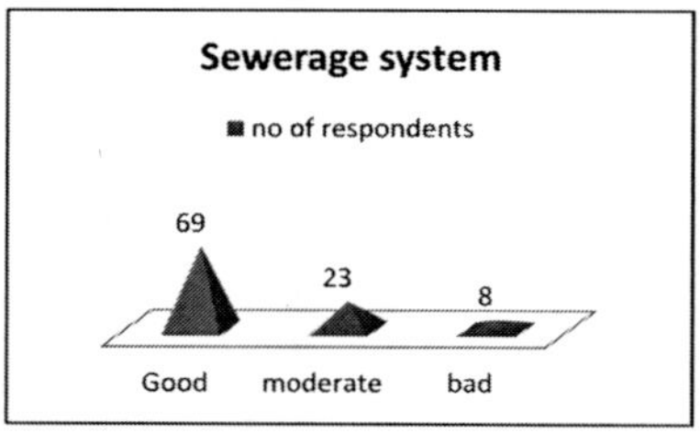

Fig. 13: Presence of Sewerage System

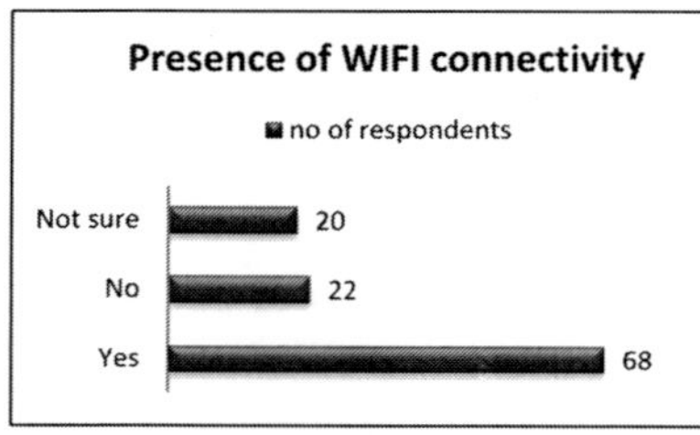

Fig. 14: Presence of WIFI

This figure (Fig. 13) rates the quality of the sewerage system. Where 69% of respondents said its good, 23% of respondent said moderate, 8% of respondents said bad. So we can observe that the overall sewerage system is good in this city.

This figure (Fig. 14) shows the presence of WIFI connectivity as perceived by the respondents. Where 20% of respondents were not sure about the, 22% of respondents are said no and 68% of respondents are said yes, there is availability of good wifi. So, we can say that higher percentage respondents are positive about the presence of good WIFI connectivity in the area.

This figure (Fig. 15) describes the presence of a good banking facility in the city. Here, 84% of respondents have said yes, there is a good banking facility in the area. 9% of respondents are said no and 7% of respondents are said no idea. So, we can conclude that large no. of respondents agrees with presence of good banking facility.

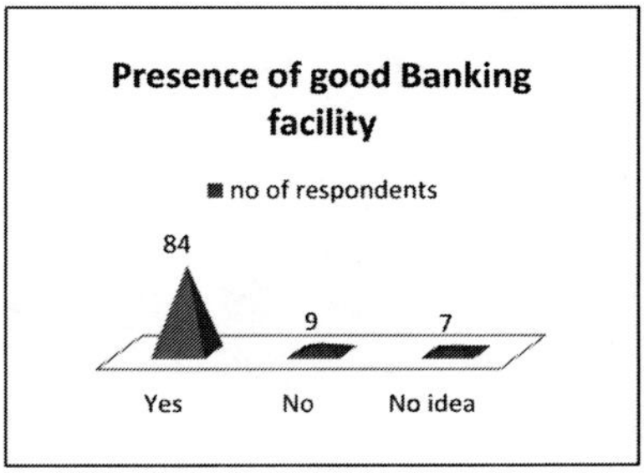

Fig. 15: Presence of Banking Facilities

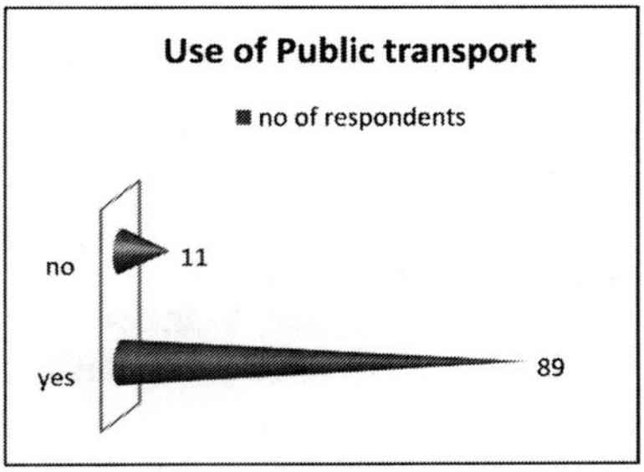

Fig. 16: Use of Public Transport by People

Source: Primary Survey

This diagram (Fig. 16) presented about the use of public transport. Here 11% of respondents said no, they don't use public transport and 89% of respondents are said yes. So, we can conclude that high percentages of respondents are using public transport.

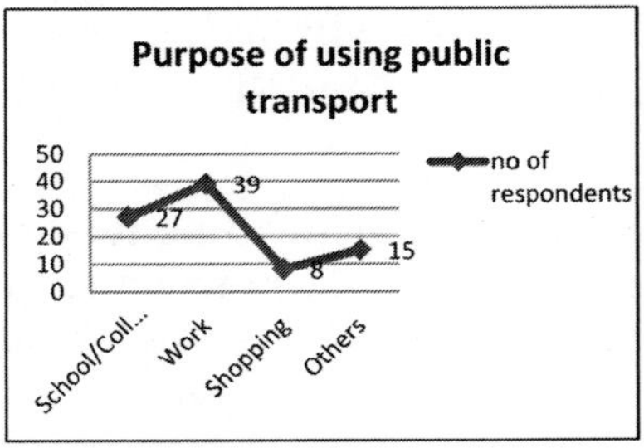

Fig. 17: Purpose of Using Public Transport

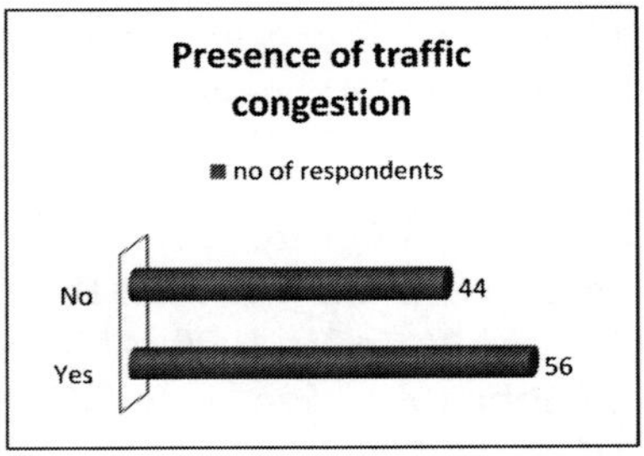

Fig. 18: Presence of Traffic Congestion

Source: Primary Survey

This figure (Fig. 17) discussed the purpose of using public transport. Here, a majority of 39% of the respondents use public transport for working purpose, followed by school/ college (27%), shopping (8%) and others (15%).

This figure (Fig. 18) discussed the presence of traffic congestion. Where 44% of respondents were negative and said no, there aren't any traffic congestions but 56% of respondents have said yes it is a big issue. So, we can conclude that more or less traffic congestion is present in this city.

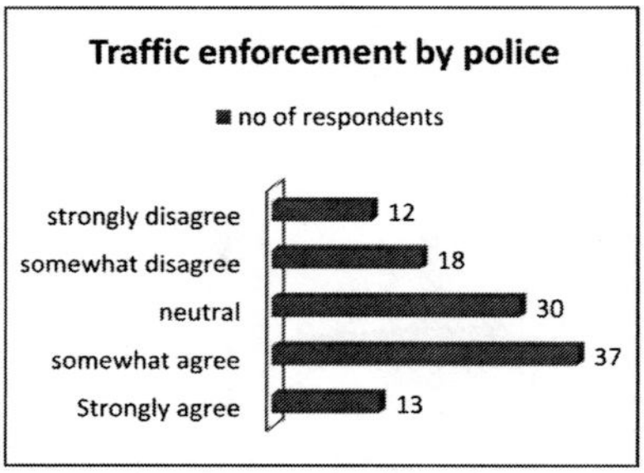

Fig. 19: Traffic Enforcement by Police

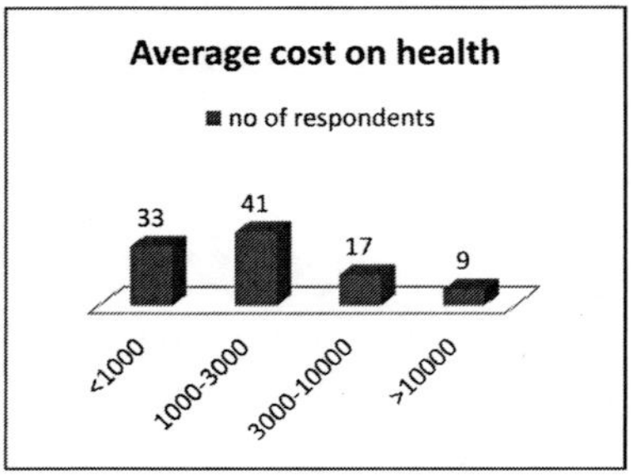

Fig. 20: Average Cost on Health

Source: Primary Survey

This figure (Fig. 19) stated about the availability of proper traffic enforcement by police. Here, around 37% of the respondents somewhat agreed that proper traffic enforcement is available, followed by neutral (30%), those who somewhat disagreed (18%), those who strongly agreed (13%) and those who strongly disagreed (12%). So we can conclude that more or less traffic is enforced by police in this city.

This diagram (Fig. 20) informed about the average per month cost on health of the people of Vizag, where 33% said it's less than Rs.1000, 41% said it is between Rs. 1000-3000, 17% has a range of Rs.3000-10000 and 9% is having more than Rs. 10000.

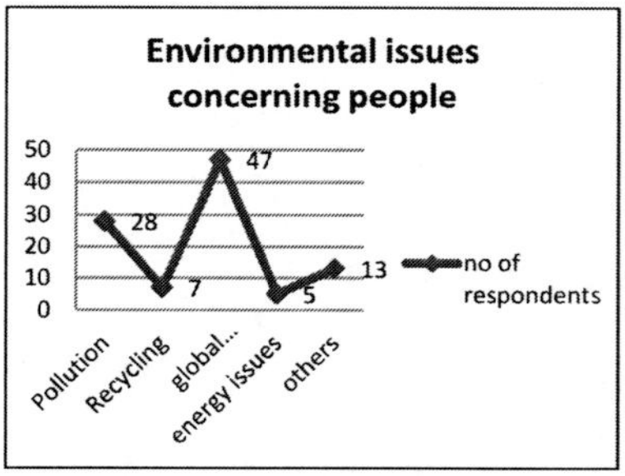

Fig. 21: Environmental Issues of people

Fig. 22: Waste Management practices by people

Source: Primary Survey

This diagram (Fig. 21) represented the environmental issues concerning people in the area. Here, 28% of respondents said pollution is the main problem, 7% of respondents said recycling is a concern, 47% of respondents said global warming leading to a rise in the average temperature, 5% of respondents said energy issues and 13% referred to other issues. So, we can conclude that excess heat due to global warming and pollution are the major issues than the other issues.

This figure (Fig. 22) informed about the waste management practices that the respondents practice themselves. Here it was observed that 17% of the respondents uses cloth bags, 8% only buy bottle drink when in need, 14% reduced paper usage, 37% of respondents said waste segregation and 24% referred to other practices.

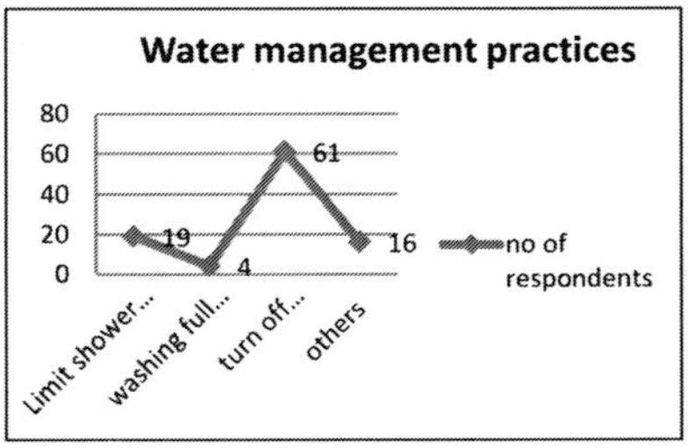

Fig. 23: Water Management Practices

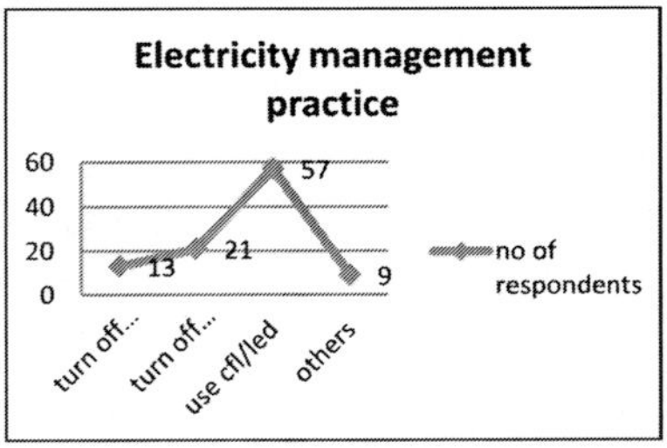

Fig. 24: Electricity Management Practices

Source: Primary Survey

This diagram (Fig. 23) discussed the water management practices performed by the respondents where 19% of the respondents take limited shower time, 4% of respondents washes full loads of laundry, 61% of respondents turn off unused taps and 16% of respondents said other practices. So, overall there is an awareness of water conservation among the respondents.

This data (Fig. 24) informed about the electricity management practices. Where 13% turn off unused lights, 21% turn off unused electronics when not in use, 57% use CFLs/LEDs and 9% using other practices.

8.12 Findings of The Study

1) In the Vizag city maximum people goes to beach for their recreation & majority of the people is travelling either by private vehicles or by public vehicles.
2) There are not much problems as such related to water supply except for water cuts and the electricity bill of the people of Vizag normally exceeds 1000 bucks per month.
3) The percentage of plastic waste is higher than other waste but it can also be said that waste segregation is properly done in Vizag city.
4) The waste processing is rightly done in this city. The people of Vizag use quite a wide number of appliances.
5) More respondents agreed with the presence of good internet connection in the area and also mobile internet users are higher percentage than the broadband and other sources of internet users.
6) There are presence of urban renewal mission in this city, as programmes like HRIDAY, BSUP, IHSDP, JNNURM and AMRUT are very much effective in changing the urban landscape of the city.
7) Higher percentage of respondents are positive about the presence of good WIFI connectivity in the area. The overall network speed is also good in this city.
8) Beach is most preferred form of recreation in the city along with that, a large no. of respondents agree with presence of good banking facility but there is a presence of less number of ATMs.
9) Here, high percentages of respondents are using public transport where a majority of the public uses it for working purpose followed by schools and colleges.
10) Here, more or less traffic congestion is present in this city and also the traffic enforcement by police in this city is average.
11) Here, excess heat due to global warming and pollution are the major issues than the other environmental issues.

12) There is overall an average level of awareness among the respondents regarding waste management practices, water and electricity conservation.

13) The northern part of Andhra Pradesh is having good transport accessibility with respect to Vizag, but the southern parts of the state has a relatively average to poor transport accessibility.

8.13 Limitations

1) One of the main problems that are faced by the people of Vizag are frequent water cuts.

2) The percentage of plastic waste is higher than other waste which needs to be addressed.

3) There are less number of ATMs in the city. It causes problems to the visiting tourists.

4) There are fair amount of traffic congestion present in the city which is really troublesome for a smart city. This problem needs to be addressed.

5) The police enforcement in the area is average as seen from the research as there are no strict traffic enforcement as such.

6) In some areas the sewage system is average or even below average. The local government should take actions.

7) Among environmental problems faced by the locals there are problems of excess heat during the summer months and there are pollution related problems as well.

8) Environmental awareness among people should be more than what it is at present for maintaining sustainable Urbanism.

9) Road connectivity to other parts of the state should improve with respect to Vizag.

8.14 Suggestions

1) A perennial source of water should be taken up to supply water to the households without frequent water cuts.

2) Desalinization plants should be set up in order to supply fresh water to the households from the brackish sea water.
3) Use of plastic wastes should be minimized and in order to do that the government at first should restrict the use of plastics with strict policy implementation and encourage using of cloth, fiber or jute bags for daily use.
4) The number of ATMs should be increased, for that locals, government and the Banks should work together.
5) In order to limit traffic congestions there should be constructions of flyovers and the conditions of traffic signals and enforcement should be improved.
6) The local governments should improve the sewage conditions of certain areas of the city. Open drains should be closed as it becomes a living place of many disease spreading mosquitoes and other pests.
7) There should be more plantation programs which should be followed throughout the city which will not only help to regulate the excess heat but also will help to control the level of pollution in the inner parts of the city.
8) Overall awareness should be increased among the people so that they use more eco-friendly and sustainable mode of living. For that, individuals, NGOs, educational institutions as well as government should step forward.
9) Transport connectivity via roadways should be improved by the government as Vizag is one of the most important city with respect to industries, port and other facilities. A better network connectivity can ensure better resource allocation.

8.15 Conclusion

After been observed all the aforesaid things it can thus be concluded that Visakhapatnam, popularly known as Vizag City is one of the most important district city of the state of Andhra Pradesh. Since the city is growing day by day it is important to have a look at the planning of the city as with increase of Urbanization there will be an increase in Urban problems. Despite of the fact that the administration is constantly working for the betterment of the City as well as the people residing in it, there are some notable problems which is can be seen. A proper scientific and sustainable planning of the city will help it in the future to become one of the most smart, developed and liveable cities of not only India but also of the world.

References

Mir, M.S., Rao, K.K. and Hunt, J.D., (2010). "Space development modeling of urban regions in developing countries". *Journal of urban planning and development*, 136(1), pp.75-85.

Raparthi, K., 2018. "Assessing the role of urban planning policies in meeting climate change mitigation goals in Indian cities". *Journal of Urban Planning and Development*, 144(2), p.05018005.

Tong, H., Shi, P., Bao, S., Zhang, X. and Nie, X. (2018). "Optimization of Urban Land Development Spatial Allocation Based on Ecology-Economy Comparative Advantage Perspective". *Journal of Urban Planning and Development*, 144(2), p.05018006.

Zubizarreta, I., Seravalli, A. and Arrizabalaga, S., (2016). "Smart city concept: What it is and what it should be". *Journal of Urban Planning and Development*, 142(1), p.04015005.

Part-II
Issues of Urban Environment and Sustainability

9

Temporal Land Use Change Pattern of Kaptai Lake and surrounding area using Remotely Sensed Data, Bangladesh

Md. Mujibor Rahman[1] and Md. Al Amin[2]

Abstract: Kaptai Lake and it surrounding area has become a very important place due to its natural resources, the largest man-made freshwater body in Bangladesh which generates a significant share of Bangladesh's power supply by using hydro-power. Over the past few decades water level and forest cover depletion has become a main problem here because of human intervention. Studies have been done to assess the water level and land cover, vegetation health and surface temperature changing in this important area. In order to perform "change detection" Landsat satellite images, belonging to 1976, 1989, 2005 and 2018 years have been used. Three land cover classes were used via "regions of interest" to perform the "maximum likelihood" algorithm of supervised classification system. From last 42 years land cover analysis the rate of decrease water level 10.48% in 1976 to 9.55% in 2018, others increase (paved surface) 10.66% in 1976 to 24.28% in 2018 where vegetation decrease 79.80% in 1976 to 65.23% in 2018 respectively. To extract NDVI values are initially performed by ENVI Classic 5.3 remote sensing software to classify NDVI maps. The present study shows that from last

[1]Professor Environmental Science Discipline, Khulna University, Khulna 9208, Bangladesh. Email: mujib@es.ku.ac.bd
[2]Research Associate of Environmental Science Discipline, Khulna University, Bangladesh. Email: ahmedprince101023@gmail.com

29 years vegetation health categories such as sparse vegetation, moderate vegetation and dense vegetation areas changed from 13.04%, 13.04% and 47.83% in 1889 to 19.32%, 19.83% and 21.36% in 2018 respectively which indicate vegetation health decrease greatly in Kaptai sub-basin. This study has been made to estimate surface temperature using ArcGIS 10.5 software over Kaptai sub-basin, using Landsat 5 and 8 satellite data. The study shows that last 29 years change of maximum temperature which indicate paved surface temperature is increased greatly from 26.2512°C in 1989 to 29.5969°C in 2018 where minimum temperature which indicate vegetation cover temperature is increased in little rate from 16.1037°C in 1989 to 17.4765°C in 2018 respectively. This study is a small preliminary effort to look into the land cover change pattern of Kaptai sub-basin which might be useful as a starting point for further in depth spatial study of these problem to figure out possible remedies.

Keywords: *Kaptai Lake, Temporal Land use change, DEM, Water level change, LULC, Vegetation health, NDVI, Surface temperature change, Remote Sensing, GIS.*

9.1 Introduction

Man-made lakes affect the environment in many ways. Some of these effects are landscape and land-use/land-cover changes, loss of habitat for existing species due to flooding, and settlement of the new inhabitants in the flooded area (Dale et al., 2011). Man-made lakes can also change groundwater levels and, consequently, cause a decline of ambient species sensitive to groundwater level disturbances (Antonicet al., 2001). Kaptai Lake is one of the most important freshwater body which is the largest man-made fresh water resource in the South-East Asia as well as in Bangladesh (ARG, 1986). This lake is a Sub-basin of Karnaphuli River and was primarily created for hydro-electrical power generation with an installed capacity of 230 MW. It is the only hydropower source in Bangladesh; about 5% of the electricity consumed in the country is produced there (pinakiat al., 2003). Although Kaptai Lake primarily created for hydro-electric power generation, now the Kaptai Lake contributes significantly to the production of freshwater fish, flood control, tourism and agriculture. At present Kaptai sub-basin is suffering from many problems.The present status of Kaptai sub-basin is totally have a bad impact on development in this region because of conflict. The ecological damage of the lake recently assessed shows that water pollution due to use of fertilizers and pesticides used in lake adjacent crop fields polluting lake water (Galib, 2009). Forest depletion and reservoir sedimentation has already become a serious problem for Kaptai Lake (Chowdhury, 1992). Replacing the forest cover with shifting cultivation, increasing soil erosion which is eventually contributing large amounts of sedimentation to the reservoir posing a serious threat to the power plant as well as navigability (UNEP, 2002).

With the advancement of technology, reduction in data cost, availability of historic spatio-temporal data and high resolution satellite images, GIS and Remote Sensing techniques are now very useful for conducting researches like land cover change detection analysis and predicting the future scenario (Das, 2009). Temporal land-use-change patterns are the result of the complex interaction between the human and the physical environment (Li and Hao, 2003). Now-a-days, Satellite based earth observation and monitoring has become a very scientific and effective tool to detect and monitor land cover changes (Roy and Saha, 2016).

The digital elevation model (DEM) provide a solid technical foundation for the development of a digital hydrological model that can be used for watershed extraction and topographic analysis (Mantelli et al., 2011). Digital Elevation Models (DEM) provides basic information on elevation of Earth's surface and are freely available from ASTER (Advanced Space borne Thermal Emission and Reflection Radiometer) data - a mission of JAPAN (Srivastava and Mondal, 2012).

Land use and land cover change is a major issue of concern with regards to change in the global environment

(Qian et al., 2007). Change detection is the process of identifying differences in the state of an object or phenomenon by observing it at different times (Singh, 1989). According to Ref. (Maseket al., 2000), land use and land cover changes respond to socio-economic, political, cultural, demographic and environmental conditions and forces which are largely characterized by high human populations.

Remote Sensing technology is one of the most beneficial tools to study spatial and temporal changes of vegetation health. The vegetation health includes only planted land, i.e., grass, trees (Aly, 2007; Singh, 2013). Loss of vegetation health and plant species diversity reduces resistance of soil erosion and soil fertility (Berendseet al., 2015). The normalized difference vegetation index (NDVI) is representative of the various spectral vegetation indices (Rouse el al., 1974). The concept of the NDVI technique is based on the principle that healthy vegetation has low reflectance rates of the electromagnetic spectrum's visible side because of chlorophyll (Campbell, 2002).

Surface temperature is a basic determinant of the terrestrial thermal behavior, as it controls the effective radiating temperature of the Earth's surface (Zhang et al., 2008). The retrieval of the surface temperature from remotely sensed TIR data has attracted much attention, especially from Landsat-8 TIR bands. Landsat-8 carries two sensors, i.e., the operational land imager (OLI) and the thermal infrared sensor (TIRS); the Landsat-5 Thematic Mapper (TM) which has a 120-m resolution (Vidal, 1991).

Kaptai Lake is a sub-basin of Karnaphuli River has become a very important place due to its geographic location. It is general impression that changes the water level and elevation of Kaptai sub-basin, land cover changes of Kaptai sub-basin area, vegetation health change in area decreased substantially and also temperature changes influence land cover over 42 years. To look into these issue it is necessary to map the trend of water level and land cover change (1976-2018), vegetation health and surface temperature changes

(1989-2018) in the Kaptai Lake and its surrounding areas using remote sensing technology and spatial functionalities technique in Geographical Information System (GIS). There is no study found that worked on temporal land cover change pattern mapping from satellite imagery at high resolution in Kaptai watershed. Mainly found survey based and laboratory based experiments of Kaptai Lake and its surrounding area not remotely sensed using data based experiments in present.

9.2 Objectives

The aim of the study is to detect temporal land use change pattern of Kaptai sub-basin area over times with the following specific objectives:

- To detect change of water body and land cover area of Kaptai sub-basin from 1976 to 2018;
- To assess the changes in vegetation health from 1989 to 2018; and
- To show surface temperature variation relationship with others characters of Kaptai sub-basin from 1989 to 2018.

Kaptai Lake which situated in most of Rangamati District and some part in Khagrachhari District is the largest man-made freshwater body in Bangladesh which is sub-basin of Karnaphuli River (Fernando, 1980). Though created primarily for hydro-electric power generation, it contributes to produce significant quantity of freshwater fishes, navigation, flood control and agriculture, etc. Kaptai sub-basin for the purpose of this study is considered to be bounded within a rectangle with its upper left comer at 92°00' E longitude and 23.40° N latitude and the lower right corner at 92.30° E longitude and 22.20° N latitude. Kaptai reservoir was created with the construction of an earth dam across the Karnaphuli River at Kaptai, about 70 km upstream from the estuary of Chittagong, in 1955 for production of hydro-electricity, which came into operation in January 1962 (BPDB, 1985). It is covering an area of approximately 58 300 ha (68 800 ha at full surface level). The maximum and mean depths of the reservoir are 35 m and 9 m, respectively, mean annual water level fluctuation is 8.14 m and the water reserve is 524.7×106 m^3

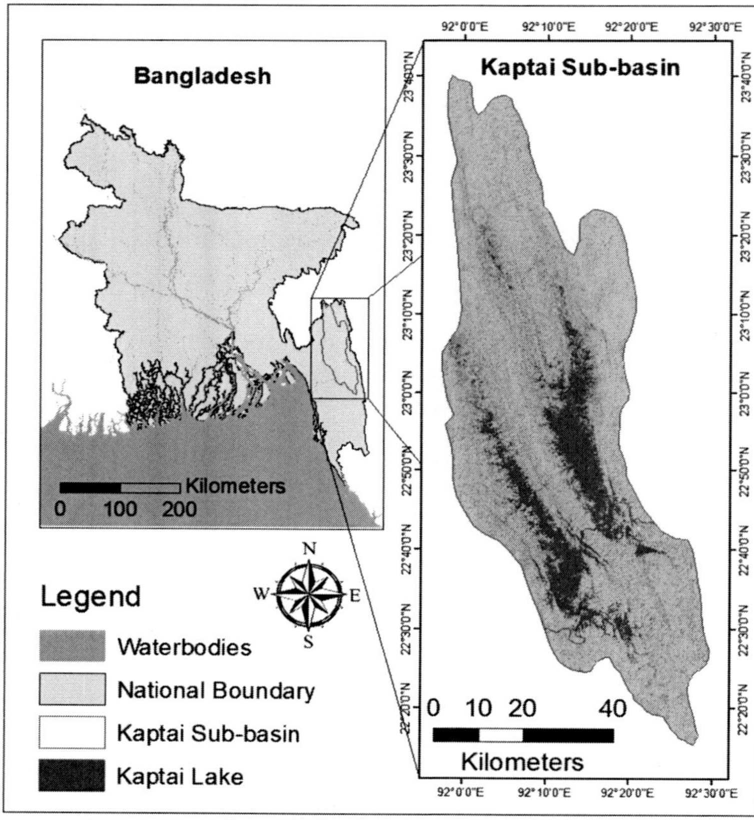

Fig. 1: Location of The Study Area in the context of Bangladesh and Kaptai Sub-basin.

(Aquatic Research Group, 1986).

9.3 Materials and Methods

For the last 42 year's study, multispectral, multi-temporal LANDSAT and ASTER satellite data of Kaptai sub-basin were acquired between 1976 and 2018. All the LANDSAT and ASTER images have been taken from USGS Earth Explorer. The 1976 images is Landsat 2 (MSS) and 1989 and 2005 images are TM image and the 2018 is OLI-TIRS image both having a resolution of 30 meters. The 2011 images to demarcate of study area using Digital Elevation Model (DEM) from ASTER satellite having a resolution of 15 meters. All the satellite images were brought to Universal Transverse Mercator (UTM) Zone 45N projection and World Geodetic System 1984 (WGS-84) datum. Table shows the list of data acquired along with their date of production, resolution and source. The Landsat images used in this thesis were collected as "level 1 data" from the website of Earth Explorer hosted by the United States Geological Survey (USGS). Because of Landsat 2 MSS satellite has no Band 4 - Near Infrared (NIR); Band 5 -Shortwave Infrared (SWIR) and also Band 10 - Thermal Infrared (TIRS); Band 11 - Thermal Infrared (TIRS) 2 which can estimate NDVI and surface temperature of Kaptai sub-basin, that's why vegetation health and surface temperature of Kaptai sub-basin is estimated from 1989 to 2018 for 29 years with Landsat 5 (Band 4 and 5) and Landsat 8 (Band 10 and 11).

Table – 1
Different Satellite Data Used in This Study

S.No.	Data Type & ID	Study Type	Study year	Scale	Source
1	ASTER (MSS)	digital elevation model (DEM) for Study area	2011	15m	Earth Explorer, USGS
2	Landsat 2	Water level and land cover change	1976	60m	Earth Explorer, USGS
3	Landsat 5 (TM)	Water level and land cover change; NDVI and Surface temperature	1989 and 2005	30m	Earth Explorer, USGS
4	Landsat 8 (OLI-TIRS)	Water level and land cover change; NDVI and Surface temperature	2018	30m	Earth Explorer, USGS

All the satellite imagery was geo-referenced using the Ground Control Points (GCPs) collected from the field using a standard GPS device. Three distinct GCPs were chosen for each image. The geometric error was checked for each image using the following equation,

$$RMS_{error} = \sqrt{\left(x' - x_{orig}\right)^2 + \left(y' - y_{orig}\right)^2} \quad \text{... (1)}$$

Where, x' = latitude of the image
y' = longitude of the image
x_{orig} = original latitude of the ground
y_{orig} = original longitude of the ground

Table – 2, shows the average root mean square error for each data.

Table – 2
RMS Error during Geo-Referencing

S.No.	Corresponding Year of Image	RMS Error in Acquired Data
1	1976	0.176985
2	1989	0.002271
3	2005	0.00155
4	2018	0.000085

Study Area Demarcation: The first part of data processing in this research was carried out in ArcGIS 10.5 to demarcate study area of the present study from Digital elevation model (DEM) provide good terrain representations and are commonly used in watershed modeling. ASTER is the one type of DEM used in the current study. An advanced multi-spectral imager called Advanced Space borne Thermal Emission and Reflection Radiometer (ASTER)the spatial resolution can be categorized into 3 groups: VNIR (visible and near-infrared)-15 meter, SWIR (short wave infrared)-30 meter, TIR (thermal infrared)-90 meter. Here, an ASTER DEM of a resolution of 30 m was taken on October 02, 2011 covering the Kaptai sub-basin area for present study was acquired. To create Kaptai watershed four ASTER satellite image are used by mosaicking from ENVI Classic 5.3 software. The Digital Elevation Model (DEM) was created from the TIN using the 3D Analyst tool of ArcMap. It was ensured that the DEM created was free of sinks before further use. Sinks are erroneous depressions that occur as some cells in the DEM assume values that are lower than the neighboring cells. This is caused by the interaction between the algorithms that create the DEM and the data itself. The DEM is a grid of elevation cells where each cell holds the elevation value of the terrain space the cell covers. The study area is not the whole portion of the image. So, to avoid complexity the image are resized using the map coordinates of the study area which generated from DEM ASTER. After that and before the classification process the exact study is area map is digitized using the ROI tool of ENVI Classic 5.3 in order to build a mask band. A mask band let us run any operation only within the masked area. So making is essential to calculate the water level and land cover change statistics, vegetation health monitoring and surface temperature maps.

Water Level and Land Cover Changes: A supervised classification method were applied to the rectified and enhanced multispectral data to analyze different terrain and structure characteristics. For this supervised classification, the Maximum Likelihood (MLC) decision rule, was used. In this study, totally, three LULC classes were established as vegetation, water body and others (building, concrete area, bare soil). The classified maps for 1976, 1989, 2005 and 2018 images are presented in Fig. 2. Envi Classic 5.3 supports both supervised and unsupervised classification of images. Here for better result the "Maximum Likelihood" algorithm of supervised classification. The classification method works upon the preselected ROI. Based on the Landsat band metrics (Near infrared RGB: band 4, 3, 2; and Natural color RGB: band 7, 4, and 2) and personal observation the study area is classified with 3 ROI.

Vegetation Health Monitoring using NDVI: For vegetation health monitoring between 1989 and 2018 year need to assess NDVI (Normalized Difference Vegetation Index). In ENVI Classic 5.3 has NDVI option from which can generating NDVI Map directly. Basically NDVI differencing is a technique which demonstrated the best vegetation change detection. NDVI is calculated from the visible and near infrared light reflected by vegetation. NDVI is calculated from these individual measurements as follows (Arulbalaji and Gurugnanam, 2014):

$$NDVI = \frac{NIR - VIS}{NIR + VIS} \quad \text{... (2)}$$

Where, NIR = spectral reflectance in the near-infrared band, where light scattering from the canopy dominates (0.725–1.1μm); and

VIS = reflectance in the red (visible) band, chlorophyll-absorbing portion of the spectrum (0.58 to 0.68μm).

To see the gradually change of vegetation health, need to extract Normalized Difference Vegetation Index (NDVI) histogram. When ENVI Classic 5.3 generating NDVI maps of 1889 to 2018, from which need to extract NDVI histogram. NDVI histogram range would be between -1 and +1, where increasing positive values indicate increasing green vegetation and negative values indicate non-vegetated surface features such as water, paved surface.

Estimate Surface Temperature: To carry out this research work, have used ArcGIS 10.5 for surface temperature retrieval, procedure for each and every step involved in this process is shown in this procedure. Landsat 8 and 5 satellite images are freely available for research purpose, and can be easily downloaded by accessing the USGS (United States Geological Survey) website. Details of procedure carried out for producing LST and vegetation index maps by using ArcGIS 10.5 Imagine image processing software. Estimation of surface temperature method is divided into some several parts: original DN to TOA value conversion, study area boundary extraction using DEM, then NDVI extraction and last average surface temperature by cell statistics for automatic mapping. The full process of estimation of surface temperature are given below for Kaptai sub-basin as follows:

- **Conversion:** digital number (DN) to Top of Atmosphere (TOA) Radiance;
- Top of Atmosphere (TOA) Brightness Temperature;
- Normalized Differential Vegetation Index (NDVI);
- Land Surface Emissivity (LSE);

- Calculate Land Surface Temperature (LST); and
- Average surface temperature by cell statistics.

These methods are applied to determine the LST from Landsat TM5 and OLI8 data. The results are compared with the values of temperature acquired by the thermal spectrometer of sensor.

9.4 Results and Discussion

9.4.1 Land cover of Kaptai sub-basin for different times

Fig. 2, showing the land cover distribution of Kaptai sub-basin for 1976, 1989, 2005 and 2018 years in which three categories are present in different color like others in red color, water body in blue color and vegetation area in green color which indicate different land cover types. These map are generated from Maximum likelihood classification, then

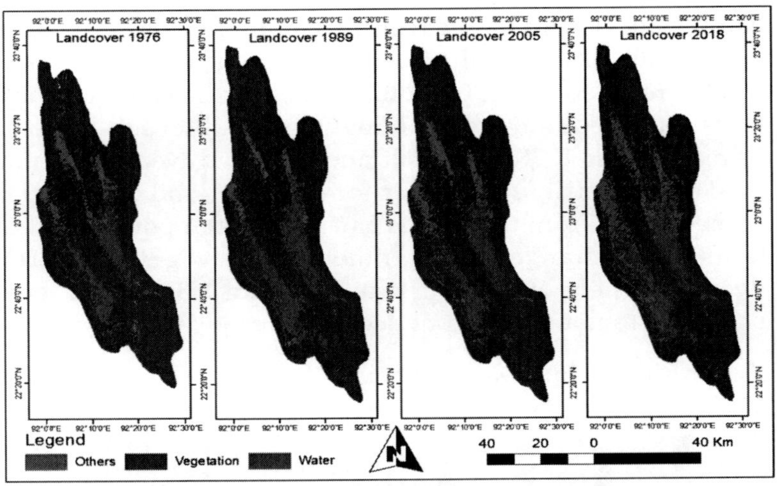

Fig. 2: Land Cover of Kaptai Sub-basin for 1976, 1989, 2005 and 2018.

generated from statistic values which present in Table – 3. Land cover distribution of Kaptai sub-basin maps is given below:

In land cover map 1976, showing the "others" which mean

settlement area, barred land and non-vegetative area (Red color) which visually little that's mean 1976 there is settlement and human activity in Kaptai lake and its surrounding area is little, but vegetation area is dominating that time. In land cover map 1989, showing red color is increasing slowly and also increase blue color. That means green color decrease is little. From land cover map 2005 and 2018, showing red color increasing rate more than past year 1976 and 1989. That's mean green color decrease more than past study years. But blue color not much visually change in land cover map.

The static land cover distribution for each study year as derived from the maps are presented in the table below:

From Table – 3 shows, in 1976 land class pixel values for vegetation occupied only 803487 of the total values which indicate 79.80 % of the total land cover. But with respect to vegetation areas the water body and others scenario of the Kaptai sub-basin's land cover distribution values are 96201 and 107302 of the total values which indicate 10.48%, and 10.66% respectively of the total land cover. This indicate the fact that vegetation area dominating in Kaptai sub-basin at its mark. From 1976, 1989, 2005 and 2018 study year also show land cover distribution values for different land cover types respectively. From the values can see the temporal trend of land cover change which indicate that vegetation area decrease where others increase noticeably. But water level change rate not so much noticeable in study year.

In Fig. 3, shows a comparison between the patterns of

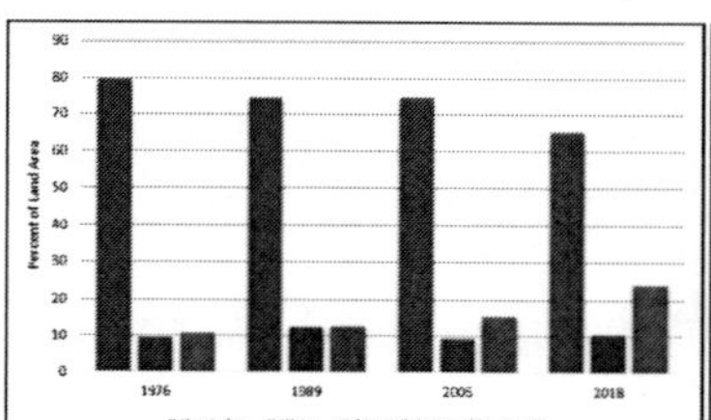

Fig. 3: Land Cover Change Pattern of 1976, 1989, 2005 and 2018

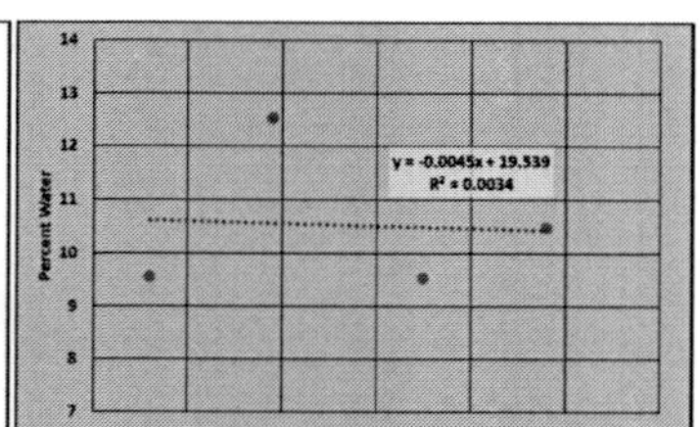

Fig. 4: Water Level Change Pattern on Temporal Basis

Table – 3

NDVI classification for different land cover types of 2006, 2009, 2012 & 2015

Land Cover	1976		1989		2005		2018	
Categories	No. of Pixel	No. of Pixel in (%)	No. of Pixel	No. of Pixel in (%)	No. of Pixel	No. of Pixel in (%)	No. of Pixel	No. of Pixel in (%)
Water Body	96201	10.48	604849	12.54	459492	9.53	505480	9.55
Vegetation	803487	79.80	3605063	74.77	3614835	74.97	3145020	65.23
others	107302	10.66	611762	12.69	747347	15.50	1170597	24.28

land cover in both time windows. Here the water body shows a stability in cover while vegetation cover show gradual decrease most in the figure, from 80 to 65 where others (Built up and barren soil) fluctuates.

In Fig. 4, shows water level change pattern trend of Kaptai Lake from 1976 to present which express by Regression Co-efficient (R^2). It is a statistic used in the context of statistical models whose main purpose is either the prediction of future outcomes or the testing of hypotheses, on the basis of other related information. In this study of water level of Kaptai Lake of $R^2 = 0.0034$ which very less than value 1. Because if Regression Co-efficient value is very much less than 1 value, then the change rate very less on temporal basis and near

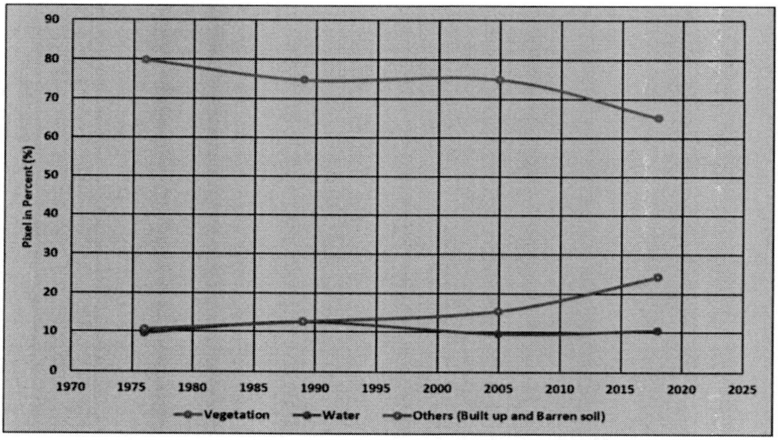

Fig. 5: Temporal Land Cover Change Pattern

future also. So the water level change of Kaptai Lake is not noticeable in near future, but also it decrease its water level day to day because of land slide, soil erosion because of decrease of vegetation cover and sedimentation which is tensed for Kaptai sub-basin area's natural environment.

In Fig. 5, shows the different cover types change pattern distribution from 1976 to 2018 study year in line chart. It shows a comparison between the patterns of land cover in both time windows. Here vegetation cover shows gradual decrease where others (built up and barren soil area) gradually increase most in the figure in present and near future. If the present condition will continue with human activity, urbanization, soil erosion, landslide and deforestation. So vegetation areas and water body in Kaptai sub-basin decrease where others dominate greatly which indicate that natural environment of Kaptai sub-basin gradually decrease. The water level change not so much noticeable in Kaptai Lake, but it also have to consider of Kaptai water body level has maintained to continue hydroelectric power generation, navigation, freshwater source and tourism.

9.4.2 Vegetation Health Monitoring of Kaptai Sub-basin over Time

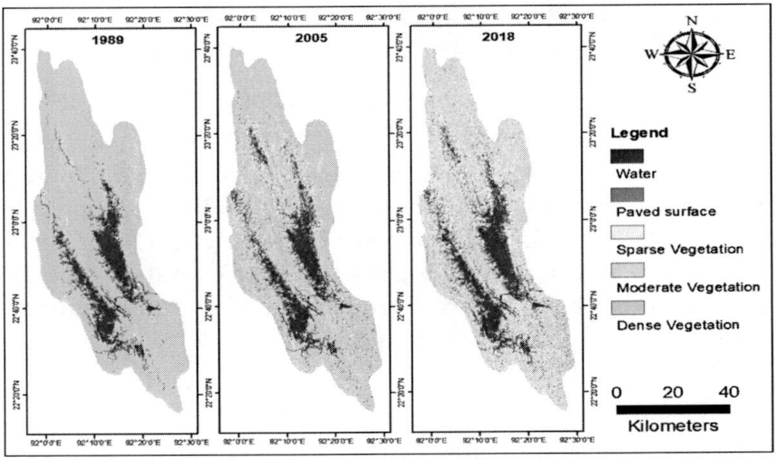

Fig. 6: Vegetation Health Classification Map of 1989, 2005 and 2018 of Kaptai Sub-basin.

Fig. 6, showing the vegetation health classification maps in different color which indicate water, paved surface and vegetation health class into three categories (sparse vegetation, moderate vegetation and dense vegetation) which is given below:

In Fig. 6, showing the vegetation health classification map of 1989, 2005 and 2018 of Kaptai sub-basin categories in different color like others include water body in blue color and paved surface in pink color. But mainly focus on sparse vegetation in yellow color, moderate vegetation in light green

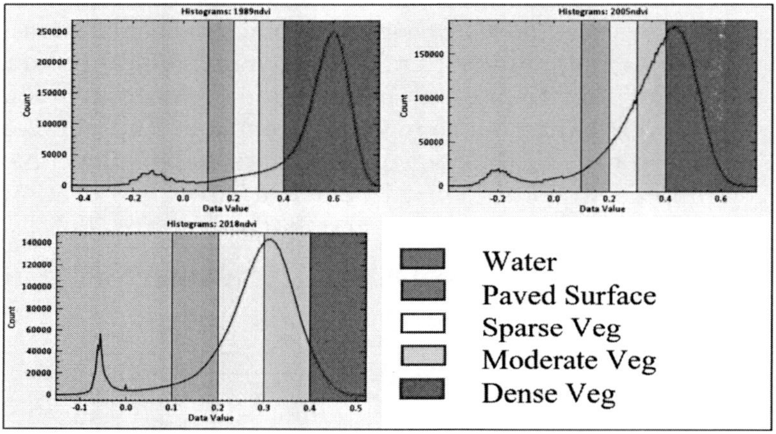

Fig. 7: NDVI histogram result from ENVI Classic 5.3 of 1989, 2005 and 2018

color and dense vegetation in green color in visually. In map we see vegetation health decreasing gradually in Kaptai sub-basin. Especially in 2018 map showing very shocking visual vegetation health decreasing scenario of vegetation cover of Kaptai sub-basin where can see sparse vegetation and moderate vegetation color dominate and dense vegetation cover in very small portion in that area.

In Fig. 7 shows NDVI histogram result from ENVI Classic 5.3 of 1989, 2005 and 2018 which indicates dense vegetation NDVI value more than 0.4 to 0.52 cover and green color area decrease greatly, moderate vegetation NDVI value spread of histogram more than 0.3 to less than 0.4 and Sparse vegetation NDVI value spread from more than 0.1 to less than 0.2 where light green and yellow color in histogram spread little of total vegetation areas in Kaptai sub-basin of study year. In 1989, highest pick of NDVI pixel value found on 0.6 value which means this time dense vegetation cover dominate greatly in Kaptai sub-basin area. In 2005, highest pick of NDVI pixel value found on 0.44 value which means this time dense vegetation cover decrease and getting covert into moderate vegetation cover in Kaptai sub-basin area. In 2018, highest pick of NDVI pixel value found on 0.31 value which means this time moderate vegetation cover dominate and dense vegetation cover is found in small portion in Kaptai sub-basin area.

The vegetation health classification for each study year as derived from NDVI values are presented in the table below:

Table – 4
Vegetation Health Classification for 1989, 2005 & 2018.

Land Cover Classification	Surface Feature	NDVI Value	Percent of Pixel (%) 1989	2005	2018
Non-vegetation Class	Water	<0.1	15.66	14.62	13.02
	Paved Surface	0.1-0.2	10.43	14.73	26.47
Vegetation Health Class	Sparse Vegetation	0.2-0.3	13.04	14.67	19.32
	Moderate Vegetation	0.3-0.4	13.04	14.68	19.83
	Dense Vegetation	>0.4	47.83	41.3	21.36

Table – 4 shows Kaptai sub-basin's vegetation health classification which estimate from NDVI values of 29 years (1989-2018). In 1989 paved surface occupies only 10.43% which very less than of half of total cover area of Kaptai sub-basin. This indicates the fact that anthropogenic activity of Kaptai sub-basin is very little that time. The vegetation health class occupying 13.04% of sparse vegetation and moderate vegetation and 47.83% of dense vegetation land cover indicates vegetation area fairly dominate in Kaptai sub-basin in 1989, especially dense vegetation is found almost half amount of land cover. Where after 29 years in 2018 study year paved surface occupies 26.47% which indicates the fact that human settlement are increasing gradually in Kaptai sub-basin. The vegetation health class occupying 19.32% sparse vegetation, 19.83% moderate vegetation and 21.36% of dense vegetation land cover indicates vegetation health greatly decease in Kaptai sub-basin in 2018 which not well for natural environment as well as wetland ecosystem.

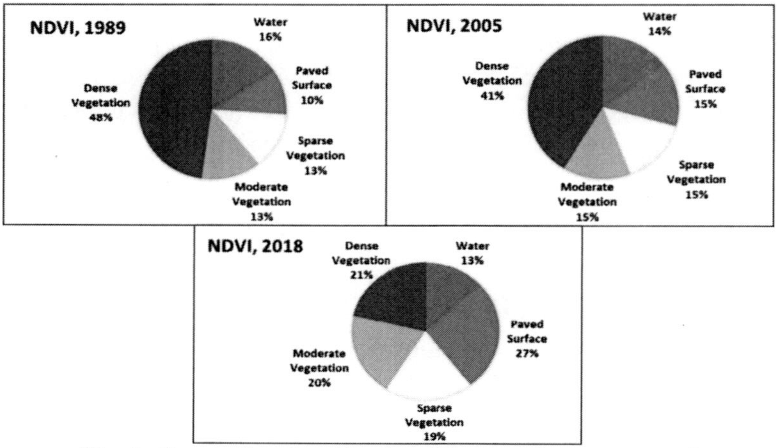

Fig. 8: Vegetation health classification from NDVI of 1989, 2005 and 2018

In Fig. 8 shows sparse vegetation 13%, moderate vegetation 13% and dense vegetation 48% of total 73.91% vegetation areas in Kaptai sub-basin of 1989 study year. In 2005, sparse vegetation 15%, moderate vegetation 15% and dense vegetation 41% of total 70.65% vegetation areas in Kaptai sub-basin. In 2018, sparse vegetation 19%, moderate vegetation 20% and dense vegetation 21% of total 60.51% vegetation areas in Kaptai sub-basin.

9.4.3 Assessment of Surface Temperature over Time in Kaptai Sub-basin

In this study to estimate of surface temperature of different years in Kaptai sub-basin is taken same month (November of last week of winter season, because to get error less, clear, cloud free satellite images) satellite images from Landsat 5 (TM) and 8 (OLI) so that the analysis of surface temperature can do result with perfectly, because different season of month give different surface temperature yearly .If taken different seasonal month satellite image to analysis in this study which create different result of surface temperature.

Fig. 9, showing three different year surface temperature

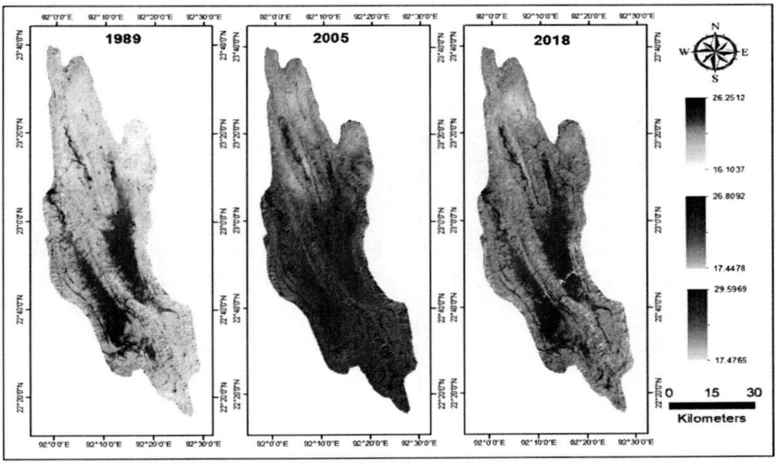

Fig. 9: Surface Temperature Map of 1989, 2005 and 2018 of Kaptai Sub-basin

of 1989, 2005 and 2018 of Kaptai sub-basin with maximum and minimum temperature in Degree Celsius (°C) which analysis from ArcGIS 10.5 where deep yellow, blue and red color region of map indicate maximum temperature which indicate water body and paved surface (concrete surface, built-up area and barren soil) and light yellow, blue and red color region of map showing minimum temperature which indicate vegetation cover and forest area of Kaptai sub-basin is given below:

The surface temperature change in degree celsius (°C) for each study year as derived from the values are presented in the table below:

Table – 5
Surface Temperature Change in Degree Celsius (°C) of 1989, 2005 and 2018 Kaptai Sub-basin

Year	Maximum Temperature (°C)	Minimum Temperature (°C)
1989	26.2512	16.1037
2005	26.8092	17.4478
2018	29.5969	17.4765

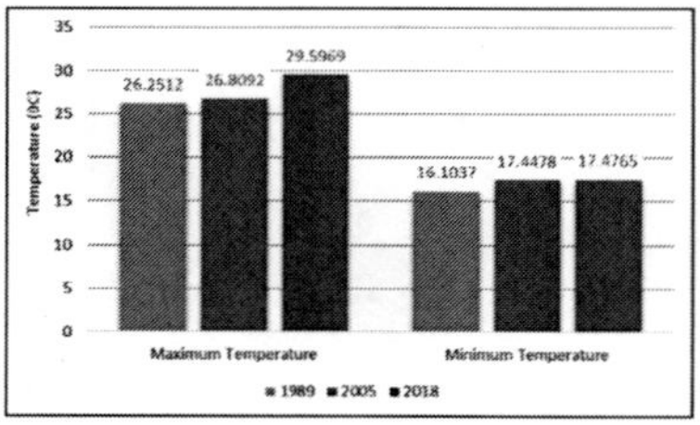

Fig. 10: Surface Temperature Change in (°C) of 1989, 2005 and 2018

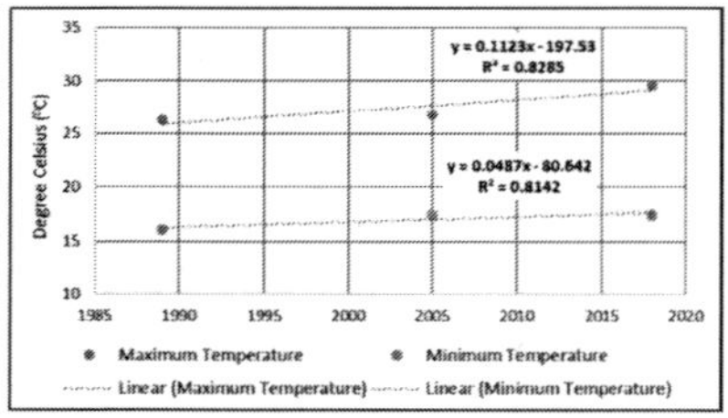

Fig. 11: Change Trend of Surface Temperature in (°C)

Table – 5, mainly focus on surface temperature change of study area of 1989, 2005 and 2018. This table showing that in 1989, maximum temperature is 26.2512 °C and minimum temperature is 16.1037 °C which indicates past 29 years ago from present the temperature was average of vegetation cover area. But in 2018, maximum temperature is 29.5969 °C and minimum temperature is 17.4765 °C which indicates temperature getting high noticeably and anthropogenic activities in paved surface (concrete surface, built-up area and barren soil) also increase in Kaptai sub-basin.

Fig. 10, shows the variation of surface temperature of trend over time from 1989 to 2018 changes of maximum temperature is noticeably high in paved surface (concrete surface, built-up area and barren soil) which also indicate paved surface increase greatly where minimum temperature change in vegetation cover not noticeable which also indicate these region decrease.

9.4.4 Change Trend of Surface Temperature of Kaptai Sub-basin Area

Regression co-efficient analysis was performed to examine the relationship between real-time ground and satellite data in the study area using infrared thermometer measurements. In the study, also tested the use of maximum and minimum values temperature measurements for regression co-efficient analysis (Table – 5). It is experienced that there is significant difference in the case of use of minimum or maximum values of temperature measurements.

Maximum values increased the correlation, whereas the minimum values also increase the correlation almost at the same rate for all spectral ranges. In Fig. 11, can see maximum temperature regression co-efficient value is R^2 = 0.8285 and minimum temperature regression co-efficient value is R^2 = 0.8142 are almost close to regression co-efficient value 1 which indicate the changing rate of surface temperature in present and near future is high and this rate will be continue if the anthropogenic activity and human settlement increase. Because when regression co-efficient value is close to 1 which express changing rate is high and value is very less than 1 then changing rate is low.

9.5 Conclusion

In this study, temporal land use change pattern of Kaptai Lake and its surrounding area is assessed using satellite remote sensing data. From the result of water level changing rate is decreasing very slowly which not noticeable, although the increasing rate of soil erosion, land slide and sedimentation create low depth of water level of Kaptai Lake day to day which is not good news. The analysis of land cover concluded that land cover change detection statistics clearly shows decreasing trend for all land covers except the "others" (Built up and barren soil area) with increasing trend of highest magnitude which is damaging to natural environment. From static values of 2018 there is present very less dense vegetation cover and dominate moderate and sparse vegetation cover in Kaptai sub-basin. Monitoring of vegetation health from vegetation health classification is evident of health reduction of vegetation cover in Kaptai sub-basin. Therefore, it can be concluded that convert of forest and vegetation cover into agricultural land and paved surface and other environment pollution are damaging to natural environment specially vegetation health. If this rate of changing vegetation health continues, the consequences will be more harmful for the environment. Change of surface temperature shows increasing trend for this area which indicated increase of paved surface area of Kaptai sub-basin. Surface temperature changing rate of Kaptai sub-basin is very high after 2005 study year to present which also negative effect for natural environment.

References

Antonic, O.; Hatic, D.; Krian, J. and Bukovec, D. 2001. Modelling groundwater regime acceptable for the forest survival after the building of the hydro-electric power plant. *Ecol. Modell.,* 138: 277-288. Available from: doi: 10.1016/S0304-3800(00)00408-7.

Aquatic Research Group (ARG). 1986. Hydrobiology of the Kaptai Reservoir, Final Report, FAO/UNDP Contract No. DP/BGD/79/015-4F1. *Institute of Marine Science, University of Chittagong, Bangladesh,* 192.

Aly, A.A. 2007. A Holistic Ecosystem Approach for Sustainable Management of Land and Water Resources in Siwa Oasis. PhD Thesis, Faculty of Agriculture, Alexandria University, Egypt.

Berendse, F.; Ruijven, J.; Jongejans, E. and Keesstra, S.D. 2015. Loss of plant species diversity reduces soil erosion resistance of embankments that are crucial for the safety of human societies in low-lying areas. *Ecosystems,* 18: 881-888.

BPDB. 1985. Karnaphuli Hydro Station. Bangladesh: Bangladesh Power Development Board, Kaptai, Rangamati Hill Tracts. *BPDP report,* 20.

Chowdhury, J. 1992. Draft Working scheme of Chittagong hill tracts south forest division for 1989-90 /0 1993-94, Vol. l. *Bangladesh Forest Department, Working Plans Division, Chittagong.*

Campbell, J.B. 2002. Introduction to remote sensing. *CRC Press.*

Dale, V.H.; Efroymson, R. A. and Kline, K. L. 2011. The land use-climate change-energy nexus. *Landscape Ecol.,* 26: 755-773. Available from: doi: 10.1007/s10980-011-9606-2.

Das, T. 2009. *Land Use/Land Cover Change Detection: an*

Object Oriented Approach, Münster, Germany. Thesis: Master of Science in Geospatial Technologies, Institute for Geoinformatics, University of Münster, Germany.

Fernando, C.H. 1980. The fishery potential of man-made lakes in South East Asia and some strategies for its optimization. In: Soerianegara, S. (ed.), Biological Resource Management for Economic Development in Southeast Asia. *Indonesia: BIOTROP Tenth Anniversary Special Publication,* 25-38.

Galib, S. 2009. On-line document, Retrieved on May 27, 2019. Web (URL) address: <URL: http://en.bdfish.org/2009/11/kaptai-lake/>

Li, L. and Hao, Z.C. 2003. The automated extraction of catchment properties from digital elevation models. *Adv. Earth Sci.,* 18: 251-256.

Mantelli, L.R.; Barbosa, J.M. and Bitencourt, M.D. 2011. Assessing ecological risk through automated drainage extraction and watershed delineation. *Ecol. Inform.,* 6: 325-331.

Masek, J.G.; Lindsay, F.E. and Goward, S. N. 2000. Dynamics of urban growth in the Washington DC metropolitan area, 1973-1996, from Landsat observations. *International Journal of Remote Sensing,* 21: 3473-3486.

Pinaki, R. and Monirul. A. 2003. Kaptai cries for fresh water. Retrieved on May 26, 2019. Available from: The Daily Star. May 26, 2003.

Qian, J.; Zhou, Q. and Hou, Q. 2007. Comparison of pixel-based and object-oriented classification methods for extracting built-up areas in aridzone. *In: ISPRS Workshop on Updating Geo-Spatial Databases with Imagery & the 5th ISPRS Workshop on DMGISs,* 163-171.

Roy, B. and Saha, P. 2016. Temporal Analysis of Land Use Pattern Changes in Chittagong District of Bangladesh using Google Earth and ArcGIS. *Annual Int'l Conference on Chemical Processes, Ecology & Environmental Engineering (ICCPEE'16) April 28-29, 2016 Pattaya*

(Thailand). 40-45.

Rouse, J.W.; Haas, R.H.; Deering, D.W. and Sehell, J.A. 1974. Monitoring the vernal advancement and retro gradation (Green wave effect) of natural vegetation. *Remote Sensing Center, Texas A&M Univ., College Station,* 1978-4.

Srivastava, V.K. and Mondal, K. 2012. Evaluation of Digital Elevation Models (DEMs) generated from ASTER and SRTM data: A case study of flat alluvium terrain of BakeshwarFujisada, H. 1994. Overview of ASTER instrument on EOS-AM1 platform. *Proceedings of SPIE,* 2268: 14-36.

Singh, A. 1989. Digital Change Detection Techniques Using Remotely Sensed Data. *International Journal of Remote Sensing,* 10 (6): 989-1003.

Singh, B.G. 2013. Detection of land use and land cover change with Remote Sensing and GIS: A case study of Punjab Siwaliks. *Int. J. Geom. Geosci.,* 4: 296-304.

UNEP. 2002. State of Environment Bangladesh 2001. United Nations Environment Program, Dhaka. On-line document, Retrieved on May 24, 2019. Web (URL) address: <http://wwwrrcap.unep, orgllc/cdibtmlfcountry rep/bangladetresults.htm>

Vidal, A. 1991. Atmospheric and emissivity correction of land surface temperature measured from satellite using ground measurements or satellite data. *Int. J Remote Sens,* 12: 2449-2460.

Zhang, R. et al. 2008. Two improvements of an operational two-layer model for terrestrial surface heat flux retrieval. *Sensors,* 8: 6165-6187.

10

Assessing the Impact of Land Use/ Land Cover Change on Land Surface Temperature by using Satellite Data: A case study of Guwahati City, Assam

Chandana Sarkar[1], Bhalindar Singh[2] and Dr. Bimal Kumar Kar[3]

In recent times increase in temperature of growing urban areas is becoming a serious environmental concern for urban planners and especially in developing countries like India. Rapid urbanisation and consequent fast transformation of land use/land cover change profoundly impacts biodiversity and ecosystem function, as well as local and regional climate. These changes led to the formation of urban heat island effect and urban temperature rise. The situation is same as in Guwahati city, since last few decades unprecedented urban growth coupled with sharp transformation of land use/land cover pattern brought significant changes in land surface temperature in and around the city area. Therefore the study attempts to examine the impact of land use/land cover changes on land surface temperature in Guwahati city by employing multi temporal satellite data. Hence the temperature data extracted seasonally (Summer and winter) from the Landsat 5 TM and Landsat 8 OLI TIRS over the period 1990-2020.The study reveals that the LST increases 0.030°C/year and 0.087°C/

[1]Research Scholar, Department of Geography, Gauhati University. Email: sarkarchandana272@gmail.com
[2]Assistant Professor, Department of Geography, Kampur College. Email: bsnagaon@gmail.com
[3]Professor, Department of Geography, Gauhati University. Email: bimalkar@gauhati.ac.in

year during winter and summer periods respectively and significant LST difference exist over different LU/LC units. The result of the study revealed that the built up and barren land area has high surface temperature (31.42°C), (29.91°C) and forest cover and water body area has experienced low surface temperature (22.37°C), (21.17°C). Furthermore, a linear regression analysis is amplified to quantify the relationship between LST, NDVI and NDBI in the city.

Keywords: *LU/LC change, NDBI, NDVI, LST Change, Urban heat island effect.*

10.1 Introduction

Over the last few decades' rapid urbanization along with multiplicity of economic activities have led to growing demand of land use/land cover changes and land surface temperature variations in most of the developing countries especially in India. Urbanization process is accompanied with harsh transformation of natural land surfaces comprising of vegetation and pervious surface into built-up and impervious surfaces (Tan et al. 2010; Mathew et al. 2016; Pal and Ziaul 2016). The uncontrolled and unplanned urban growth has led to serious issues on climate and the local environment (Bhat et al. 2017). Along with rapid changes of land use/land cover urban growth also responsible for various environmental problems like air pollution, greenhouse gas emission, water pollution, urban heat island effect and so on (Shao et al. 2006; Chan and Yao, 2008). Urban heat island is a phenomena where by an urban area is significantly warmer than its surroundings rural area due to high concentration of impervious surfaces (Xie and Zhou, 2015). Considerably, the expansion of built up area alters the natural landscapes to built-up areas affect the amount of humidity in the air, which is related to atmospheric temperature (Ibrahim 2017). Moreover the impermeable built-up surfaces are characterised by high thermal conductive materials that has an immense impact on surface energy budget. The crucial problem is that impervious built up surfaces store solar heat during the day and re-radiate from afternoon until late night, and as a result, Land Surface

Temperatures (LST) rises substantially (Argueso et al. 2013; Imran et al. 2018, Jacobs et al. 2018). Therefore, land use and land cover (LULC) is identified as one of the key aspects of climatic change in both global and regional levels (Jahan et al. 2012; Nagarajan and Basil 2014; Grimm et al. 2008). The multifaceted interactions between human and physical environments lead to the process of LULC change (Manandhar et al. 2010; Huang et al. 2012). So, Understanding the trends of LULC change will be very helpful in the land use planning and environment management of a region (Zhao et al, 2013; Li et al, 2018). At present , researchers can effectively characterise and examine the dynamics of LU/LC with the developments of Geographical Information Science (GIS) and Remote Sensing (RS) (Choudhury and Mishra, 2016; Tran et al. 2017). In addition to LULC, land surface temperature (LST) is another imperative parameter which has a significant impact on the environment due to rapid urbanization (Govind & Ramesh, 2019). A lot of studies have been carried out to assess the impact of LULC on LST (Devadas and Rose, 2009; Ogawa et al. 2012; Jalan and Sharma, 2014; Babazadeh and Kumar, 2015; Grover and Singh, 2015;Choudhury et al. 2019; Imran et al. 2021).

During the past few decades urbanization is taking place at faster rate in most of the developing countries particularly in India. Almost all the metropolitan cities in India experiencing the modification of LULC change associated with urbanisation, which tends to bring about changes in energy budget and creating the urban heat island (UHI) condition. It thereby slowly contributes to rising temperature of urban environment and brings about a complex microclimatic condition with far reaching implications to the urban dwellers. Guwahati is one of the fast growing million plus city in Indian state of Assam and largest city in north-east India. Rapid urban growth along with fast transformation of land use/land cover has brought about significant changes in LST. In last decades drastic changes in land cover with decline in forest area and water bodies due to concentric human activities enhance the heat emission of land surfaces and atmospheric temperature. Therefore a comprehensive understanding about changing dynamics of land use/land cover is necessary to monitor and analyse its environmental influence in the area. Against the background the present study made an attempt to explore the pattern of land use/ land cover changes induced by urbanisation and industrialisation in the city area and to examine the impact of land use/land cover changes on the variation in LST of different land use/land cover classes in the city area.

10.2 Study Area

Guwahati city, the largest and fast growing metropolitan city in Indian state of Assam located at southern bank of river Brahmaputra and towards the south eastern side of Kamrup district (Fig. 1). Geographically, the city area extends from 91°38' E to 91°51'E longitude and from 26°5'N to 26°12'N latitude with an area of 216.79 km^2. At present, the city is governed by Guwahati Municipal Corporation with comprised of 31 no. of wards. The northern side of the city is bounded by mighty river Brahmaputra and in the southern side is surrounded by hillocks which are in extension of Khasi

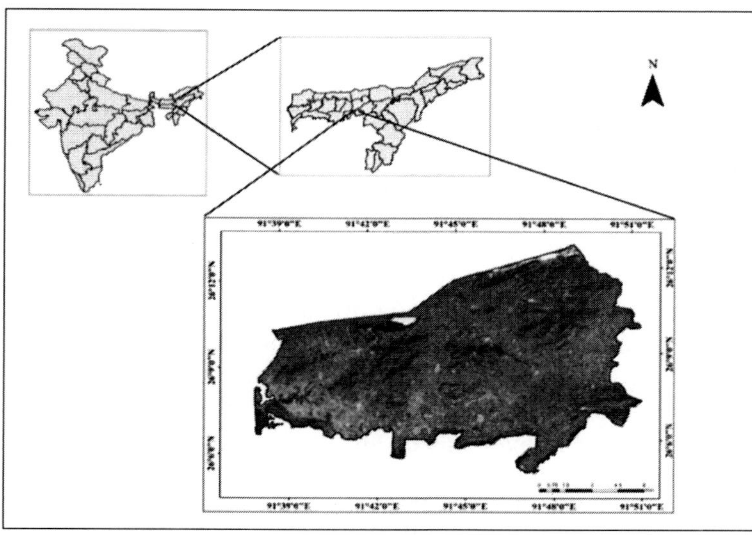

Fig. 1: Location Map of the Study Area (Guwahati City)

hills. In the west and the south west there is the Rani Reserve Forest, Deepar Beel wet land and the alluvial tracts of the Brahmaputra plain. The city has an undulating topography, with an elevation varying from 49.5 to 55.5 m above from the mean sea level. The city is characterized by a warm humid and temperate climate with annual rainfall is (3038mm/year) concentrated during the summer monsoon months from July to October. The temperature varies between 12°C and 14°C in winter to 30–37°C during a wet summer season. The total population of the city is 9,62,334 (according to 2011 Census) with sex ratio of 931 females per 1000 males and population density of 4393 persons/km^2.

10.3 Data Base and Methodology

The study is exclusively based on secondary data. For this purpose two cloud free Landsat images were acquired from the United States Geological Survey (USGS) website (Table – 1). Further, in order to make the images usable, the acquired images were pre-processed by the through radiometric and geometric corrections. For the purpose of analysis, two soft wares, viz. Arc GIS 10.1 and ERDAS IMAGINE 2015 were used. Since the objective of the study is to understand the impact of land use/land cover change on Land surface temperature in urban areas, Normalised difference vegetation index (NDVI) and Normalised difference built up index (NDBI) were calculated by the formulae 6 and 7.

Table – 1
Remote Sensing Data Sets used in The Present Study

Satellite	Resolution	Path/Raw	Observation Date
Landsat 5 TM	30 m	139/42	6 Feb, 1990
Landsat 8 OLI TIRS	30 m	139/42	11 Feb, 2020

Source: Landsat Data Collected from USGS Earth Explorer.

Further land surface temperature of Guwahati city was derived from Landsat 5 TM for the year 1990 and Landsat OLI TIRS imagery for the year 2020 and four Landsat images (Two images for summer and two images for winter) were downloaded from the USGS website with zero per cent cloud coverage. Moreover, Landsat 5 TM band-6 is the thermal band and Landsat OLI TIRS imagery denotes 10 &11 band as thermal bands. So derivation of temperature from TM and OLI TIRS imageries have different steps in converting digital values into spectral radiance which have been discussed below:

Step 1: Conversion of band 6 digital values to spectral radiances from Landsat TM 5

The following formula has been used to convert the band 6 digital values into radiance values (Landsat Project Science Office, 2002):

$$L\lambda = \frac{LMAX\lambda - LMIN\lambda}{QCALMAX\lambda - QCALMIN\lambda} \times (QCAL-QCALMIN) + LMIN\lambda \quad \text{... (1)}$$

Where, Lλ is the atmospherically corrected cell value as radiance, QCAL is the digital value of imagery, LMINλ is the spectral radiance scales to QCALMIN, LMINλ is the spectral radiance scales to QCALMAX,QCALMIN is the minimum quantized calibrated pixel value (typically 1), and QCALMAX is the maximum quantized calibrated pixel value (typically 255).

For conversion of band 10 and 11 digital values to spectral radiances from Landsat OLI, the following formula has been used:

$$L\lambda = ML \times QCAL + AL \quad \text{... (2)}$$

Where, Lλ is the TOA (top of atmosphere) spectral radiance, ML is the radiance multi band X, QCAL is the quantized and calibrated standard product pixel value, and X is the band number. Here ML and AL are band-specific multiplicative rescaling factor and band–specific additive rescaling factor respectively.

Step 2: Conversion from spectral radiance to at satellite brightness temperatures

Emissivity corrections have been applied to radiant temperature according to the land cover nature by Artis and

Carnahan (1982).

$$T = \frac{K_2}{L_n\left(\frac{K_1}{L_\lambda}+1\right)} -273.15 \qquad \text{... (3)}$$

Where, T represents at-satellite brightness temperature in Kelvin (K), L_λ represents at-satellite radiance in W/(m^2 sr μm). For Landsat-5 TM, K_1 = 607.76, K_2 = 1260.56 for band 6, and For Landsat 8 OLI K_1 for band 10 and 11 are 774.8853 and 480.8883 respectively, and K_2 for band 10 and 11 are 1321.0789 and 1201.1442 respectively. Values of K_2 and K_1 were obtained from metadata file. The values of thermal constant for Landsat TM and Landsat OLI are then converted from Kelvin (K) to °C (Where 0°C = 273.15 K) (Pal and Ziaul, 2016).

Step 3: Emissivity has been calculated by using following equation:

$$E = 0.004\left(\frac{NDVI - NDVImin}{NDVImax - NDVImin}\right)^2 +0.986 \qquad \text{... (4)}$$

Therefore, spectral emissivity is corrected by the equation (4) (Synder et al, 1998; Weng et al., 2004).

Step 4: Land Surface Temperature (LST)

The following equation is used to derive LST

$$BT/1 + W^*(BT/P)^*L_n\ (E) \qquad \text{... (5)}$$

Where, BT represents the at-satellite brightness temperature, W is the wavelength of emitted radiance, P=h* c/s (1.438×10–2 m K), h is the Planck's constant (6.626×10–34 Js), s is the Biltzmann constant (1.38×10–23 J/K) and is the velocity of light (2.998×108 m/s).

Calculation of Normalized Difference Vegetation Index (NDVI)

NDVI and NDBI have been extracted to establish the relationship with LST through spatial indices of the study area by the following way:

To extract NDVI the method has been applied by Townshend and Justice (1986)

$$\text{NDVI} = \frac{(\text{NIR band} - \text{Rband})}{(\text{NIR band} + \text{Rband})} \quad \text{... (6)}$$

Where, NIR is the DN value from the near infrared band and R is the DN value from the red band. Hence, the NDVI value ranges between 0 and 1. The values near to 0 indicate low vegetation cover and the values close to 1 indicate high density of vegetation.

Calculation of Normalized Difference Built-up Index (NDBI)

NDBI is calculated by using the method by (Zha et al. 2003), where the values closer to 0 indicate low density of built-up area and the values near to 1 indicate high density of built-up area.

$$\text{NDBI} = \frac{\text{MIR band} - \text{NIR band}}{\text{MIR band} + \text{NIR band}} \quad \text{... (7)}$$

Where, MIR is the DN value from the middle infrared band and NIR is the near infrared band.

Land Use/Land Cover Mapping

A supervised classification scheme has been used for the purpose of image classification by using maximum likelihood algorithm method. One hundred thirty spectral signatures from the study images have been collected and merged for detecting each individual class properly. Further image classification was used to define the land use/land cover types into five classes, namely, agricultural land, barren land, forest, built-up and water body. Accuracy assessment has been made through confusion (error) matrix only for 2020 image. A total of 250 sample sites from Google earth pro and ground verification were selected for accuracy assessment. Overall

Table – 2

Confusion (Error) Matrix for 2020 LU/LC Change Map of Guwahati City

Classified Image Categories	Agricultural Land	Barren Land	Forest	Built-up	Water Body	Row Total	User's Accuracy
Agricultural Land	49	0	0	0	0	49	100%
Barren Land	0	50	0	0	1	51	98.03%
Forest	1	0	50	1	1	53	94.33%
Built- up	0	0	0	49	0	49	100%
Water Body	0	0	0	0	48	48	100%
Colum Total	50	50	50	50	50	250	
Producer's Accuracy	98.00%	100%	100%	98.00%	96.00%		
Overall Accuracy		98.40%					
Kappa Co-efficient		0.98					

Source: Computed by the Authors.

accuracy of the LU/LC map was 98.40 per cent and Kappa coefficient was 0.98 (Table – 2).

10.4 Results and Discussion

Land Use and Land Cover Change

LU/LC map for the years 1990 and 2020 have been prepared to quantify the magnitude of land use/land cover changes in the city area. Growing population pressure and expanding commercial and functional activities contributed to significant changes in land use/land cover pattern in the city since prolonged period (1990-2020).

Table – 3
Area Under Different Land Use/Land Cover Categories in Guwahati City, 1990-2020

Land Use/	1990		2020	
Land Cover Categories	Area in km^2	Area in %	Area in km^2	Area in %
Agricultural Land	65.58	35.46	45.06	24.36
Barren Land	48.38	26.16	27.40	14.82
Forest	50.56	27.34	43.10	23.31
Built-Up	9.75	5.27	59.88	32.38
Water Body	10.67	5.77	9.48	5.13

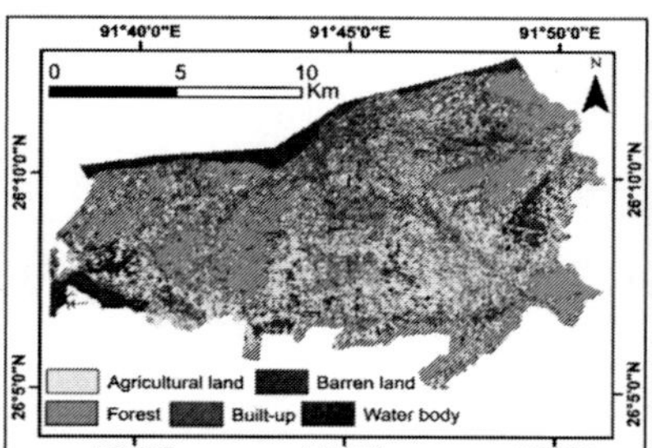

Fig 2: LU/LC Map of Guwahati City,1990

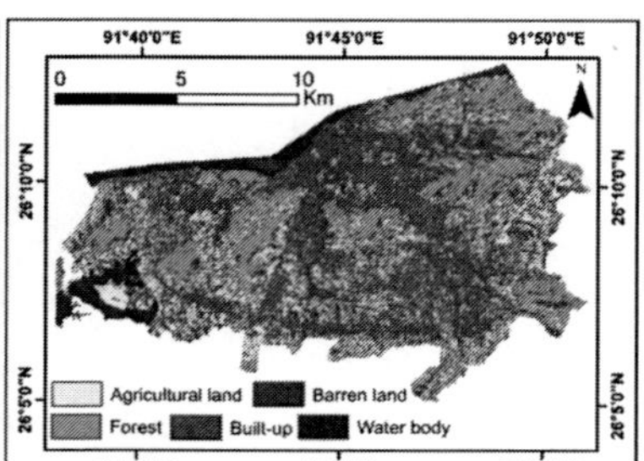

Fig 3: LU/LC Map of Guwahati City, 2020

Sources: Calculations based on data from LANDSAT United State of Geological Survey, LANDSAT-5 TM and Landsat-8 OLI TIRS (1990 &2020).

In 1990 the major portion of land use was found to be agricultural land (35.46 per cent) and barren land (26.16 per cent) in the region. Forest areas are usually located at the hill area which are designated as the reserve forest (RF) and protected areas in the city. In recent years mushrooming growth of informal settlements in the hilly areas caused huge loss of forest areas due to growing population pressure in city core and increasing demand of land in plain areas of the city. The share of built-up area to geographical area in 1990 was only 5.27 per cent, which has increased to 32.38 per cent in 2020. The development of the city had been such that during a period of around three decades (1990-2020) the proportion of built-up area witnessed a marked increase from 9.75 km^2 to 59.88 km^2.It is worth noting that the expansion of built-up land in the city had been at the expense of corresponding decrease in area under agriculture, forest and barren land during 1990-2020 (Table – 3). Further, the study reveals that the area under water body in the city has slightly decreased from 5.77 per cent to 5.13 per cent during the period (1990-2020) due to infilling of low-lying area to residential area in the city. Accordingly, lack of suitable residential land in city core has contributed to expansion of city area and increasing rate of informal settlements in low-lying areas of western and south-western parts of the city (Fig. 3). Over the years, the process of buying and selling of usurped land intensified and most government lands including forest lands, hills and wetlands came under informal occupation by land mafia and were thereafter surreptitiously sold to business or corporate groups (Mahadevia et al., 2014). Besides, currently the city growth has also been seen along the national highway NH 37 where many new commercial and residential complexes have emerged. This type of sudden growth in the built-up area is also causing decline in the agricultural land and forest cover. Therefore, growth of the city has shown clear sprawling towards along the national highway connecting a number of census towns and villages, such as North Guwahati, Amingaon, Narengi, Khanapara, Basistha, Mirza etc.

Spatial Analysis of NDVI

The NDVI represents the coverage and health of vegetation in an area. The NDVI of a Landsat image is generated from the red and near infrared bands. It is a widely-used vegetation index calculated by using equation (6). The value of NDVI ranges from +1 to -1. The positive values are representative of healthy green vegetation and the negative NDVI values indicate non-vegetative cover. In the year 1990 the maximum NDVI or vegetative greenness in Guwahati city was primarily found in north-western and north-eastern

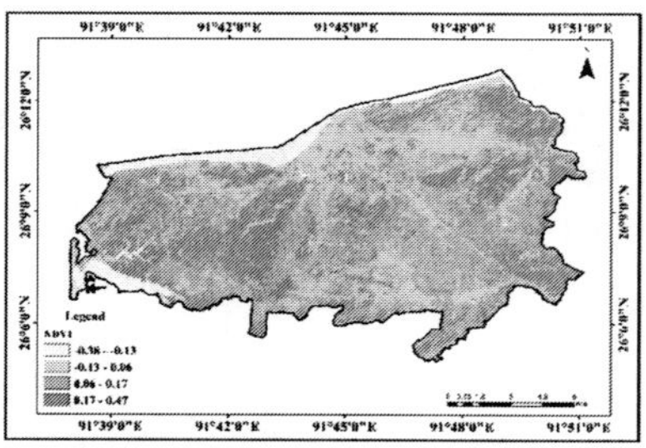

Fig 4: NDVI Map of Guwahati City, 1990

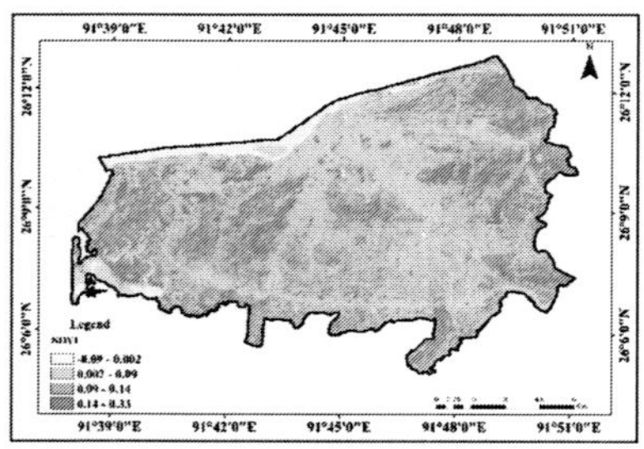

Fig 5: NDVI Map of Guwahati City, 2020

parts of the city ranging from 0.17 to 0.47 (Fig. 4). Whereas, central part of the city has seen highly concretized and therefore has the least NDVI value of (-0.38 to -0.13).

The southern part of the city also records negative vegetative index ranging from 0.06 to -0.13 due to the presence of agricultural waste land and barren land. In later period huge transformation in NDVI has been seen during 1990-2020. For instance, the expansion of built up areas and construction of road and railway networks have greatly influenced the NDVI of the Guwahati city, particularly in the north-western and south-eastern parts of the city, where the vegetative index witnessed a mark decline during 1990-2020, excepting a few patches (Fig. 5). This is indicative of concretization of few patches of green zones in the dense built-up zones of the city. Owing to the imbalance in the built-up and natural land cover in the central and southern parts of the Guwahati city, it largely records negative NDVI. Thus, it is observed that the vegetation covered areas in the city have weakened the effect of UHI (Xiong et al. 2012). Further, a small patch of high NDVI of 0.14 to 0.33 is found in Maligaon and Gotanagar area at Nilachal hill located at north-western part of the city. Other prominent green patches of NDVI ranging from 0.09 to 0.14 correspond to Assam national state Zoo at Zoo hill, Kalapahar and Ramsa hill at north eastern part in the city.

Spatial Analysis of NDBI

The Normalised Difference Built up Index (NDBI) is commonly used as an indicator to extract built up land from urban areas (Liu and Zhang, 2011; Zha et al., 2003; Ghosh and Siddique, 2018). Hence, spatial pattern of (NDBI) of

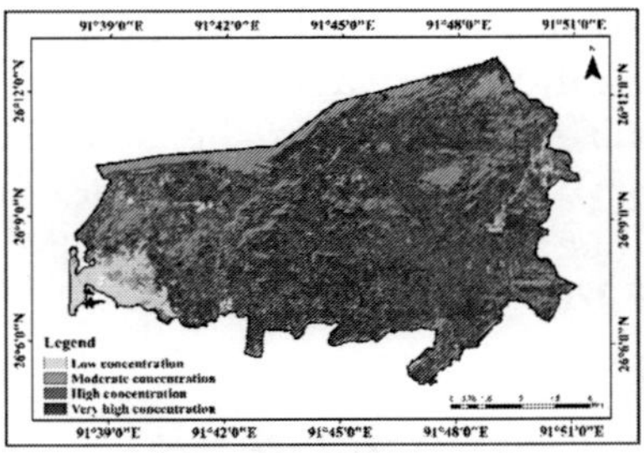

Fig. 6: NDBI Map of Guwahati City, 1990

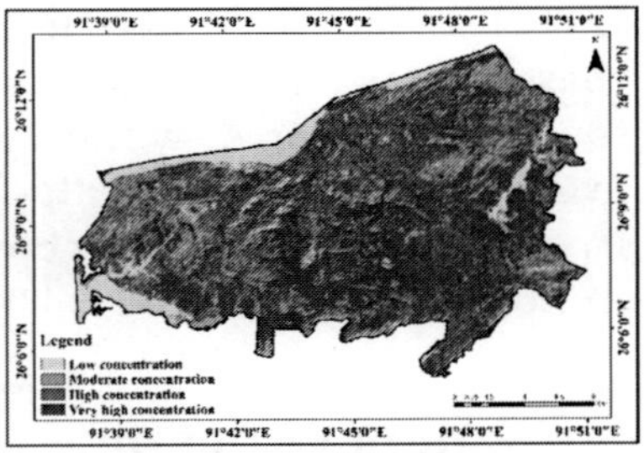

Fig. 7: NDBI Map of Guwahati City, 2020

Guwahati city is depicted in the Fig. 6 and Fig. 7. In the early 1990s high value of NDBI was distributed in urban and dense residential areas particularly in Fancy Bazar and Pan Bazar area of the city (Fig. 6).

Hence, the thickly populated and concrete zones in the central part of the city act as the city core possessing a very high concentration of NDBI in northern part of the city. The low concentration of NDBI was mainly observed particularly in hilly areas and outskirts of the city with dense vegetation cover. In 2020s, after a passage of 30 years a huge transformation occurred and increasing trend of NDBI values have been evident towards the north-western, south-eastern and southern-most periphery of the city. Besides city core high Normalized Difference Built up Index values are also recorded in various parts of the suburbs including, Beltola, Sijubari, Jyoti kutchi-Dakshingaon, ISBT and Basistha area in the city (Fig. 7). Thus, the spatial patterns of built-up areas illustrate increasing NDBI trend towards north to south and south-eastern parts of Guwahati being covered with less vegetation, which indicative of the fact that the city is expanding rapidly towards the periphery due to extreme population pressure and increasing demand of land at city core.

Spatial Analysis of Temperature

Land surface temperature distribution map of Guwahati city in different points of time have witnessed the change in LST distribution across the city. Hence, in order to show the seasonal variations in LST two different images of each year (during summer & winter) were acquired on the basis of availability of suitable data for 1990 and 2020. It is evident that LST in Guwahati city has been displaying an increasing trend during the period 1990-2020.

Table – 4
Mean LST of Different LU/LC categories in Guwahati City (1990-2020)

Date/Year	Built-up (°C)	Barren Land (°C)	Forest (°C)	Water Body (°C)	Agricultural Land (°C)	Mean LST (°C)
Jan, 1990	20.48	17.78	15.36	14.34	17.23	17.04
May, 1990	26.18	25.82	21.94	18.69	24.54	23.43
Jan, 2020	22.32	18.05	16.11	15.65	18.33	18.09
May, 2020	30.83	29.91	22.37	21.17	25.97	26.05

Source: Computed by the authors with the help of Arc GIS.

The average LST of January, which was 17.04°C in 1990, had increased to 18.09°C in 2020. On the other hand, the average LST for summer month (April) had witnessed an increase from 23.43°C to 26.05°C (Table – 4). Hence, changing pattern of LULC in a city also affects LST due to its variation bio-

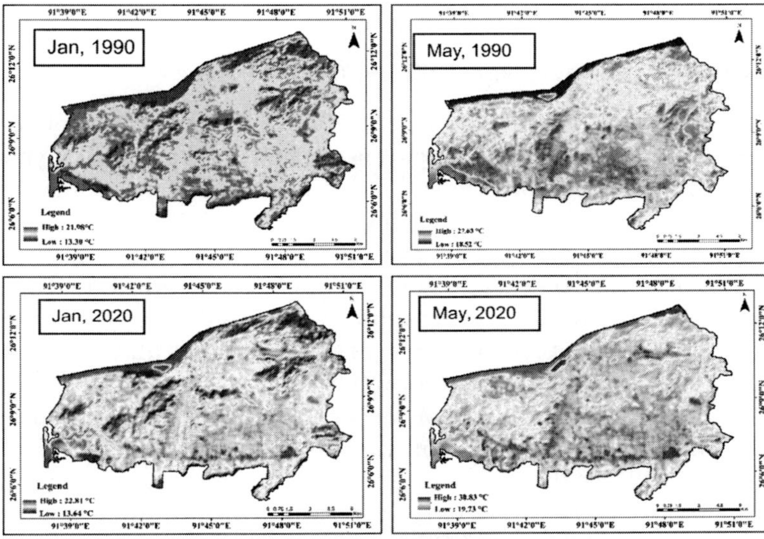

Fig. 8: Spatio-Temporal Pattern of LST in Guwahati City (1990-2020)

physical parameters (Jiang et al., 2015; Chetia et al., 2020). Accordingly, there has been an increasing trend of LST in different LULC types of the Guwahati city. Over the period (1990-2020) it is seen that the LST of built-up areas has increased from 20.48°C to 22.32°C in winter and 26.18°C to 30.83°C in Summer. Similarly, for agricultural land and barren land the LST has increased from 24.54°C to 25.97°C and 25.82°C to 29.91°C respectively during the same period. Considerably, in the case of forest and water body area also similar changes have been recorded from 15.36°C to 16.11°C in winter and 21.94°C to 22.37°C in summer and 14.34°C to 15.65°C in winter and 18.69°C to 21.17°C in summer. The highest surface temperature is mainly experienced in central part of the city having characterised by intense concrete surface, while the north-western and eastern parts of the city are relatively cooler due to the presence of dense forest cover in hilly areas of the city. Therefore, the results showed that high temperature anomalies are closely associated with built up land, densely populated areas and concrete surface. The study also reveals that LST increases gradually from the city outskirts towards the inner city core areas throughout the period (Fig. 8).

Relationship between LST, NDBI and NDVI

The relationship between LST, NDVI and NDBI has been examined by using linear regression and correlation analysis. For the purpose 30 ground control points were randomly selected and tested to obtain the correlation between the LST and NDBI and NDVI in the city. Based on these ground control points, a scatter plot was made between LST, NDBI and NDVI (Fig. 9). The results of the relationship derived from scatter plot show a strong relationship as all the values of coefficient of determination (r^2) are greater than 0.8. From the Fig. 9 it can be clearly observed that there exists a positive linear relationship between LST and NDBI over the period (1990-2020) as the built-up areas significantly absorb solar radiation that positively controls LST. Whereas, the relationship between LST and NDVI presents a negative

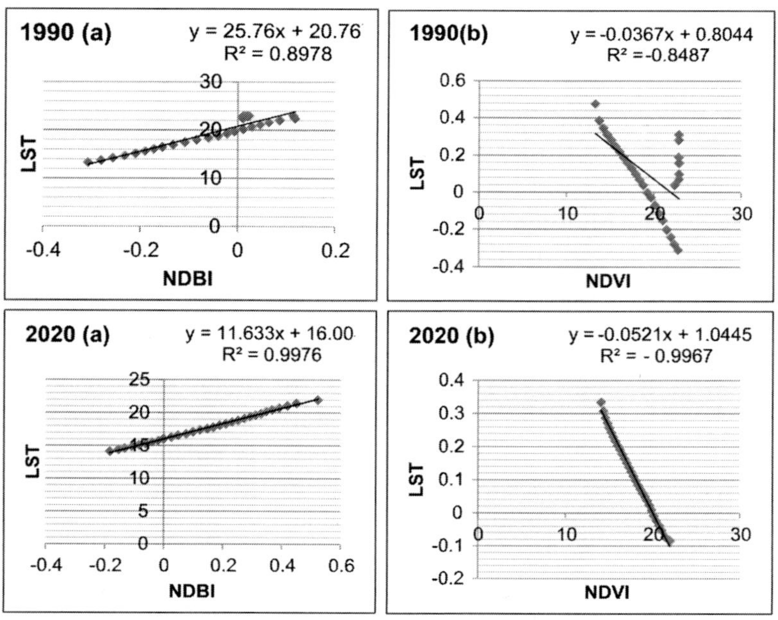

Fig. 9: Scatterplot of the Relationship between LST, NDBI & NDVI (1990-2020)

correlation, as the areas with vegetation cover keep the surface temperature lower and it is responsible for generating a cooling effect in the urban microclimate, while the concrete built-up areas add to the existing high temperature. Thus, it is evident that land surface temperature is sensitive to each land use type and its characteristics.

10.5 Conclusion

On the basis of above background it has been concluded that rapid urbanization and socio-economic development substantially altered the land use/land cover pattern of the Guwahati city. The built-up area drastically increased in the periphery particularly in western and south eastern parts of the city while substantial newly grown bareness area replaced most of the lowland and naturally vegetated areas. Expansion of urban area changed the surface radiative properties that imbalanced surface energy budget, and consequently, affected the LST with an increasing trend. Spatial distribution of maximum and minimum LST showed the increase of 0.34°C to 0.83°C in winter and 1.21°C to 3.2°C in summer during the study period (Fig. 8). Moreover it also notable that mean LST is gradually increasing from 1990 to 2020. For instance, built up and barren land area showed highest LST while forest and waterbody area showed lowest LST. This is the clear indication of the effect of climatic change. Furthermore, human thermal discomfort substantially shifted from moderate to strong heat stress during the study period. Therefore urban planners and policymakers in Guwahati city should concern about future urban expansion both horizontally and vertically and should make a proper plan for environment-friendly construction, green building, and green or cool roof technology to reduce the urban microclimate warming effect. Growth management policies should be suggested to reduce the LST-related urban heat island problem.

Conflict of Interest

Authors declare no conflict of interest.

References

Argueso, D., Evans, J., Fita, L., & Bormann, K. (2013). Temperature response to future urbanization and climate change. Clim Dyn. Available at: https://doi.org/10.1007/s00382-013-1789-6

Artis, D. A. & Carnahan, W. H. (1982). Survey of emissivity variability in thermography of urban areas. *Remote Sensing of Environment*, 12(4), 313-329.

Babazadeh, M., & Kumar, P. (2015). Estimation of the urban Heat Island in local climate change and vulnerability assessment for air quality in Delhi. *European Scientific Journal,* 7881(June), 55-65.

Bhat, P. A., Shafiq, M. U., Mir, A. A., & Ahmed, P. (2017). Urban sprawl and its impact on landuse/land cover dynamics of Dehradun City, India. International Journal of Sustainable 283 Page 18 of 20 Environ Monit Assess (2019) 191:283 Built Environment, 6(2), 513-521. Available at: https://doi.org/10.1016/j.ijsbe.2017.10.003.

Census of India (2011).District Census Handbook, Kamrup District (Metro), Assam.

Chan,C.K., Yao, X. (2008). Air pollution in mega cities in China. Atmos. Environ., 42,1-42.

Chaudhuri, G., & Mishra, N. B. (2016). Spatio-temporal dynamics of land cover and land surface temperature in Ganges-Brahmaputra delta: a comparative analysis between India and Bangladesh. *Applied Geography,* 68, 68-83. Available at: https://doi.org/10.1016/j.apgeog.2016.01.002.

Chetia, S., Saikia, A., Basumatary, M. and Sahariah, D. (2020).When the heat is on: Urbanisation and Land Surface Temperature in Guwahati, India, *Acta Geophysica.* Available at: https://doi.org/10.1007/s11600-020-00422-3.

Choudhury, D., Das, K. & Das, A. (2019). Assessment of land use and land cover changes and its impact on variations of land surface temperature in Asansol-Durgapur

Development Region. *The Egyptian Journal of Remote Sensing and Space Sciences,* 22, 203-2018.

Devadas, M. D., & Rose, L. A. (2009). Urban factors and the intensity of Heat Island in the city of Chennai. In: Proc. of the seventh International Conf. on Urban Climate, p. 3-6.

Ghosh, S. and Siddique, G. (2018). Change Detection of built -up areas applying built-up index for Chandannagar city. *International Journal of Technology Research and Management,* 5(4), 1-7.

Govind, N.R. & Ramesh, H. (2019). The impact of spatiotemporal patterns of land use land cover and land surface temperature on an urban cool island: a case study of Bengaluru. *Environ. Monit.* 191(283), 1-20.

Grimm, N.B., Faeth, S..H, Golubiewski, N.E., Redman, C.L., Wu, J., Bai, X. & Briggs, J.M. (2008). Global change and the ecology of cities. Science 319(5864),756-760.

Grover, A., & Singh, R. (2015). Analysis of urban heat island (UHI) in relation to normalized difference vegetation index (NDVI): a comparative study of Delhi and Mumbai. *Environments,* 2(4), 125-138. Available at: https://doi.org/10.3390/environments2020125.

Huang, J., Pontius, R. G., Li, Q., & Zhang, Y. (2012). Use of intensity analysis to link patterns with processes of land change from 1986 to 2007 in a coastal watershed of southeast China. *Applied Geography,* 34, 371-384. Available at: https://doi.org/10.1016/j.apgeog.2012.01.001.

Ibrahim GRF (2017) Urban land use land cover changes and their effect on land surface temperature: case study using Dohuk City in the Kurdistan region of Iraq. *Climate* 5(13).Available at: https://doi.org/10.3390/ cli5010013.

Imran, H.M., Kala, J., Ng, A., Muthukumaran, S. (2018). Effectiveness of green and cool roofs in mitigating urban heat island efects during a heatwave event in the City of Melbourne in southeast Australia. J Clean Prod.Available at: https://doi.org/10.1016/j.jclepro.2018.06.179.

Imran, H. M., Hossain, A., Islam, A. K. M.S., Rahaman, A.,

Bhuiyan, Md. A. E., Paul, S. & Alam, A. (2021). Impact of land cover changes on land surface temperature and human thermal comfort in Dhaka City of Bangladesh. *Earth Systems and Environment*. Available at: https://doi.org/10.1007/S41748-021-00243-4.

Jacobs, S., Gallant, A., Tapper, N., Li, D. (2018). Use of cool roofs and vegetation to mitigate urban heat and improve human thermal stress in Melbourne, Australia. *J Appl Meteorol Climatol.* Available at: https://doi. org/10.1175/JAMC-D-17-0243.1

Jahan, M. (2012). Impact of rural urban migration on physical and social environment: the case of Dhaka city. *Int Soc Dev Sustain* 1(2),186-194.

Jalan, S., & Sharma, K. (2014). Spatio-temporal assessment of land use/land cover dynamics and urban heat island of Jaipur city using satellite data. International Archives of the Photogrammetry, Remote Sensing and Spatial Information Sciences - ISPRS Archives, XL-8(1), 767-772. https://doi. org/10.5194/isprsarchives-XL-8-767-2014.

Jiang, Y., Fu, P. and Weng, Q. (2015). Assessing the impacts of urbanisation associated land use/land cover change on land surface temperature and surface moisture: a case study in the Midwestern United States. *Remote Sens.* 7(4), 4880-4898.

Landsat Project Science Office, (2002). Landsat 7 science data user's handbook. Goddard Space Flight Centre, Nasa, Washington, DC. URL: http://ltpwww,gsfc.nasa.gov/IAS/handbook/handbook_toc.html,

Li, B., Wang, W., Bai, L., Wang, W., & Chen, N. (2018). Effects of spatio-temporal landscape patterns on land surface temperature: a case study of Xi'an city, China. *Environmental Monitoring and Assessment*, 190(7), 419. Available at: https://doi. org/10.1007/s10661-018-6787-z.

Liu, L. and Zhang, Y. (2011). Urban heat island analysis using the Landsat TM data and ASTER data: A case study in Hong Kong. *Remote Sensing,* 3, 1535-1552.

Mahadevia, D., Desai, R., & Mishra, A. (2014). City Profile: Guwahati. Working Paper 24.

Centre for Urban Equity, CEPT University, Ahmedabad.

Manandhar, R., Odeh, I., & Pontius, R. G. (2010). Analysis of twenty years of categorical land transitions in the lower hunter of New South Wales, Australia. *Agriculture, Ecosystems and Environment,* 135, 336-346.

Mathew, A., Khandelwal, S., & Kaul, N. (2016). Spatial and temporal variations of urban heat island effect and the effect of percentage impervious surface area and elevation on land surface temperature: study of Chandigarh city, India. *Sustainable Cities and Society,* 26, 264-277.Available at: https://doi. org/10.1016/j.scs.2016.06.018.

Nagarajan, M. & Basil, G. (2014). Remote sensing-and GIS-based run of modelling with the effect of land-use changes (a case study of Cochin corporation). Nat Hazards 73(3):2023-2039.

Ogawa, K., Gurjar, B. R., Kikegawa, Y., Mohan, M., Kandya, A., & Bhati, S. (2012). Urban heat island assessment for a tropical urban airshed in India. *Atmospheric and Climate Sciences,* 02(02), 127-138.Available at : https://doi.org/ 10.4236 /acs.2012.22014.

Pal, S., & Ziaul, S. (2016). Detection of land use and land cover change and land surface temperature in English Bazar urban centre. *Egyptian Journal of Remote Sensing and Space Science,* 20(1), 125-145. Available at: https:// doi.org/10.1016/j. ejrs.

Shao, M., Tang, X. Zhang, Y., Li, W. (2006). City clusters in China: air and surface water pollution. Front. Ecol. *Environmen.,* 4,353-361.

Synder, W.C., Wan, Z., Zhang, Y. and Feng, Y.Z. (1998). Classification-based emissivity for land surface temperature measurement from space. *Int J Remote Sens,* 19(14), 2753-2774.

Tan, K. C., Lim, H. S., MatJafri, M. Z., & Abdullah, K. (2010). Landsat data to evaluate urban expansion and determine land use/land cover changes in Penang Island, Malaysia. *Environmental Earth Sciences,* 60(7), 1509-1521.Available at: https://doi.org/10.1007/s12665-009-0286-z.

Townshend, J. R. & Justice, C.O. (1986). Analysis of the dynamics of African vegetation using the normalized difference vegetation index. *Int J Remote Sens,* 7(11), 1435-1445. Available at: https://doi.org/10.1080/01431168608948946.

Tran, D. X., Pla, F., Latorre-Carmona, P., Myint, S. W., Caetano, M., & Kieu, H. V. (2017). Characterizing the relationship between land use land cover change and land surface temperature. ISPRS *Journal of Photogrammetry and Remote Sensing,* 124, 119-132.Available at: https://doi.org/10.1016/j. isprsjprs.2017.01.001

Weng, Q., Lu, D. & Schubring, J. (2004). Estimation of land surface temperature-vegetation abundance relationship for urban heat island studies. *Remote Sensing of Environment,* 89(4), 467-483.

Xie, Q. & Zhou, Z. (2015). Impact of urbanization on Urban Heat Island effect based on TM imagery in Wuhan, China. *Environ. Eng. Manag. J.* 14(3),647-655.

Zha,Y., Ni,S. & Yang, S. (2003). An effective approach to automatically extract urban land use from TM imagery. *Journal of Remote Sensing,* 7, 37- 40.

Zhao, R., Chen, Y., Shi, P., Zhang, L., Pan, J., & Zhao, H. (2013). Land use and land cover change and driving mechanism in the arid inland river basin: a case study of Tarim River, Xinjiang, China. *Environmental Earth Sciences,* 68(2), 591-604.Available at: https://doi.org/10.1007/s12665-012-1763-3.

11

Towards Eco-Sustainability: Scope and Significance of Designing Green Buildings for Urbanizing Kerala, India

Dr. T.K. Prasad[1] *and Jishnu J.S.*[2]

Abstract: Growth of urbanization coupled with frequent disasters affecting the State, Kerala requires more sustainable and resilient housing practices. Kerala with its peculiar geographic location, sandwiched between the magnificent Western Ghats and vast expanse of Arabian Sea, the land availability for developmental activities are restricted to a great extent. The steady rate of urbanization is much more pronounced in Kerala because there is no distinctive rural urban demarcation. In context of Kerala it is very important to build the assets in such a way that they are resilient to disasters as well as eco-sustainable. Green buildings and disaster resilient structures in the cities are promoted as they are sustainable and reduces the intensity of damage to the environment. The study focuses on the sustainable construction of flood resilient amphibian housing using materials with lesser carbon emissions. Carbon footprints of materials in the construction are estimated and new replacement of the construction material is reviewed in this study. The study proposes engineered bamboo and wood as a replacement material that has less amount of carbon

[1]Department of Geography, Kannur University, Kerala. Email: tkprasadgeo@gmail.com

[2]Former Post Graduate Student, Kannur University, Kerala. Email: iishnuis321@gmail.com

emission and will contribute to the sustainable aspect. Life cycle assessment emission is taken into account for the comparison of the carbon footprint.

Key Words: *Eco-Sustainability, Green Building, Amphibian Housing, Carbon footprint, Flood resilient, Life cycle assessment.*

11.1 Introduction

The term resilience is very relevant to the current scenario in Kerala as we are frequented with natural disasters especially floods, landslides and cyclones from 2018, where its intensity and magnitude is changing towards an unpredictable level. Most of the urbanization activities are expected to happen in the developing countries where emerging economies like India witness an unprecedented urban growth. There are large influx of people moving from rural parts of the country towards the urban area which results in congestion and haphazard development. The climate change and its associated negative effects are already worsening the situation. All cities are becoming more urbanized where majority of the population are expected to live in cities. By 2025, cities will need infrastructure, ports, water and residential buildings to cater to the needs of its growing population (Dobbs et al. 2012).

All the cities in the world are moving towards achieving sustainable development goals, particularity SDG 11 which aims on building inclusive and sustainable urbanization. A new emerging concept towards achieving this goal is green infrastructure, which enhance and contribute urban sustainability. It is also considered as an important aspect in mitigating climate change and adaption, there by offering an enhanced resilience for the city. It can also improve resilience through flood risk management and conservation of biodiversity. In several European cities it has become the part of flood management plan and in India, Ahmadabad the impact of flood was reduced by riverfront projects from Sabarmati River (Mell 2017). Green infrastructure is a milestone in developing countries which can serve as a guide to the use of environmental resources carefully and effectively to tackle the environmental problems (Zuniga-Teran et.al). In India Green Infrastructure is a critical component in all 100 smart cities initiative introduced by the Government of India.

Climate change is a crisis which the entire world is battling and its impacts are evident across the world. According to reports by UNEP (United Nations Environment Programme), CO_2 emissions climbed to 9.95 $GtCO_2$ (United Nations Environment Programme, 2021). The construction industry consumes more than 40% of the world's resources, requires 40% of global energy, emits 30% of greenhouse gas emissions and uses 25% of the global water supply (UNEP 2016). In the case of building construction, approximately 80% of carbon dioxide emissions are caused by mortar, commercial concrete, wall materials, steel and doors and windows. In a conventional RCC (Reinforced Cement Concrete) building in India, cement constitutes more than 60%, followed by concrete masonry blocks, ceramic tiles and bricks (Kurian et al., 2021). As a result, CO_2 emissions from buildings should be identified and analysed for sustainable development. India stands third as the emitter of greenhouse gases after China and US and is in a vulnerable position to climate change (The Carbon Brief Profile: India, 2019). In India, cement, ammonia, and iron and steel production contributed to more than 80% of total emissions. The cement industry alone accounts for over half of all IPPU (Industrial Processes and Product Use) related emissions. Therefore while designing cities and buildings resilience, climate change adaptation, disaster management and sustainability forms the major agenda.

This paper checks the need for a new alternative in place of the traditional materials used in the construction and at the same providing a stable and safe housing for flood prone areas in the state. The paper will serve as an eye-opener for all stakeholders to get convinced that Green House Gases

(GHGs) can be minimized in the lifecycle of a building by changing certain traditional methods and materials. The paper will check the emissions involved in the Life Cycle Assessment (LCA) of the materials used for typical constructions in Kerala. It also looks for materials which are contributing maximum emissions in the life cycle of a residential building. This study will help to lead the building sector toward a more sustainable development in future, particularly in the context of Kerala.

11.2 Objectives

The main objectives of this study are as follows:

- To understand the feasibility of construction of flood resilient housing using eco-friendly materials.
- To test the suitability of amphibious architecture in Kerala to decrease loss of livelihood and property in flood deluge.
- To estimate the carbon footprint of houses built using traditional construction materials like cement, bricks and mortars etc.,
- To suggest an eco-friendly alternative material for cement that can reduce the carbon footprint and emissions of green house gases thereby leading to sustainable construction.

11.3 Methodology

The research paper will check the emissions involved during the Life Cycle Assessment (LCA) of the materials used for typical constructions in Kerala. A carbon footprint is the overall amount of Green House Gas (GHG) emissions that an individual, organization, event or product emits both directly and indirectly (Center for Sustainable Systems University of Michigan, 2021). This carbon footprint is calculated by adding all the emissions resulting from each stage of the product or service lifetime. The stages mainly involve the production of material, manufacturing, usage and the end of life. This is calculated in carbon dioxide equivalent (CO_2 eq). By estimating the carbon footprint of each material, a comparative study can be done based on the traditional using materials in the construction and the newly proposed materials. The life cycle assessment (LCA) is a popular tool for calculating carbon footprints.

11.4 Study Area

Kerala lies between the north latitude of 8°17'30" N and 12°47'40" N and east longitudes of 74°27'47" E and 77°37'12" E (Fig. 1). It covers around 1.2 per cent of India's geographical area. Physiographically the state the can be divided into three geographical regions– 1) Highlands 2) Midlands 3) Lowlands. (Fig. 2). The Highlands have an average elevation of 900 m which slopes down from the Western Ghats. Anamudi (2695 m), the highest peak of South India is located in highland portion of Western Ghats in Kerala. Midland land lies between the coastal plain in the west and highlands of the east. The area lying between 300 m to 600 m falls under this zone. Steep slopes are covered with natural vegetation of wet and semi evergreen forests. Soil is dominated by gravelly loam, residual laterite and red loam. The sea bound regions are the lowlands. It is made of coastal plains, estuaries made by rivers and extensive network of backwaters. Kerala's

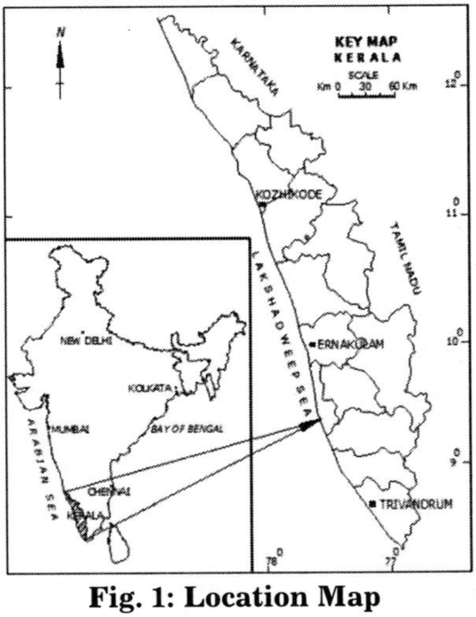

Fig. 1: Location Map

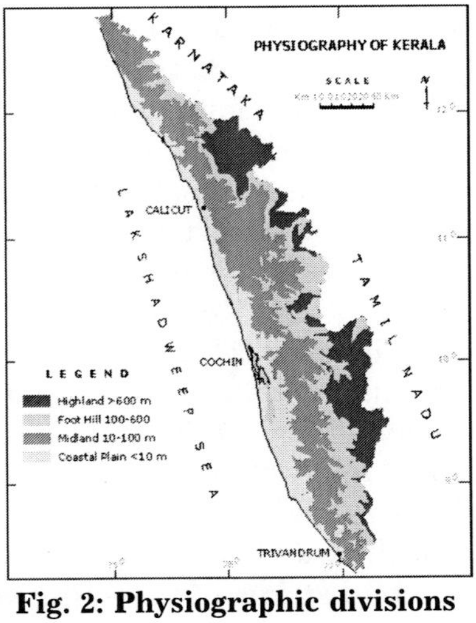

Fig. 2: Physiographic divisions

coastal stretch runs for a distance of 580 km in length. The shoreline is parallel over a great part of length in accordance with the district boundaries but in certain areas indentations, cliffs and projections are present. The width of the coast is narrower in the northern and southern portion of the State, with its maximum width in the central region. About 40 percent of Western Ghats lies in Kerala.

Among the 44 rivers of Kerala 41 originates from the Western Ghats. It is home for the moist deciduous and evergreen forest of Kerala there by becoming a global biodiversity hotspot. The mountains of the Western Ghats and their characteristic features influence the monsoon weather pattern that mediates the warm tropical climate of the State. They also play a significant and important ecological function in sequestration of atmospheric carbon dioxide. With its unique geographical setting and high HDI parameters it was worth calling Kerala God's own country.

11.5 Results and Discussions

Kerala: Disaster Vulnerability

With its changing dynamics of climate given by its coastal location and steep gradient along the Western Ghats state is vulnerable to all kind of disasters. Though geographically we have abundance of forest and maritime resources the availability of land for developmental activities are very much restricted due to irregular topography and limited availability of plain areas. It makes the coastal plains and river flood plains of Kerala the most densely populated making them vulnerable to disasters. Western Ghats are the strong foundation for the ecology of Kerala, but unfortunately the reckless developmental activities happening in the ecologically sensitive highlands of Kerala especially the mining activities beyond the permitted scale and range is critically weakening the stability of the Western Ghats. The state received unusually high rainfall between June 1, 2018 and August 19, 2018. It was the worst flood the state has witnessed in nearly a century. All 14 districts of the state were placed under the red alert displacing millions of people. According to the reports one sixth of the total population had been directly affected. The Central Government had declared it a Level 3 Calamity or calamity of severe nature. Thirty five out of the fifty four dams within the state opened their shutters unanimously for clearing the way for gushing flood waters. About 14.5% of the land area is susceptible to floods and for certain area the proportion is as high as fifty percent. The highland districts are faced with increased threats of landslides as the rain water makes the soil saturated and making it susceptible to move downslope. The state for the past few years faces a pre-monsoon drought and post monsoon flood condition. It is further predicted that State will be vulnerable to more floods, landslides, sea level rise, cyclones in coming years, which are induced by climatic changes induced by anthropogenic forces

Re-Build Kerala initiatives and eco-sustainability

Especially in a State like Kerala where topography is highly variable but the population density exceeds its carrying capacity, it will be detrimental to move forward without a clear management strategy. Instead of claiming an edge over the less advantaged geopolitical contexts within the country, it is time Kerala examined how the state has failed the vulnerable populations within it. Taking cognizance of their inherent and newer vulnerabilities, substantial investments are needed to nurture inclusive and resilient communities where no one is left behind (Global Sustainable development Report 2019). It is essential to explore the options associated with more sustainable materials to reduce the environmental degradation.

Rebuild initiative of Kerala Government is a unique approach adopted in order to bring about a perceptible change in the citizen's life by building infrastructures that are of high standards in technology and at the same time ecologically efficient. The RKDP constitutes the State's strategic roadmap for a Green and Resilient Kerala. They give priority to investment programs that are critical for resilient and sustainable recovery and rebuilding of the State. It aims towards rebuilding of Kerala in a way that addresses key drivers of floods and other natural disasters and climate change risks and strengthens preparedness against future disasters.

Kerala has 3.463 crores of the population with 4.91% of population growth in 10years (Census Organization of India, 2011). The housing necessity is also increasing at a higher pace and it is the needful time to evaluate the emission in the construction segment. In terms of human development, high population density and urbanization lead to high per capita energy consumption and, as a result, carbon intensity. The population density is 859 persons per square km, one of the highest in the country. If green technology is not integrated into the development process, there is a danger of huge carbon footprints. The countries that have pledged to achieve net-zero emissions have progressed significantly in the last year, accounting for almost 70% of global CO_2 emissions which also include India which is the third country producing carbon emissions. GHG (Green House Gas) emissions from the energy, industry, agriculture and waste sectors accounted for 58%, 22%, 17%, and 3% of net CO_2 eq emissions, respectively (Government of Kerala and Department of Environment and Climate Change, 2014).

Concept of Amphibian Houses

Amphibious structures are characterized by the fact that they have a buoyant foundation, which helps them to float on the water when there is a rise in the water level and remain fixed on the ground during normal conditions (Fig. 3). It is designed to float only when the flood waters rises (Fig. 4). They are fixed in a particular place with the help of vertical guidance posts. They can float on top of any level of water but is restricted to the height of the guidance post. The main components of amphibious houses are wet dock and debris unit which control the inflow of debris, mud and rock, buoyant foundation which helps to float on water, guidance post that makes the house move up and down during the inflow of flood waters and flexible utility connections to bring in water, electricity and bring out waste water. They retain their ground connection even during flood times. The foundation of the house can be made using traditional

Fig. 3: House resting on ground

Fig. 4: House floating in flood waters

Source: www.buoyantfoundation.org

materials eco-friendly materials like bamboo or recyclable plastic barrels which will help in achieving eco sustainability and less carbon emissions. Bamboo and wood for construction can also help in reducing the overall weight of the building there by putting less pressure towards the land.

In urban areas where most of the housing construction happening in the coastal and flood plain regions, amphibious foundation can be an effective low cost strategy that offer resilience for flood related damages and speedy recovery from disasters. This was a tremendous hit in Bangladesh as the country is coping with severe flooding and submergence of low lying lands due to climate change. It proved to be successful for urban slum dwellers in the country.

Several developed countries like the United States, United Kingdom, Ireland are transitioning to wood or bamboo with engineered properties as a construction material thereby reducing carbon emission. Carbon emissions from conventional building materials are involved in several stages like manufacturing, transportation, construction, operational and demolition stages. Significant emissions are observed during the manufacturing process of conventional materials like cement, steel and bricks. The main research question is whether the replacement and transition to the new material wood and bamboo will bring the desired results by effectively reducing carbon foot print. After fixing the problem statement and hypothesis, we checked the possibilities of various alternative construction materials that can replace cement in construction. Various materials like Pulverized Fuel Ash, Ground Granulated Blast-furnace Slag a by-product of Iron and Steel Industry, Silica Fumes, Limestone Fumes, Alternate fuels, Green Concrete, Ashcrete etc., was considered as a suitable alternative. But later it was found that it does not have a substantial reduction in CO_2 emissions and some are not meeting the criteria for becoming a suitable alternative. The major data collection and comparison was done based on various research papers and links collected. Information gathered from all sources concluded that prefabricated wooden and engineered bamboo structures are the best alternative if demand and supply balance is being properly met.

Buildings account for up to 45% of global energy consumption and carbon emissions, implying that they are the most significant contribution to anthropogenic climate change (Fig. 5). Load-bearing and reinforced concrete (RCC) frame structures made of traditional materials such as

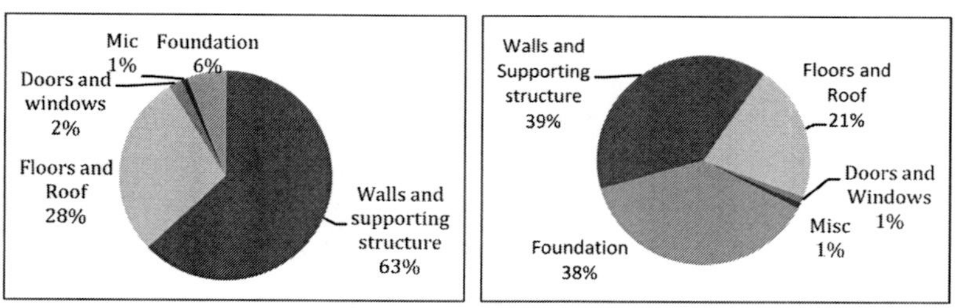

Fig. 5: Share of materials in conventional buildingsin India (Praseeda, Reddy and Mani, 2016)

cement, steel, aggregates, burnt clay brick, concrete blocks, and so on are used in urban housing in India. (Praseeda, Reddy and Mani, 2016). Most of the residential building has

RCC floor or roofs, monolithic walls, stone masonry, soil block masonry and rammed earth.

Traditional Materials Used for Construction in Kerala

The total carbon footprint of a residential building has been estimated by the authors in the paper (Kurian et al., 2021) with the help of BIM (Building Information Modelling). For the analysis, the researchers used a residential three-storey building with an RCC framed structure located at

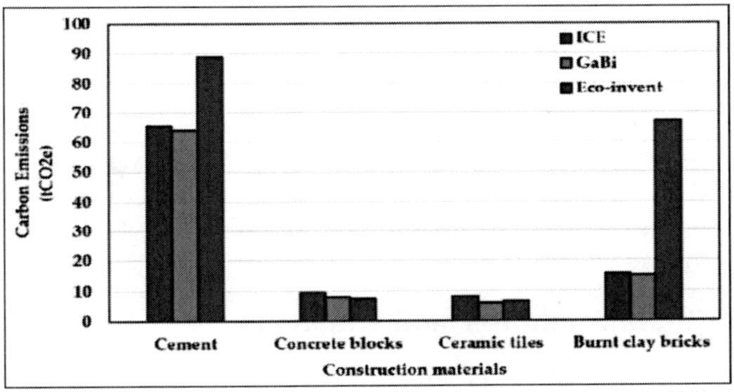

Fig. 6: Carbon Emission of Materials Traditional Building (Kurian et al., 2021)

Kakkanad, Ernakulam, Kerala, India. The climate of the location has a humid and warm climate with a maximum temperature of 38°C. The total area of the building is 720 sq.m with an RCC flat roof of 125 mm and a masonry wall of 200 mm. The traditional materials used in construction in Kerala are Cement, Concrete Blocks, Ceramic Tiles and Burnt clay bricks (Fig. 6).

As per the paper (Kurian et al., 2021), more than 60% are cement followed by masonry blocks at 9.4%. Brick and ceramic tiles constitute about 15.7% and 8.1% respectively. The carbon emissions of materials as estimated from different databases like ICE, GaBi and Eco-invent are shown in figure. The paper estimates the maximum total carbon emission of the materials at construction states as 98.65 tCO_2eq. The carbon emission produced during the transportation, operational and destruction stages of the building are also stated in the paper as follows:

- Construction stage = 98.65 tCO_2eq
- Transportation Stage = 0.854 tCO_2eq
- Operational Stage = 550.24 tCO_2eq
- Destruction Stage = 9.865 tCO_2eq
- Total = 659.6 tCO_2eq

For the transportation for the shipping of material, trucks were used and carbon emission is observed. In the operational stage, the energy consumption of 7240 kWh is used. In the operational stage, the main energy is utilized for the cooling, warming, AC, supply of water. 10% of the emission in the construction stage is taken as the emission observed during the destruction stage. The total emission from the house was 659.6 tCO_2eq. As per the research, it was concluded that the residential building will produce 916 kg CO_2eq/m^2 of carbon emission (Kurian et al., 2021).

11.6 Findings and Recommendations

Concrete which is the mixture of cement, gravel sand water and aggregate is one of the most consumed substances in the world after water. The study further reveals that more than 60% of the material in the building has cement as its major component. Replacing cement with alternative high performance low cost eco-friendly material in construction will solve the problem. It is proposed in this paper that construction can be done with the help of engineered bamboo materials and prefabricated wood material (Fig. 7). This can also be applied to amphibious flood resilient structure which will be innovative, sustainable and eco-friendly with less carbon footprint. Flood, landslides and torrential rain have become recurring phenomena in Kerala during every monsoon period. When weather became extremely unpredictable many residents started losing their properties and paid a heavy price in repairing and reconstructing fully or partially damaged homes. This had taken a serious toll on the financial security for many families, especially the

Fig. 7: Wooden houses (left) built at Kannur, Kerala (Paithal Hill Resorts–Camilsons Group Website, 2020) and Flood resistant bamboo house in Kadathuruthy Kottayam–(onmanorama.com, 2019).

marginalized or vulnerable section of the population. In order to cope up with the changing climatic conditions innovative design and structures were required to minimize the damage. The construction sector in Kerala was also facing a shortage of traditional materials like rocks, metals, cement and the prices of available materials were not affordable to the common man.

This led to the search of further suitable, cost effective and environment friendly materials, which led to the construction of amphibious house in Vazhappilly, Ernakulam district by P Gopalakrishanan Achari. The air tanks installed in the foundation is what helps the house rise (www.onmanorama.com). Materials like brick, mud, rock or cement were avoided. The walls are made of multi wood sheets and the structure is made of steel GI pipes. With further research and innovation steel pipes can be replaced by more sustainable materials which can contribute to less carbon emission and increased sustainability. It is a cost effective construction approximately Rs 1600 per square feet and also demands less labour force and less time for the completion of the project. This type of structure can be constructed in any land

Fig. 8: Working model of amphibious house in Kerala
Source: https://www.thebetterindia.com/(November 29, 2019)

regardless of the soil or rock condition because the weight exerted on the land is much less due to light weight materials used in the construction.

Carbon Footprint of Wooden Houses

The total reduction of the carbon emission in percentage with respect to the conventional building is as follows:

- Carbon emission of conventional concrete building = 916 kg CO_{2eq}/m^2.
- Carbon emission of wooden building = 353 kg CO_{2eq}/m^2.
- Percentage of reduction = $\frac{916 - 353}{916} \times 100 = 61.46\%$
- Carbon emission of bamboo building of a single storey house = 80 kg CO_{2eq}/m^2.
- Percentage of reduction = $\frac{916 - 80}{916} \times 100 = 91.26\%$
- Carbon emission of bamboo building of a double storey house = 39 kg CO_{2eq}/m^2.
- Percentage of reduction = $\frac{916 - 39}{916} \times 100 = 95.74\%$
- Carbon dioxide emission (kg)/per 1 ton of material is–450 for engineered bamboo
- $1m^3$ engineered bamboo substituting concrete/steel can save more than 3 ton of CO_2 to be released into atmosphere
- 1 hectare of bamboo planted = 1000 tons of CO_2 saved

Padilla-Rivera and Balnchet have evaluated the carbon footprint of a wooden building using the life cycle assessment. In the study, the authors examine the reduction of the GHG emission from the building by replacing the steel and concrete building with timber structures. The building is a timber-based structure with four storeys with a total area of 1512.3 sq.m. The authors have also compared the carbon emission from different countries. It is observed that the emission from wooden construction ranges from 275kg CO_{2eq}/m^2 to 353 kg CO_{2eq}/m^2. In this case, 75% of the carbon emission is emitted during the fabrication. It is followed by transportation with

13%, construction at 1% and waste disposal of 11%. (Padilla-Rivera and Balnchet, 2017).

Bamboo can be used as a durable building material when it is industrially processed and engineered. It will also reduce the stress on existing resources and will gradually reduce deforestation. The bamboo strips is the building block which can be used to produce all kind of building materials like beams, panels etc. The main characteristic features of bamboo are its tensile strength, shrinking, fire resistant, compressive strength, flexural bending strength, shearing strength and its elasticity. Including transport, processing and production bamboo has negative carbon foot print which almost negative half a ton of CO_2 per ton of building material produced, which is much less than other sustainable materials. It has a high rate of carbon dioxide absorption and it releases 30 percent more oxygen than other tress. In a study done by

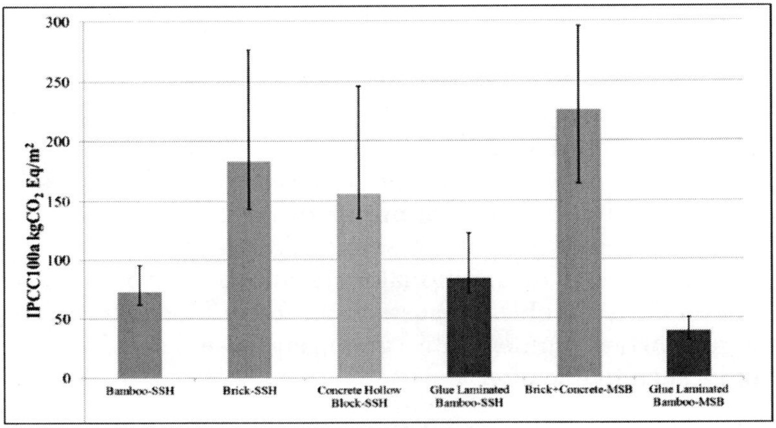

Fig. 9: Environmental impact in $kgCO_{2eq}$
SSH: single-storey House; MSB: multi-storey building.

Escamila et al, it was found that bamboo-based buildings have the lowest environmental impact for both Single-story houses (SSH) and Multi storied buildings (MSB) (Fig. 9). By contrast, brick/concrete (Br+Con)-based buildings have the highest environmental impacts. In the case of single-storey buildings, both bamboo-based buildings have very similar emissions per square meter: close to 80 CO_{2eq}/m^2. The bamboo-based multi-storey building has the lowest environmental impact of all in the sample, only 39 CO_{2eq}/m^2 (Escamila et al, 2018).

11.7 Conclusion

This paper aims to provide an alternative to conventional residential houses in Kerala that use materials like cement, concrete blocks, ceramic tiles and burnt clay bricks. The study proposes the use of engineered bamboo structures and prefabricated wood material as an alternative to traditional materials. A typical house in Kerala has 916 kg CO_{2eq}/m^2 of carbon emission. The carbon emission of a bamboo houses is 80 kg CO_{2eq}/m^2 and the wooden houses ranges from 275kg CO_{2eq}/m^2 to 353 kg CO_{2eq}/m^2. There has been a total reduction of 95.74%, 91.26% and 61.46% in carbon emission from bamboo and wooden structures respectively. Traditionally bamboo and wood has been used as a construction material and has the advantage of being renewable and fast growing. The research can further be broadened and studied by implementing the recommended amphibian flood resilient housing structure which will help in identifying the necessary drawbacks and limitations. Identification of suitable sites for bamboo and timber plantation can be initiated to ensure the sustainable utilization of resources. Thus in the long run the replacement of traditional materials and introduction of new efficient, durable and sustainable materials can transform our urban environment into a green, energy efficient, resilient and a sustainable one.

References

Architectural Digest India (2020) Wood in Architecture: 5 stunning homes built by top architects in India, Architectural Digest India. Available at: https://www.architecturaldigest.in/content/wood-inarchitecture-5-stunning-projects-built-by-top-architects-in-india/ (Accessed: 14 November 2021).

BBC, T. S. (2019) Could wooden buildings be a solution to

climate change?–BBC Future. Available at: https://www.bbc.com/future/article/20190717-climate-change-wooden-architecture-concreteglobal-warming.

Census Organization of India (2011) Kerala Population 2011 - 2021. Available at: https://www.census2011.co.in/census/state/kerala.html.

Center for Sustainable Systems University of Michigan (2021) 'Carbon Footprint Factsheet', Encyclopedia of Ecology, Pub. No. C. doi: 10.1016/B978-0-12-409548-9.10752-3.

Excerpted from a paper presented at the *Road Map Towards a Flood Resilient Urban Environment* International Conference on Urban Flood Management sponsored by UNESCO-IHP and COST Action C22, 25-27 November 2009, Paris, France.

Gan, W. et al. (2019) 'Dense, Self-Formed Char Layer Enables a Fire-Retardant Wood Structural Material', Advanced Functional Materials, 29(14). doi: 10.1002/adfm.201807444.

Government of Kerala and Department of Environment and Climate Change (2014) 'Kerala State Action Plan on Climate Change', pp. 1-153. Available at: http://www.moef.gov.in/sites/default/files/KERALA STATE ACTION PLAN ON CLIMATE CHANGE.pdf.

Kurian, R. et al. (2021) 'Estimation of carbon footprint of residential building in warm humid climate of india through BIM', Energies, 14(14). doi: 10.3390/en14144237.

Leal Filho, W., Azul, A. M., Brandli, L. L., Özuyar, P., Wall, T., & Springer International PublishingVerlag (Eds.). (2020). *Sustainable Cities and Communities: With 62 Tables*. Springer.

NautiyalPromode and Kant Raman (2021) 'INDIA TIMBER SUPPLY AND DEMAND 2010 - 2030'.

Padilla-Rivera, A. and Balnchet, P. (2017) 'Carbon footprint of pre-fabricated wood buildings', (June 2018), pp. 88-95. doi: 10.5151/sbds-issd-2017-015.

Praseeda, K. I., Reddy, B. V. V. and Mani, M. (2016) 'Embodied and operational energy of urban residential buildings in

India', Energy and Buildings, 110, pp. 211-219. doi: 10.1016/j.enbuild.2015.09.072.

Simon, D and Arfvidsson, H. and Anand, G. and Bazaz, A. and Fenna, G. and Foster, K.and Jain, G. and Hansson, S. and Evans, L.M. and Moodley, N. Developing and testing the Urban Sustainable Development Goal's targets and indicators-A five-city study. Environ. Urban. 2016, 28, 49-63

Songkarn Kongsricharoen. (2019). The Analysis Carbon Footprint of TDG Bamboo Laminated Column. *International Journal of Engineering Research & Technology (IJERT), Volume 8* (Issue 11).

The Carbon Brief Profile: India (2019). Available at: https://www.carbonbrief.org/the-carbon-briefprofile-india.

United Nations Environment Programme (2021) Building sector emissions hit record high, but low carbon pandemic recovery can help transform sector - UN report. Available at: https://www.unep.org/news-and-stories/press-release/building-sector-emissions-hit-recordhigh-low-carbon-pandemic.

Zea Escamilla, Edwin & Habert, Guillaume & Correal, Juan & Archila, Hector & Echeverry, Juan & Trujillo, David. (2018). Industrial or Traditional Bamboo Construction? Comparative Life Cycle Assessment (LCA) of Bamboo-Based Buildings. Sustainability. 10. 3096. 10.3390/su10093096.

Zuniga-Teran, A. A., Staddon, C., de Vito, L., Gerlak, A. K., Ward, S., Schoeman, Y., Hart, A., & Booth, G. (2020). Challenges of mainstreaming green infrastructure in built environment professions. *Journal of Environmental Planning and Management, 63(4)*, 710-732. https://doi.org/10.1080/09640568.2019.1605890

12

A Geo–Environmental Study on Solid Waste and its Management in Calangute Beach Town, North Goa, India

Subhanita Ghosh

Abstract: Fundamental concept of solid waste management in Goa includes household waste and similar substance collected by waste collection authority of Municipal Council. Solid waste in Goa includes a large percentage of vegetable wastes and small amount of papers, plastics, rubbers, glass and metal etc. Urban activities and growth are constantly putting pressure on an already burdened environment infrastructure. Depends on population and economic condition of Goa it is clear that an enormous amount of waste is going to be generated. An analysis has been carried out to find out road network for solid waste site and the shortest route for transportation. The collection, transportation, disposal and treatment of solid waste in Calangute and its adjacent area are maintained in a very well manner. Two colour dustbins are used for dry and wet waste in Calangute and those dustbins are also maintained in a very good way. In Calangute and its adjacent area there has to be a systematic improvement in various factors like institutional arrangement, financial provision, appropriate technology, human resource development, awareness, policy and legal framework for solid waste management system.

[1]Former Post graduate student, Department of Geography and Applied Geography, University of North Bengal, Darjeeling, West Bengal. Email: subhanitaghoshs@gmail.com

Keywords: Municipal Solid Waste, Plastic Waste, E Waste, Solid waste problem, Solid waste management, Measurement, Waste treatment.

12.1 Introduction

Much of our knowledge of ancient civilizations, as well as more contemporary times, has been derived from the solid waste discarded by the people of those times. In ancient cities, waste was seldom a problem—it simply accumulated until the city was levelled in a war and a new community was built on top of the rubble. The debris of war, as well as the discards of bygone eras and civilizations, provide a rich history of lifestyle and cultural development For example, archaeologists are currently digging in the town dump of Williamsburg, Virginia, in order to obtain a more complete picture of life in colonial times. Solid wastes are all the discarded solid materials from municipal, industrial, and agricultural activities. The objective of solid wastes management (SWM) are to control, collect, process, utilize and dispose of solid wastes in an economical way consistent with the public health protection. The urban waste management system in developing countries like India consist formal and informal system. The generation of waste in Indian cities ranges from 200-870 gm/d depending upon the population and the lifestyle of people. The Municipal waste from the Indian cities contain about 40- 60% of organic matter which can be easily recycled as compost.

12.2 Area of Study

Goa is a state in western India with coastlines stretching along the Arabian Sea. Its long history as a Portuguese colony prior to 1961 is evident in its preserved 17th century churches and the area's tropical spice plantations. Goa is also known for its beaches, ranging from popular stretches at Baga and Palolem to those in laid-back fishing villages such as Agonda. Goa encompasses an area of 3,702 sq. km. It lies between the latitudes 14°53' 54" N and 15°40'00" N and the longitudes 73°40'33" E and 74°20'13" E. In North Goa under Mapusa

Municipal Council Calangute town and its adjacent area is our study area, which is famous for its beach. The beach is thelargest in North Goa and visited by thousands of domestic and international tourists alike. It lies between 15°35'30" N to 73°45'43"E.

12.3 Objectives

The main objectives of this research work are enumerated below:

- To analysis the qualitative and quantitative assessment of solid waste.
- To examine the existing solid waste management system of the study area.
- To assess existing status of generation, collection, storage, transportation, treatment and disposal method practiced in the study area.
- To estimate weight and per day waste generation in Calangute and its adjacent area.
- To provide comprehensive suggestion for future management and planning.
- To identify the major problems of solid waste.

12.4 Database & Methodology

This research work is based on both primary and secondary data collected from different sources. The primary sources of data have been collected through city and household survey, market survey, restaurant survey and industry survey of selecting the items. The random sampling design was adopted to collect the primary data on the other hand various information are collected as secondary data from various government report, net website of Goa Municipal Councils, Goa pollution control board, Central library, different book review of solid waste of Goa, different journal articles, official website and statistical bulletins of Goa.

12.4.1 Prefield:

1. First of all Calangute and its adjacent area of Goa of India is selecting for this study.

2. Minor and major dumping grounds in Goa are identified for compared study.
3. General literature survey was carried out and collection of map and secondary data for solid waste.
4. A structure of questionnaire for residential, commercial, industrial and their working staff were used to obtain information about the solid waste management.

12.4.2 Field:

The following method is taken during field survey–

1. Data are collected from both primary and secondary source.
2. As study in a populated area it becomes difficult task to conduct the primary survey. Primary data collected randomly from the residential families of the study area with the help of questionnaire prepared.
3. Relevant photographs have been taken during the field survey to illustrate the scenario more specifically.
4. Some officer expert and executive in different organisation were personally meet and interviewed.

12.4.3 Postfield:

1. Sorting of primary data.
2. This stage involves computation of master data table from the questionnaire statistical application, cartographic representation and drawing the map.
3. Cartographic techniques are used to prepare this report.

12.5 Profile of generation of Solid Waste and Management in Goa

12.5.1 Management of Municipal Solid Waste

(a) Collection of municipal solid wastes

Littering of municipal solid waste shall be prohibited in cities, towns and in urban areas notified by the State Governments. To prohibit littering and facilitate compliance, the following steps shall be taken by the municipal authority, namely- i. Organising house-to-house collection of municipal solid wastes through any of the methods, like community bin collection (central bin), house-to-house collection, collection on regular pre-informed timings and scheduling by using bell ringing of musical vehicle, ii. Devising collection of waste from slums and squatter areas or localities including hotels, restaurants, office complexes and commercial areas ;

(b) Segregation of municipal solid wastes

The municipal authority shall undertake phased programme to ensure community participation in waste segregation. For this purpose, regular meetings at quarterly intervals shall be arranged by the municipal authorities with representatives of local resident welfare associations and non-governmental organizations.

(c) Storage of municipal solid wastes

i. Storage facilities shall be created and established by taking into account quantities of waste generation in a given area and the population densities.
ii. Storage facilities to be set up by municipal authorities or any other agency shall be so designed that wastes stored are not exposed to open atmosphere and shall be aesthetically acceptable and user-friendly;
iii. Storage facilities or bins shall have easy to operate design for handling, transfer and transportation of waste.

(d) Transportation of municipal solid wastes

Vehicles used for transportation of wastes shall be covered. Waste should not be visible to public, nor exposed to open environment preventing their scattering.

i. The storage facilities set up by municipal authorities shall be daily attended for clearing of wastes. The bins or containers wherever placed shall be cleaned before they start overflowing;
ii. Transportation vehicles shall be so designed that multiple handling of wastes, prior to final disposal, is avoided.

(e) Processing of municipal solid wastes

The biodegradable wastes shall be processed by composting, vermicomposting, anaerobic digestion or any other appropriate biological processing for stabilization of wastes. It shall be ensured that compost or any other end product shall comply with standards as specified in Schedule-IV;

(f) Disposal of municipal solid wastes

Land filling shall be restricted to non-biodegradable, inert waste and other waste that are not suitable either for recycling or for biological processing. Land filling shall also be carried out for residues of waste processing facilities as well as pre-processing rejects from waste processing facilities waste shall be avoided.

12.6 Analytical Approach on Solid Waste Problem and Management in Calangute and Adjacent Area

12.6.1 Sources of Solid Waste and Different Environmental Problems due to Solid Waste

Table–1
Sources of Solid Waste in Calangute

Category	Frequency	Percentage
Plastic	33	23.91
Metal	12	8.70
Glass	14	10.14
Papers	22	15.94
Wood	6	4.35
Vegetable & Food Leftovers	45	32.61
Others	6	4.35
Total	**138**	**100**

Source: Primary data, 2020

The information has stated that (Fig. 1) out of total solid waste 33% waste are generated from vegetable and food leftovers followed by 24%, 16%, 10%, 9%, 4% and 4% are generated from plastics, papers, glass, metal, wood and other

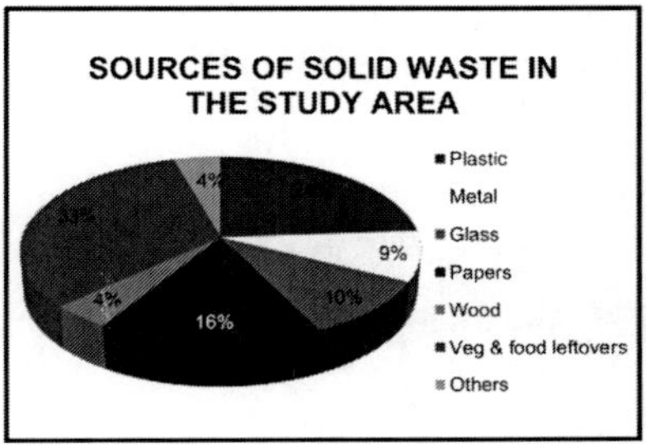

Fig. 1

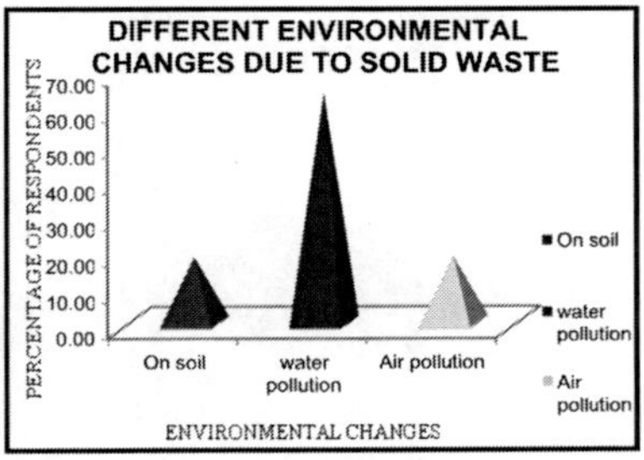

Fig. 2

Source: Primary data, 2020.

sources. So it is found that most of the solid wastes are generated from vegetable and food leftovers than that of others in the study area.

Table–2
Different Environmental Changes due to Solid Waste in Calangute

Category	Frequency	Percentage
On soil	2	18.18
water pollution	7	63.64
Air pollution	2	18.18
Total	**11**	**100**

Source: Primary data, 2020

The data has stated that (Fig. 2) the people who are agreed that environmental changes occurred due to solid waste out of them 64% people are saying that water pollution is the major reason for those changes followed by 18% and 18% people are saying that soil pollution and air pollution are the other causes for those changes respectively. So it is found that water pollution is the major cause for the environmental changes in the study area than that of other pollutions.

12.6.2 Effect of Municipal Solid Waste on Health Condition

Mapusa Municipal Council doesnot received funds from international financial sources, the Mapusa municipal Council doesnot operate Medical incineration facility, also they operate commercial centralized composting plant. Municipal council

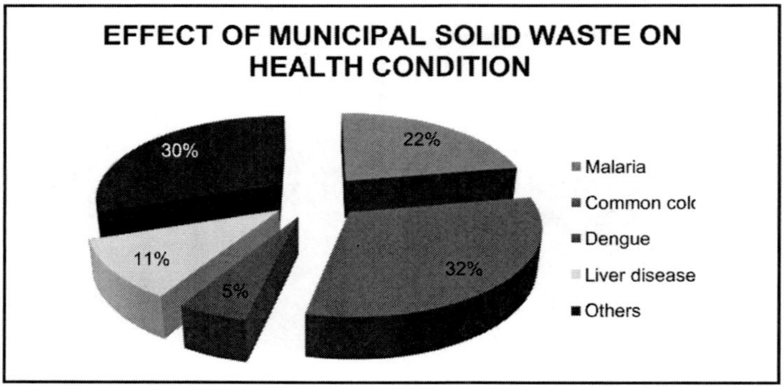

Fig. 3

also support residential composting in the area of their operation; they collect them and compost them in the composting unit, the Mapusa Municipal Council also participate in public awareness or public education programs, by using sighnboards, banners etc, the waste collection carried out by regular staffs, the total amount (approximately) of solid waste collected per day is 25 tonnes; 15 tonnes are wet waste and remaining 10 tonnes are dry waste,and street sweeping done by the municipal public workers, manually and usually at the time of morning, official waste disposal sites are maintained by municipal workers, they take the solid waste management rules of 2016: and the collection mechanism for waste and awareness on source segregation as, the Council is carrying out door to door collection of segregated waste from the household, commercial establishments and other non-residential premises etc. from all 20 wards, wherein 100% city is covered by utilizing workers or labourers employed by the Council.

The figure has stated that (Fig. 3) approximately 32% people in the study area are suffered from common cold followed by 30%, 22%, 11% and 5% people are suffered from other diseases, Malaria, Liver disease and Dengue respectively. So it is found that common cold is the disease which occurred frequently in the study area than that of others diseases.

12.6.3 Problems for Solid Waste

Table–3
Problems for Solid Waste in Calangute

Category	Frequency	Percentage
Water logging	13	68.42
water contamination	4	21.05
Others	2	10.53
Total	**19**	**100**

Source: Primary Data, 2020

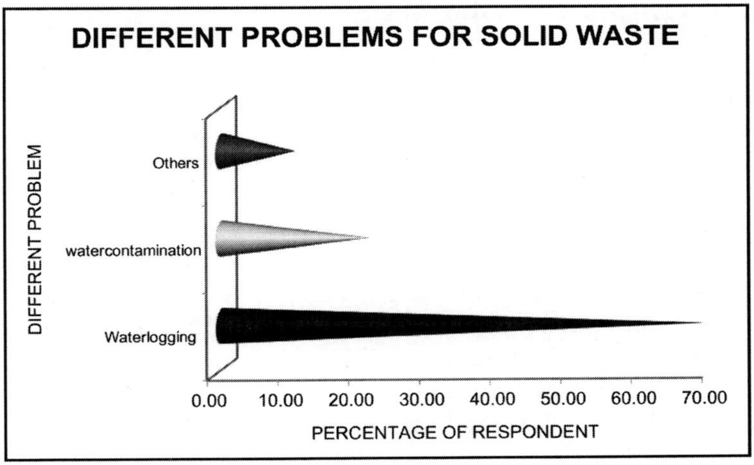

Fig. 4

Source: Primary data, 2020.

The information has stated that (Fig. 4) the people who opine that there are some problems occurred due to solid wastes out of them 68% people are saying that water logging is the major problem followed by 21% and 11% people are saying ground water contamination and other problems are occurred due to solid waste respectively in the study area. So it is found that water logging problem is the major problem than that of other problem found in study area due to solid waste.

The Council has distributed two bins (black/blue & green colour) of 10 litres capacity each to the households including commercial establishments, to segregate and store the waste at source i.e. Biodegradable (wet) waste in green colour bin and Non- biodegradable (dry) waste in black colour bin, secondary waste storage facilities and transportation of waste such as, the Council has set up 5 nos of transfer stations (M.S Enclosers) and has also developed 20 nos of open sites for secondary storage of the 240 liters bins containing the segregated waste collected from door to door, for further transportation through Municipal vehicles to the waste management facility.

12.6.4 Disposal of Solid Waste

The Council has deployed separate vehicles (13 nos) for the purpose of wet and dry waste collection; processing of Biodegradable (wet) waste such as the Council is having decentralized as well as centralized facility for treatment of the wet waste. They have different composting units; such as the centralized composting unit is located in Survey no. 145/1 situated at Assagao plateau, Assagao and the decentralized sites are near Sulabh toilet, at Dangui colony (ward no. 5); opp. Rotary garden, Dattawadi (ward no. 12); near Shantivan Crematorium at ganganagar, Khorlim (ward no. 14); at Acoi (ward no. 8); near District hospital, Peddem (ward no. 7) and near Industrial Estate, Caraswada (ward no. 4).

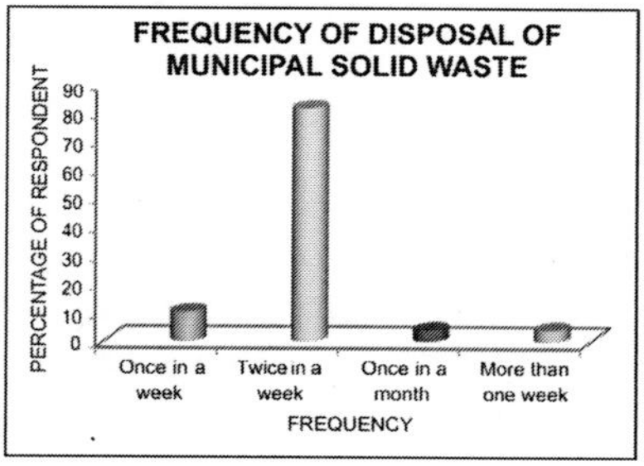

Fig. 5

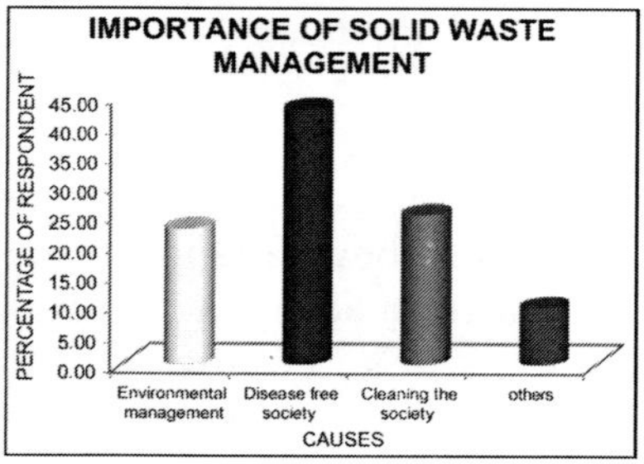

Fig. 6

Source: Primary data, 2020.

Table–4
Disposal of Solid Waste

Frequency	Frequency	Percentage
Once in a week	5	10.20
Twice in a week	40	81.63
Once in a month	2	4.08
More than one week	2	4.08
Total	**49**	**100**

Source: Primary Data, 2020.

The data has stated that (Fig. 5) approximately 47% respondents are said that the major policy for solid waste management is place individual colour basket everywhere in the municipal area followed by 17%, 11%, 10%, 9% and 7% are said that the policies which are taken by the Municipal Council to reduce the problems are regular cleaning of waste, others policies, awareness campaign, location of dumping site far away from the locality and spreading bleaching powder respectively. So it is found that the Municipal council is takes many step but using individual colour basket is very helpful in the solid waste management. The figure has stated that (Fig. 6) 43% respondents are said that importance of solid waste management is to get a disease free society followed by 25%, 23% and 9% respondents are said that cleaning of the society, environmental management and others are the importance of solid waste management. So it is found that most of the respondents in the study area thought that solid waste management has an importance for a disease free society.

12.6.5 Policies taken by Mapusa Municipal Council

The data has stated that (Fig. 7) approximately 47% respondents are said that the major policy for solid waste management is place individual colour basket everywhere in the municipal area followed by 17%, 11%, 10%, 9% and 7% are said that the policies which are taken by the Municipal Council to reduce the problems are regular cleaning of waste, others policies, awareness campaign, location of dumping

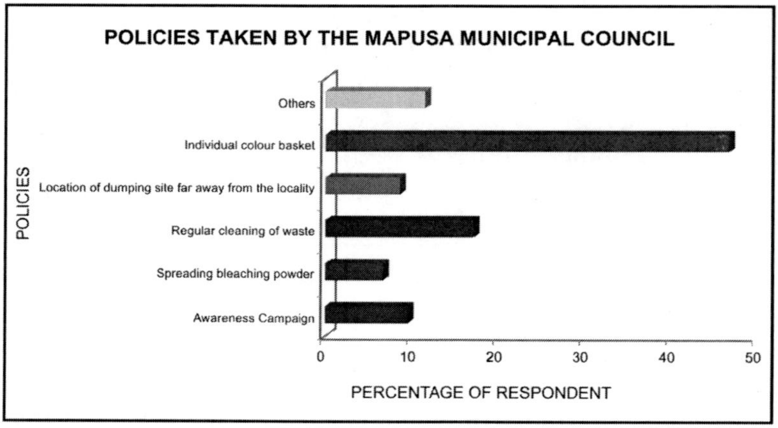

Fig. 7

Source: Primary data, 2020.

site far away from the locality and spreading bleaching powder respectively. So it is found that the Municipal council is takes many step but using individual colour basket is very helpful in the solid waste management.

12.6.6 Measures taken by Mapusa Municipal Council

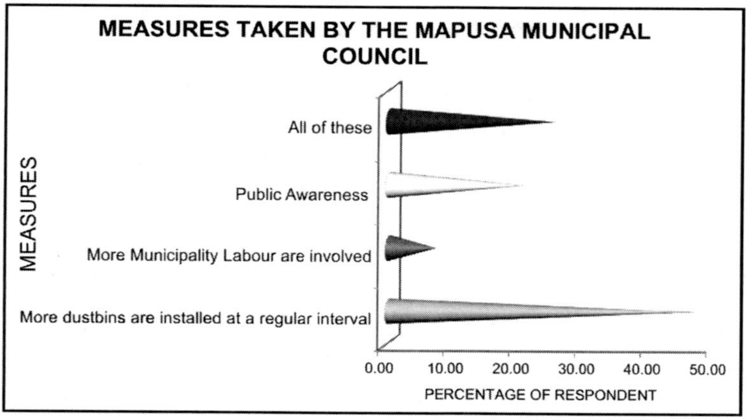

Fig. 8

Source: Primary data, 2020.

Table–5
Measure taken by the Council

Frequency	Frequency	Percentage
More dustbins are installed at a regular interval	39	46.99
More Municipality labour are involved	6	7.23
Public Awareness	17	20.48
All of these	21	25.30
Total	**83**	**100**

Source: Primary Data, 2020.

The fact has stated that (Fig. 8) 47% respondents are said that the measures that are taken by the Council are more dustbins are installed at a regular interval followed by 25%, 21% and 7% respondents are said that the measures are all of these measures, public awareness and more municipality labour are involved respectively.

So it is found that installment of more dustbins at a regular interval is more helpful than that of other measures in the study area. Calangute and its adjacent area under Mapusa Municipality in Goa is very developed. Solid waste management is a very important part of city development. City development, income level and economic activities as well as solid waste generation process are very good in residential areas as well as in commercial areas. The solid waste management is also good and well organised in Calangute and its adjacent area because the generation, collection, disposal and treatment of the solid waste of the study area are done very carefully and in a much organised manner.

12.7 Finding of the Study

- Most of the people among the respondents and their family members are adult about 25% people belongs to 30-40 years of age group, among them more than 50% people are male, 29% people among the respondents family are married and most of them about 27 % and 27% people are belongs to Schedule Caste and OBC community respectively than that of Schedule Tribe and others.

- A large number of people about 41% people are belongs to Hindu religion among the respondents of the study area, people having Degree qualification are more in numbers among the respondents, Students, businessman and the people who are engaged in tourism sector are more in number, Pucca houses are more than that of Semi Pucca and Katcha.
- Middle to higher income group of people about 48% more in numbers and the people who spend less money are more, most of the families are nuclear in nature about 92% and 96% respondents are coming from different states of India but they are reside in the study area for about 10 to 2o years and more.
- 61% respondents are settle in rented house and paid 8000 to 10000 rupees monthly rent,73% solid waste are generated from hotels and shops and remaining are from households and colour bins are used in the study area 92% dustbins are made of plastic remaining are made of metal.
- Most of the wastes are generated from vegetable and food leftovers, plastic and papers; commercial hotels and shops are paid 5000 rupees and households are paid 200 rupees per month for solid waste, according to 78% respondents solid waste has no effect in damaging the health condition and are also disagreed that the environmental changes are occurred due to solid waste.
- In the study area the wastes are managed in a very good way, according to respondents different environmental changes occurred due to solid waste, water logging problem is the major problem than that of other problem in the study area and common cold is the disease which occurred frequently in the study area than that of others diseases.
- Most of the people are encounters with different difficulties due to solid waste, health issues and

environmental pollution both are the major difficulties and disadvantages of Municipal solid waste, most of the wastes are disposed twice in a week.

- Some respondents are requesting the Municipal authority to reduce the waste and some are reporting to the Council authority to take steps regarding the problems of municipal waste, Municipal Council using individual colour basket for solid waste management, instalment of more dustbins at a regular interval is more helpful and according to respondents solid waste management has an importance for a disease free society.
- 100% respondents have the storage receptacle in their house or their compound, and also they have getting the service of collection and disposal of waste and they all are satisfied with the service according to all the respondents Municipal Council is the best to handle solid waste management in the study area.
- 100% solid wastes are disposed by the Government authority in the study area and Government waste collectors are collected the waste every day using Municipal waste collector vehicles.
- According to all the respondents Municipal solid wastes are not affecting their daily life and the atmosphere. The wastes are dumped outside the city and all the respondents are satisfied that was the suitable place for dumping.
- According to all the respondents the Government authority is taking different kinds of actions to solve the problems regarding solid waste in the study area and the problems regarding solid waste are going to be solved.
- 13.100% respondents are said that there has no role of the private voluntary organization, but Municipal Council playing a major role in the Municipal solid waste treatment.
- Different policies are taken to reduce the solid waste problem in the study area by the Government authority

and public awareness on Municipal solid waste management and other environmental problems is a perfect way to mitigate the several problems regarding solid waste.

12.8 Problems of the Study Area

- Most of the people use plastic materials in Calangute which is non degradable.
- The absence of Municipal waste collectors created problem for the residents, they suffer from mosquitoes, odour etc.
- The disturbances by the safety tanks occurred problem for the habitants in the study area.
- Sometimes the tourists who are not that much aware about the environment of the study area but they through the garbage anywhere
- Different health issues and environmental changes occurred due to solid waste in the Calangute and its adjacent area.
- Local people suffered from different types of diseases for solid waste, such as Malaria, Dengue, Common cold, Liver Disease and others.
- Different environmental changes occurred due to solid waste such as Soil pollution, Water pollution and Air pollution.
- Another problems occurred due to solid waste such as water logging, ground water contamination and others.
- Another major problem of the study area is inadequate waste collection.
- Collection coverage is careful with only 100% household received such service. But in industrial area collection coverage is still limited.

12.9 Suggestions and Recommendations

Present study reveals that there are many shortcomings in the present particles followed for management of solid waste in Calangute, Mapusa, Goa. These are mainly due to inadequate man power financial resources and machinery required for effective disposal and management of solid waste. Some of steps that can be taken for solid waste management in this locality (Calangute) are as followed–

- Management of Municipal waste rather than incurring the costs and risk of managing waste are proportional.
- There is a large gap between policy and implementation.
- Waste quantity is not measured and usually assessed on the basic number of trips made by transportation vehicles.
- Public awareness should be created at large scale for awaking people from hazards caused from improper disposal of garbage.
- Municipal authority should maintain storage facilities in such manner that these do not create insanitary condition.
- Proper maintenance of MSW transportation vehicles should be done.
- The biodegradable garbage which mainly comprises of organic materials such as kitchen, vegetable-fruit waste can be converted into valuable materials such as compost, fertilizers, biogas etc.
- High technology uses for solid waste management.
- Government policies should be applied strictly for solid waste management.
- Concern about solid waste management of Municipal Council workers.
- There is also need for development technology of recycling, treatment and other pre-plans.
- People should use paper bags, cloth bags etc.
- Decreasing the waste of city especially plastic bags.
- People should use dustbins.
- Illegal solid waste dumping should be banned by the administrative body.

- The owner of restaurant should be aware about solid waste.
- Solid wastes are utilized in different purpose by the treatment and recycling technology.

12.10 Concluding Observation

Finally it can be said that solid waste management has a vital role for environment as well as human life in Calangute and its adjacent area, Goa. Municipal Council should plan and execute the system keeping in view the increasing of the urban area and pollutions. Some points are observed by this area survey.

- Most of the people use plastic materials in Calangute which is non degradable.
- Some people are affected by different type's diseases.
- Solid wastes of Calangute and its adjacent area are well treated by the Mapusa Municipal Council.
- The collection, transportation, disposal and treatment of Solid waste in Calangute and its adjacent area are maintained in a very well manner.
- Two colour dustbins are used for dry and wet waste in Calangute and those dustbins are also maintained in a very good way.

In Calangute and its adjacent area there has to be a systematic improvement in various factors like institutional arrangement, financial provision, appropriate technology, human resource development, awareness, policy and legal framework for solid waste management system. Finally there is also developed methodology for waste management in Calangute, Goa. Primary collection of recyclable and organic waste should be given logistic support to extent possible. Therefore above this plan is successful and save for future generation in solid waste management.

References

Books:

Census Hand Book, 2011

Chawla, Romila, "Sex Tourism and Development", Sonali Publications, 2004, p. 57

District Census Handbook, South Goa, Village and Town Directory, Directorate of Census Operations, Goa.

Seth, Pran Nath, "Successful Tourism Management, Vol. I: Fundamentals of Tourism"; Sterling Publishers, 1999, p. 145.

Statistical Hand Book of Goa, 2016-17, Directorate of Planning, Statistics and Evaluation, Porvorim-Goa.

Print Media:

D'Mello (D'Souza) A Carmelita (Associate Professor, Department of Commerce, ST. Xavier's College, Mapusa-Goa), "Managing Tourism Development in Goa through Sustainable Tourism", Thesis for the award of the degree of Doctor of Philosophy, 2015.

EI Division MSME development institute - GOA, "Brief Industrial profile of North Goa District', 2016.

Kamat, Nandkumar M. (Asst. Professor, Department of Botany, Goa University, Taleigao, Goa) "Sustainable Ecotourism Planning for Happier and Wealthier Goa", Goa Today, Goa's largest and oldest English Magazine, 04 November 2015, p. 1-10.

Sawant N. Nandkumar (Associate Professor, Dept. of Geography, Parvatibhai Chowgule College, Brammer Natasha and Beech John (Coventry Business School), "Use and Abuse of Tourism: The Gaon Experience", Tourism, Culture & Communication, Vol. 5, p. 23-35, Printed in the USA, DOI: 10.3727/1098304042781508

Solomon Ranjan (NGO/ecumenical leader), "The Challenge and Prospects of Tourism in Goa Today", J&P Printers,

Bengaluru, Nov. 2009.

Websites:

www.goa/coastaltourismGOA1.pdf

www.goa/11%20hotel1%industry%20in%20goa.pdf

www.goa/12_chapter%205.pdf

www.goa-tourism.com

E: reservations@goa-tourism.com

www.facebook.com/officialgoatourism

13

Status of Solid Waste Generation & Sustainable Management in Vishakhapatnam Municipal Corporation, Andhra Pradesh, India

Barnali Biswas[1] *and Reetuparna Das*[2]

Abstract: Solid waste has become a fairly serious environmental problem particularly in the urban areas. Increasing rate of population, economic development, urbanization and industrialization have all resulted in the increase of solid waste generation. The objective of solid waste management is to control, collect, and process, utilize and dispose of solid wastes in an economical way consistent with the public health protection. In Vishakhapatnam the solid waste management is totally controlled by GVMC. It not only looks after the city but also pays proper attention solid waste management .Vishakhapatnam has proper and well planned system for solid waste management. GVMC is putting effort in controlling solid waste in the city. To reduce the quantity of toxic and hazardous chemicals and materials acquired, used, or disposed off as solid waste. There are diseases such as tuberculosis, cholera, typhoid spread due to improper management of solid waste. GVMC is trying to solve these problems in the city. Therefore in this research paper an

[1]Research Scholar, Department of Geography & Applied Geography, University of North Bengal, District: Darjeeling. Email: barnali.slg01@gmail.com

[2]Former Post graduate student, Department of Geography & Applied Geography, University of North Bengal, District: Darjeeling. Email: reetuparnadas88@gmail.com

attempt has been to point out the management of solid waste in Vishakhapatnam.

Keywords: *solid waste management, sewerage system. GVMC*

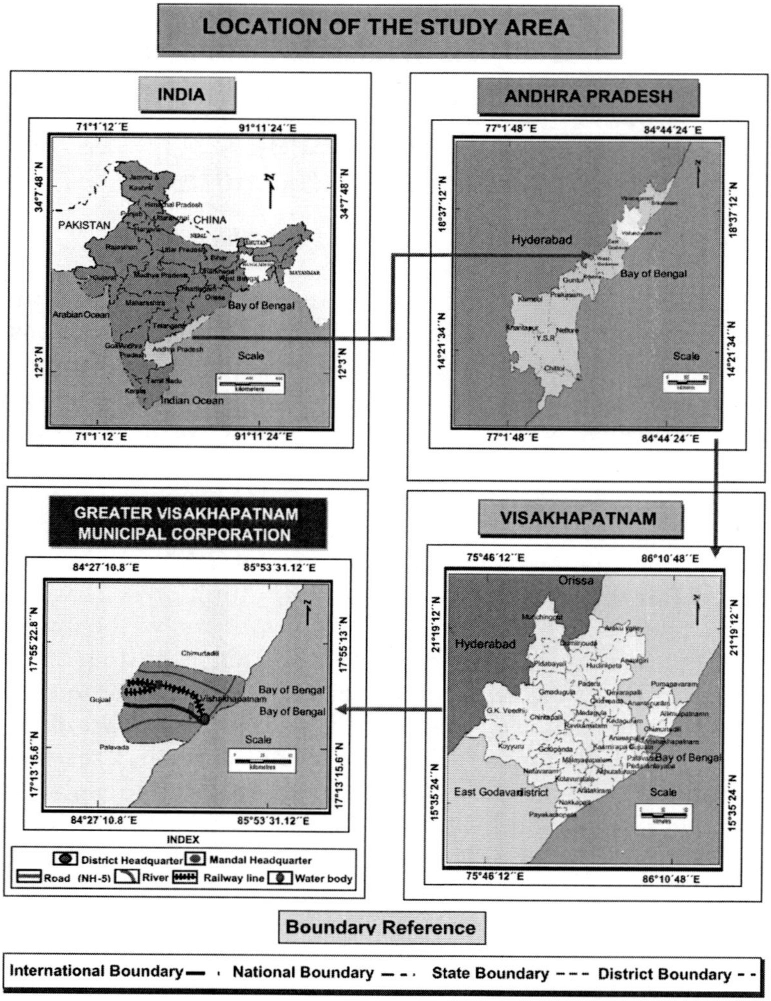

Fig. 1

Source: Oxford school of ATLAS, Vishakhapatnam urban development authority, GVMC

13.1 Introduction

The present study is carried out in the Greater Visakhapatnam Municipal Corporation area in the year 2019 to understand the solid waste management scenario in GVMC area. Municipal solid waste management is an important as it impacts health, environment and aesthetic society if it is not managed properly. Due to rapid urbanization and uncontrolled growth rate of population, solid waste management (SWM) has become acute problem in India. SWM services are rendered by municipal bodies in India. Though, it is an essential service, it is not attaining proper priority. The most common problems associated with improper management of solid waste include diseases transmission, fire hazards, atmospheric and water pollution.

13.2 Area of the Study

Vizag is located on the east coast of India, in 17°42' North latitude and 82°02' East range of hills. Based on topographical conditions, the city and its environs can be divided into four categories viz., Hilly region, Upland tracks, Rolling plains and Plains. The Kailasa and Yarada are the major hill ranges in the city. The city, appears like a small basin, is surrounded by the Yarada hill popularly known as Dolphin's nose (358m) on the side of the Kailasgiri hills on the north, with the Bay of Bengal forming the eastern wall.

13.3 Research Question

- How the solid waste management takes place in the city of Vishakhapatnam?
- How the residences of the city describe the state of solid waste?
- What are the main problems of solid waste management of the city?
- What is the level of satisfaction of solid waste management of the city?
- What is the frequency of solid waste collection of the area?
- How much amount people pay to the GVMC for the

collection service of solid waste?

13.4 Objective of the Study

- To analyze the quantity and types of Municipal solid waste generated per capita per day, in the ULB's for different sources and types of waste generated.
- To analyse the role of Greater Vishakhapatnam Municipal corporation in development of solid waste management of the city.
- To analyse the mechanism for Primary and Secondary collection of solid waste, including details of physical infrastructure such as Waste bins, Collection points, Road length covered, number of Sanitary workers employed and type of vehicles used, etc.
- To know the awareness between the people about the 3Rs i.e., Reuse, reduce and Recycle.
- Analysing the routes of the vehicles of corporation and the location of the waste bins of the city.
- To know the distance between the house and the public bins of the GVMC.

13.5 Data Base

This research work is completely based on primary and secondary data collected from different sources. Primary data was collected from household or respondent survey and hospital survey. However data based on perception about solid waste was based on respondent survey or household survey regarding the collection and dumping of solid waste in the area. Data for solid waste was collected from hospital survey also. From the hospital survey we collected data regarding solid waste management in the hospital.

13.5.1 Primary data: Primary data has been collected through questionnaire survey through predesigned questionnaire survey based on 100 samples based on respondent survey, hospital survey, official of municipality.

13.5.2 Secondary data : Secondary data has been collected through data collected from GVMC (Greater Vishakhapatnam Municipal Corporation), Andhra Pradesh pollution control board and RTO (Regional Transport Office).

13.6 Methodology

This research work is based completely on primary data and secondary data. There are different methods adopted in order to collect the data from the field. A structured questionnaire is prepared to collect the data from the field. And then computation of master data table from the questionnaire, drawing maps and cartographic representation are done in order to study the area.

Global Mapper, QGIS, Map Info softwares have been used for dizitization and drawing of maps.

13.7 Scenario of Solid Waste Management in Vizag City

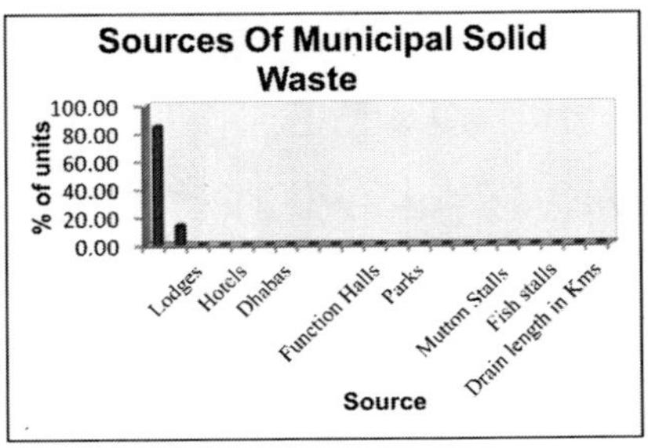

Fig. 2

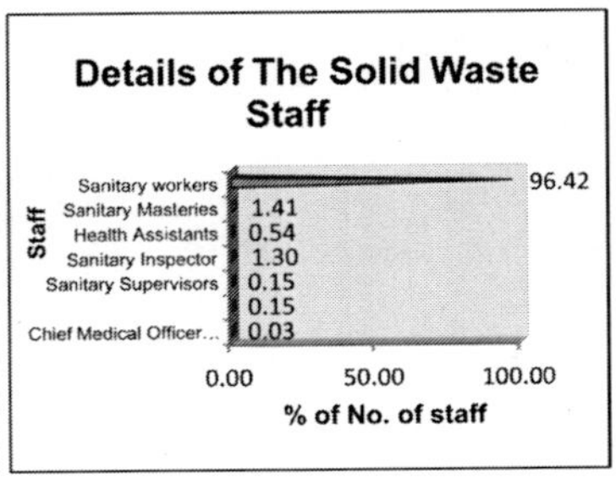

Fig. 3

Source: Greater Visakhapatnam Municipal Corporation

Fig. 2 shows that 84.38% source of solid waste came from domestic household. 13.84% from commercial establishment, 0.03% from Lodges, 0.05% from hotels, 0.01% from restaurants, 0.01% from Dhabas, 0.01% from market, 0.02% from temples, 0.03% from function halls, 0.01% from cinema halls, 0.01% from parks, 0.03% from school, 0.02% from college/universities, 0.04% from chicken stalls, 0.05% from mutton stalls, 0.01% from fish stalls, 0.65% from roads and lastly 0.81% from drains. So the most of the solid waste came from the domestic household of Vizag. In fig. 3 shows the details of solid waste management staff of public health department. Here the highest number of workers engaged in sanitary works i.e., 96.42% followed by sanitary masteries, sanitary inspector, health assistance, sanitary supervisor, Assistant Medical Officer and chief medical officer i.e., 1.41%, 1.30%, 0.54%, 0.15%, 0.15%, and 0.03%.

Fig. 4 shows that 52% of the municipal solid waste is organic waste, 23% is recyclables, 25% is inert matter. So here the maximum composition of waste is organic waste. The fig. 6 shows that 46.30% of vehicle is tricycles, used by GVMC, followed by 28.63%, 18.97%, 3.74%, 1.13%, 0.89%, 0.17%, 0.09% and 0.09% i.e., Push carts, Wheel barrows, Dumper Placers, Van, Big tippers, Mini tippers, Tractors and Dead body van.

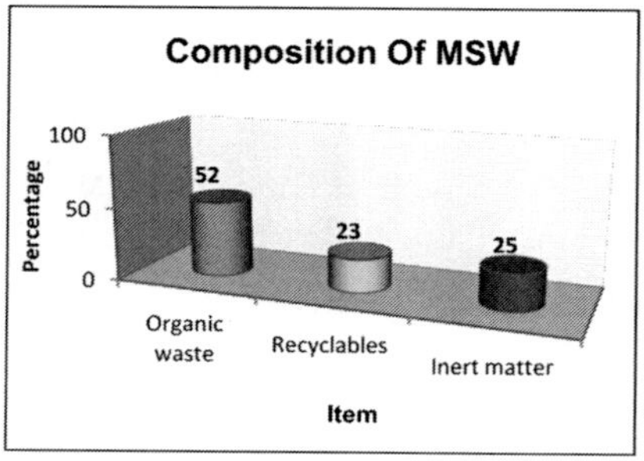

Fig. 4

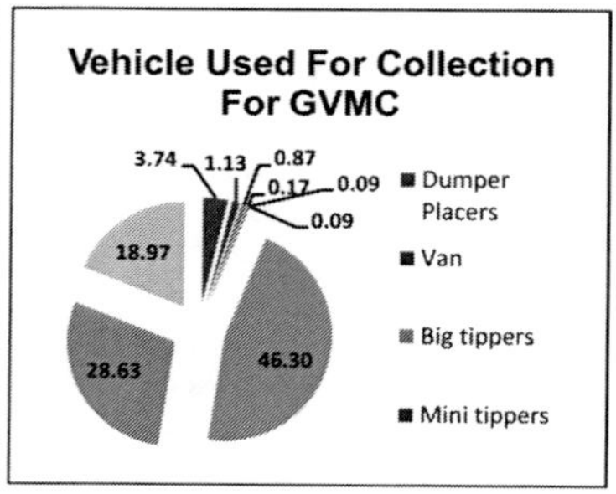

Fig. 5

Source: Greater Visakhapatnam Municipal Corporation

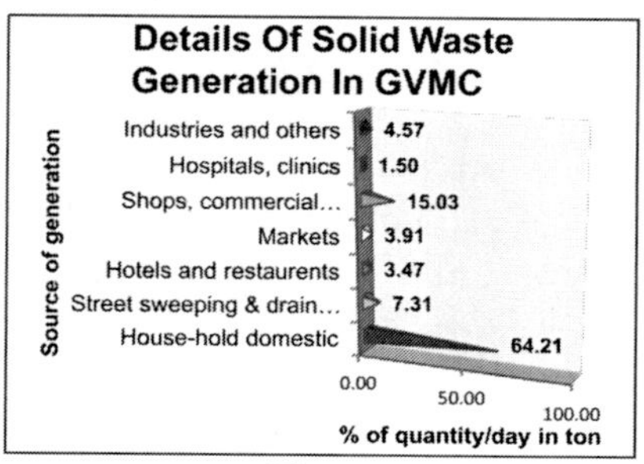

Fig. 6

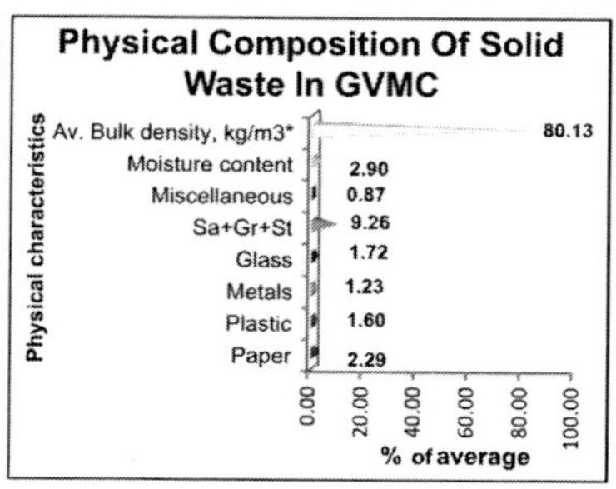

Fig. 7

Source: Greater Visakhapatnam Municipal Corporation

Fig. 6 shows the details of solid waste generation in GVMC, here highest is in house-hold domestic i.e., 64.21%, followed by 15.03%, 7.31%,4.57%, 3.91%, 3.47%, and 1.50% i.e., Shops, commercial establishments, Street sweeping & drain cleaning, Industries and others, Hotels and restaurants, Markets and Shops, commercial establishments respectively. The Fig. 7 informed about the physical composition of solid waste, the highest is in Av. Bulk density, kg/m^{3}* i.e., 80.13% followed by 9.26%, 2,90, 2.29, 1.72, 1.60, 1.23, 0.87% i.e., Sa+Gr+St, Moisture content, Paper, Paper, Plastic, Metals, and Miscellaneous respectively.

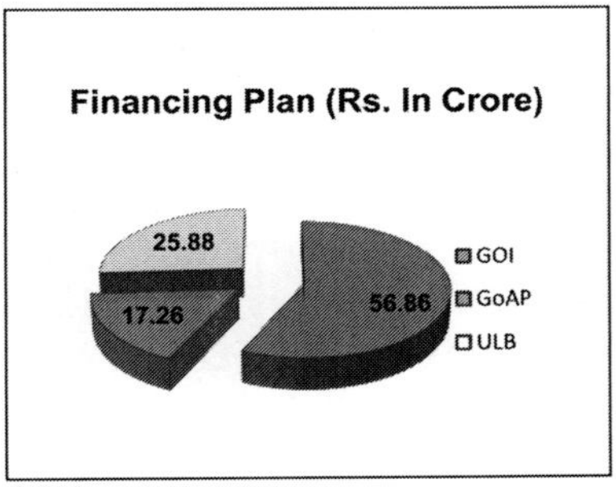

Fig. 8

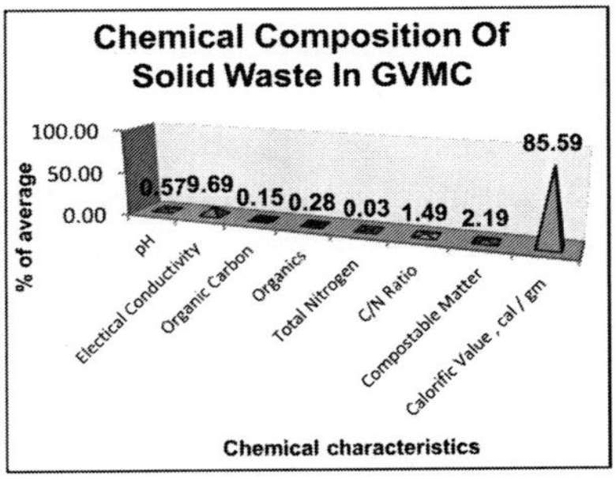

Fig. 9

Source: Greater Visakhapatnam Municipal Corporation

Fig. 8 shows the financing plan in the development of the city, here from the given data, it is clear that 56.86% financial support came from GOI, 25.88% from ULB, and

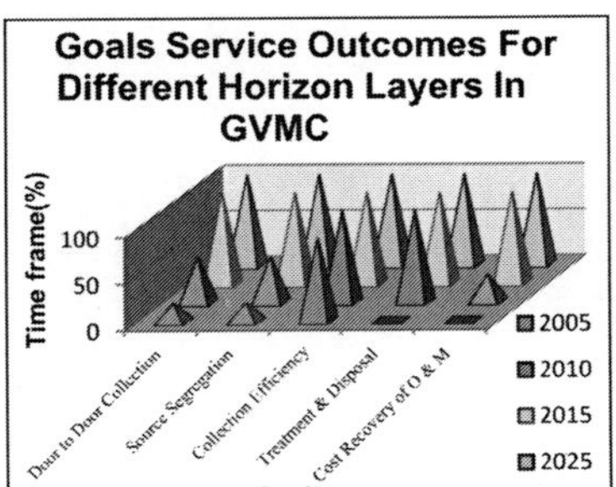

Fig. 10

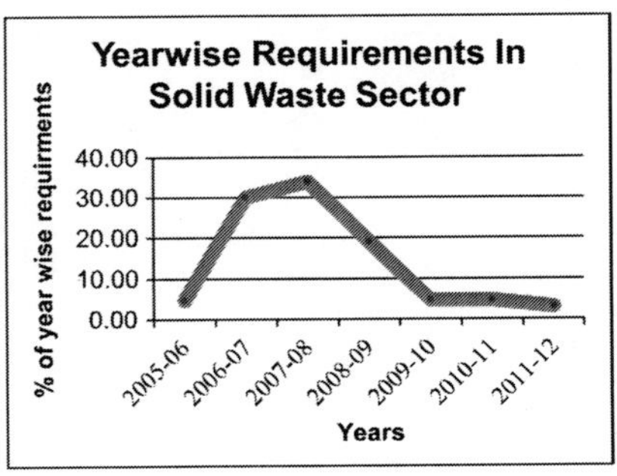

Fig. 11

Source: Greater Visakhapatnam Municipal Corporation

17.26% from GoAP. So, GOI plays a very important role in the development of the city. The Fig. 9 shows the chemical composition of solid waste in GVMC. Here the highest percentage is 85.59% i.e., Calorific Value, cal/gm. Followed by 9.69%, 2.19%, 1.49%, 0.57%, 0.28%, 0.15%, 0.03 i.e., Electrical Conductivity, Compostable Matter, C/N Ratio, pH, Organics, Organic Carbon, and Total Nitrogen respectively.

Fig. 10 shows the service outcomes for different horizon layers in GVMC. In 2005 the highest service outcomes came from Collection Efficiency, in 2010 i.e., 90%, in 2010 the 100% service outcomes came from Collection Efficiency and Treatment & Disposal. The data of 2015 and 2025 shows 100% outcomes from all the sectors like Door to Door Collection, Source Segregation, Collection Efficiency, Treatment & Disposal, Cost Recovery of O & M. Fig. 11 shows the year wise requirements in solid waste sector, here the data shows the highest requirement in 2007-08 i.e., 33.95% followed by 2006-07, 2008-09, 2005-06, 2009-10, 2010-11, and 2011-12 i.e., 29.98%,19.10%, 4.70%, 4.63%, 4.63%, and 3.01% respectively.

13.8 Perception Study on Solid Waste Problem and Its Management in Study Area

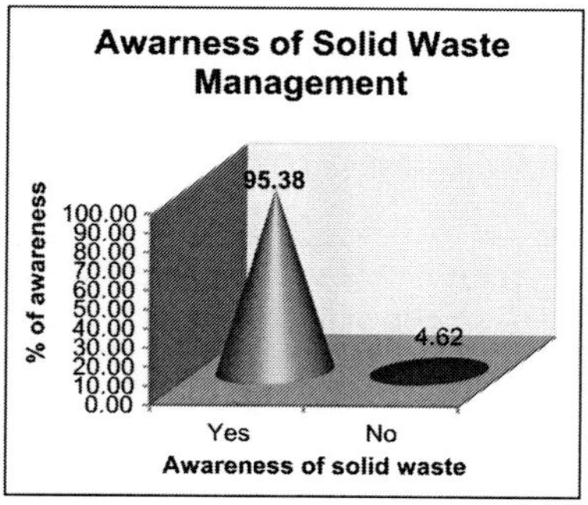

Fig. 12

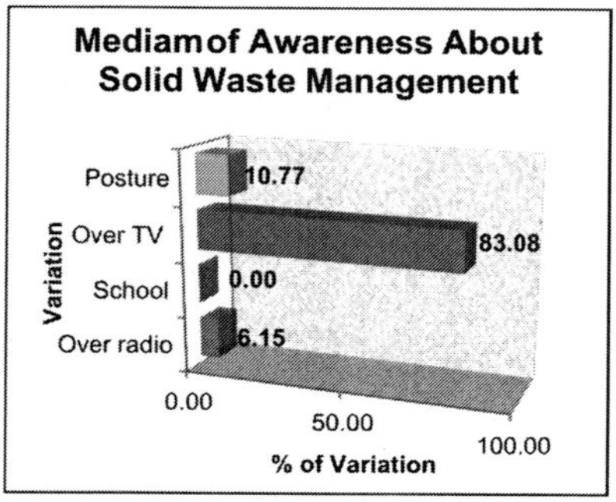

Fig. 13

Source: Primary data, February, 2019.

The Fig. 12 informed that 95.38% have heard about solid waste management and 4.62%have not heard about solid waste management. So it is clear here that maximum of the people of our study area are aware about the solid waste management. The Fig. 13 informed that 6.15% have heard over radio, 0.1% in school, 83.08% over TV and 10.77% seen in poster. So it is clear that television plays a dominant role as a medium of awareness about the solid waste management.

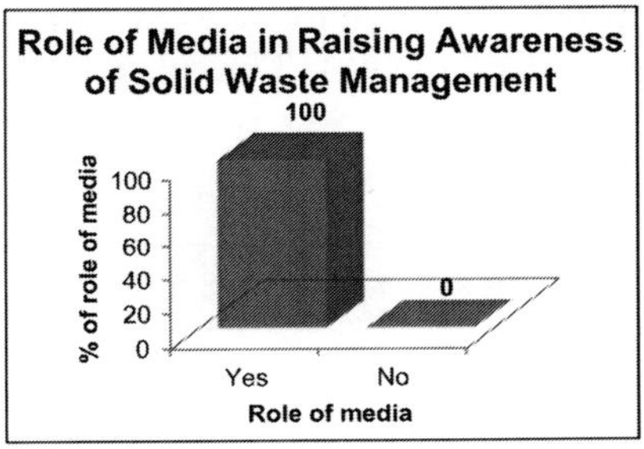

Fig. 14

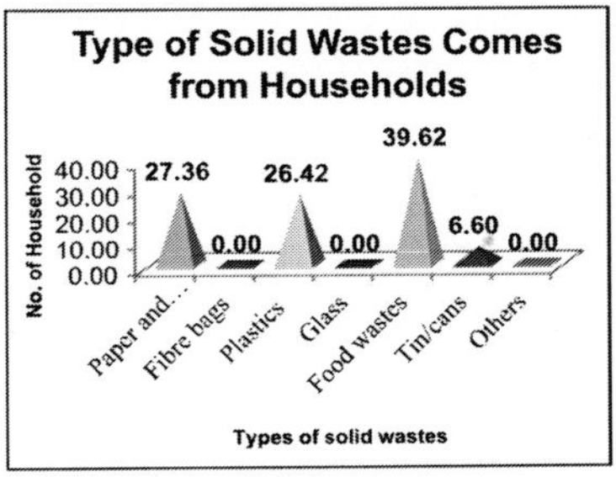

Fig.15

Source: Primary data, February, 2019

The Fig. 14 informed that there is 100% awareness about water, sanitation, and solid waste management. So it is clear that media plays an important role in raising awareness of solid waste management. The Fig. 15 informed that there are different type of waste. Out of which 27.36% as paper and cotton, 0% as fiber bags, 26.42% as plastics, 0% as glass, 39.62%as food waste, 6.60% as tins/cans and 0% others. So the highest type of solid waste is food wastes that is comes from households.

The Fig. 16 informed/that the waste is collected containers.

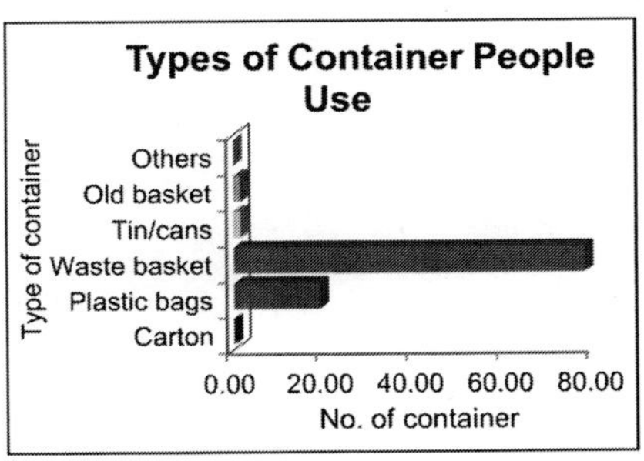

Fig. 16

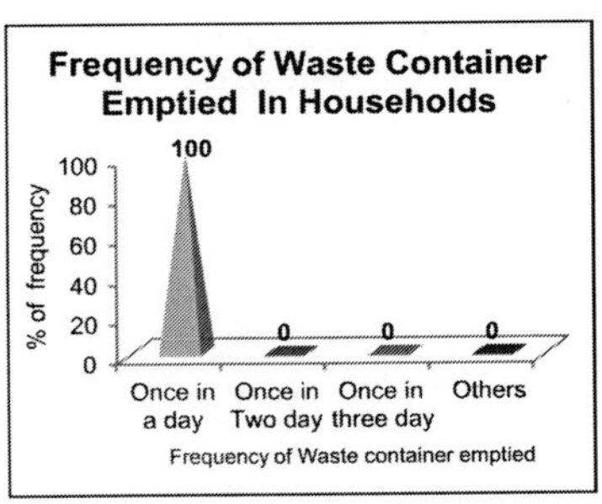

Fig. 17

Source: Primary data, February, 2019.

0% in carton, 19.05% in plastic bags, 77.78% in waste basket, 1.59% in tins/cans, 1.59% in old basket, and 0%in others. Therefore, most of the containers are categorized as carton, plastic bags, waste basket, tins/cans, old basket and others. The Fig. 17 informed that the waste is collected at different intervals. The waste is collected 100% once in a day, 0% once in two day, 0% once in three day, 0% others. Therefore, it is categorized as once in a day, once in two day, once in three day, and others.

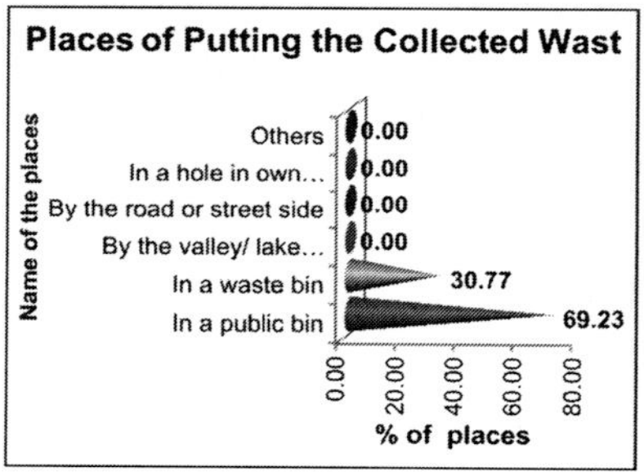

Fig. 18

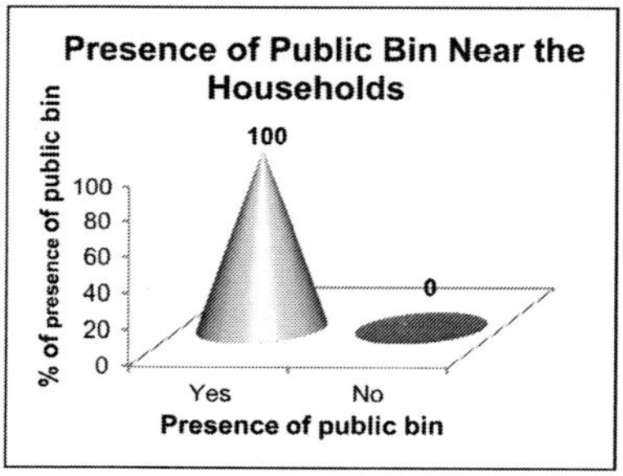

Fig. 19

Source: Primary data, February, 2019.

The Fig. 18 informed that the waste is collected in different containers/bins. 69.23% in a public bin, 30.77% in a waste bins, 0% by the valley/river/lake side/, 0% by the road, 0% in a hole in own compound, 0% others. So public is widely used in our study area and about some extent people use waste

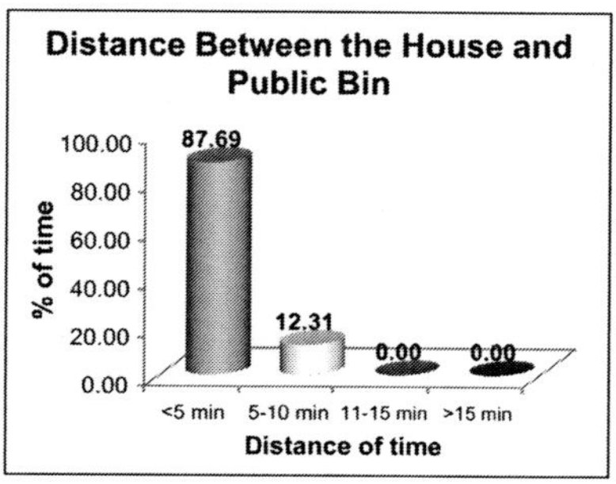

Fig. 20

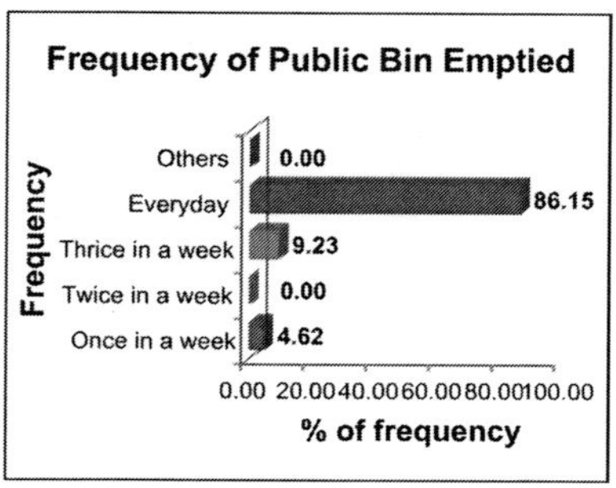

Fig. 21

Source: Primary data, February, 2019.

bin as a place of putting the collected waste. The Fig. 19 informed that there are 100%public bins near every house. So it is clear that Greater Visakhapatnam Municipal Corporation plays a very important role in context of solid waste management.

The Fig. 20 informed that 87.69%takes <5 min, 12.31% takes 5-10min, 0%takes 11-15 min, 0% >15 min. Therefore it is categorized under <5 min, 5-10min, 11-15min, >15 min. so it is clear that people of our study area get a good service of solid waste management from the corporation authority. The Fig. 21 informed that 4.62%public bins are emptied once in a week, 0% twice in a week, 9.23%thrice in a week, 86.15% everyday and 0% others. Therefore, it is categorized as once in a week, twice in a week, thrice in a week, everyday and others.

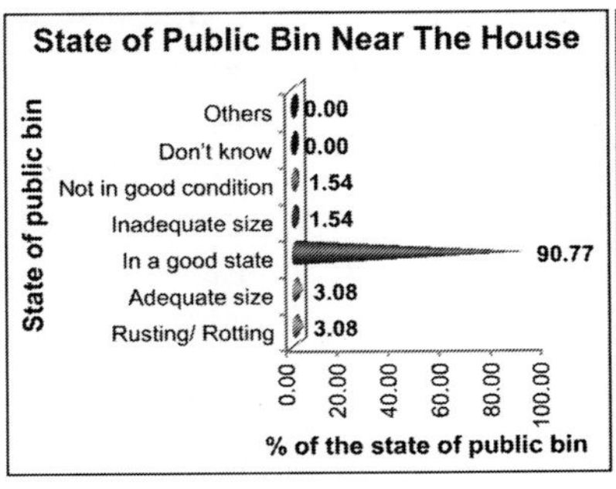

Fig. 22

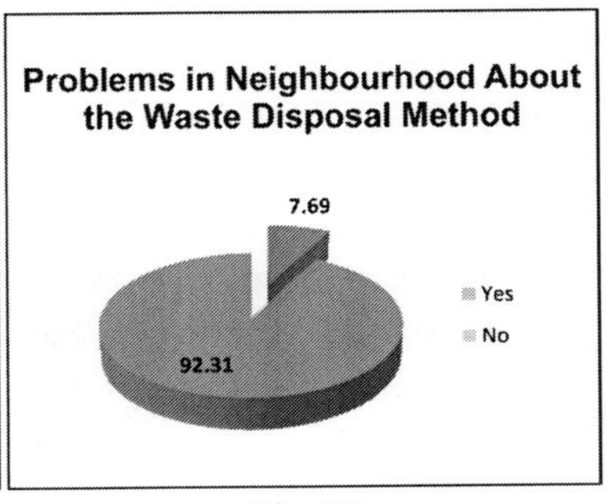

Fig. 23

Source: Primary data, February, 2019.

The Fig. 22 informed that the condition of the public bins near the house. 3.08% are rusting/rotting, 3.08%in adequate size, 90.77% in a good state, 1.54% in inadequate size, 1.54% is not in good condition, 0%dont know and0% others. Therefore, the stare of the public bins are categorized as under rusting/rotting, adequate size, in a good state, inadequate size, not in good condition, don't know and others. The Fig. 23 informed that only 7 %think that waste disposal is a problem in your neighborhood, and 92.3%think that waste disposal method is not a problem in your neighborhood

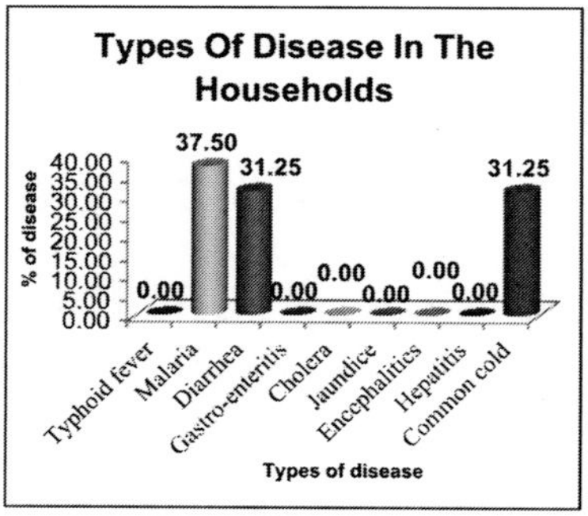

Fig. 24

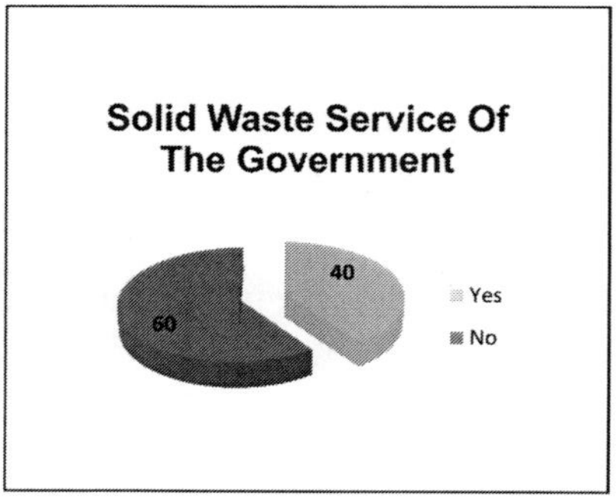

Fig. 25

Source: Primary data, February, 2019

The Fig. 24 stated that the family members have suffered from different diseases due to municipal solid waste. 0% had typhoid fever, 37.50% had malaria, 31.25% had diarrhea, 0% had gastro-enterities, 0% had cholera, 0% had jaundice, 0% had encephalitis, 0% had hepatitis, and 31.25% had common cold. Therefore, it is mainly categorized under typhoid fever, malaria, diarrhea, gastro-enteritis, cholera, jaundice, encephalitis, hepatitis, and common cold. The Fig. 25 stated that 40% think that solid waste service of the government should be better and 60% think that solid waste service of the government should not be better in the locality.

13.9 Findings, Problems, Suggestions, Conclusion

13.9.1 Findings

1. **Parking Troubles of the Vehicles:** Driving on Vizag roads is not bad enough, but finding a parking space makes some problem. People often have to travel an extra mile to find a parking spot.

2. **Severe Traffic Congestions:** In the major junction of the city face some kind of problems of traffic congestions.

3. **Rising Number of Street Vendors on Footpath:** The rising number of street vendors makes so many problems to the pedestrians and makes congestion in footpath.

4. **Solid Waste Problem of the Beach Area:** The area of

the Ramakrishna beach is so crowded than the other area. And sometimes the tourist throws the waste in the beach, which creates so many problems of solid waste.

5. **Use of Plastics:** Uses of plastics are one of the major finding in the vizag city. Some portion of people in the city till now use plastics in various purposes, not good for the environment at all.

13.9.2 Problems

1. **Rapidly Increasing Population:** As vizag is the biggest city in the Andhra Pradesh state. The population is increasing day by day which creates so many problems regarding the solid waste management in the city.

2. **Rapidly Increasing Quantity of Waste:** The increasing rate of solid waste in the urban centres due to the rise of population and the quantities and the areas to be served strain the existing SWM system.

3. **Distance between the Household and Public Bin:** The corporation of greater Vishakhapatnam is very much aware about the public bins but in some cases the distance of households and the public bin is much and create some kind of problems regarding the solid waste.

4. **Uses of Plastics:** In our study area uses of plastics is very commonly seen which is not at all good for the environment.

5. **Health Problem:** So many people of our study area face the health problem due to the solid waste. Malaria, Diarrhea is most common health problems due to solid waste.

6. **Wastes from the Fishing Ports:** As the fishing port is very important commercial part of Vizag but it is also makes so many waste which also hamper in the sea water and enhance the water pollution.

13.9.3 Suggestions

1. **Awareness About the Problem of Population Rising:** So many public awareness programmes should be taken by

the government. Because raising the population makes more problems of the solid waste.

2. **Sustainable use of Resources:** In order to secure the availability of food, drinking water. Sustainable use of the resource one of the major suggestion of the problems of inadequacy of resource.

3. **Availability of Public Bin:** The availability of public bins near to the house is a good measure to the problems of solid waste. By the help of this people does not throe there domestic waste in the roads.

4. **Raising Awareness of Plastic Hazards:** Yes use of plastic is such kind of thing which can make hazard in the future perspective. So awareness of people about the harmful effects of plastic can help to the environment. The usage of plastic should be ban

5. **Three R's (Reduce, Reuse, Recycle):** Using of waste hierarchy i.e. Reduce, Reuse, and Recycle is the guidance suggested for creating a sustainable life and a sustainable environment.

6. **Awareness of Recycling:** Rather than burning the waste, recycling is environment friendly. Burning of waste only can degrade our environment and nothing else.

7. **Uses of Mosquito Net**

In the health problem of our study area, the problem of malaria is a big issue. Using of mosquito net can reduce the problems of malaria.

13.9.4 Conclusion

Solid Waste management can be defined as the "collection, removal, processing, and disposal of materials considered waste". Waste can be put into landfills, incinerated, recycled, or composted. The most sustainable way to manage waste is to recycle and compost. It is found that with increase in the global population and the rising demand of food and other essentials, there has been a rise in the amount of waste being generated daily by each household. Waste that is not properly managed especially solid and liquid waste from household and the community and lead to the spread of infectious diseases. Therefore solid waste management is one such problem which should be taken seriously and treated in a proper manner.

References

Agarwal R, Chaudhary M and Singh J (2015): Waste Management Initiatives In India For Human Well Being, European Scientific Journal, PP 105-127.

Ahluwalia J and Patel U (2018): Solid Waste Management in India: An Assessment of Resource Recovery and Environmental Impact, Indian council for research on international economic relations, PP 1-42.

Babu V, Rao J (2013): A study on selection of landfill sites for solid waste management in the environs of greater Vishakhapatnam municipal corporation, Andhra Pradesh: A spatial technology approach, Department of geo-engineering, Andhra University, PP 2-6.

Dara P K, Reddy T B (2018): Municipal Solid Waste Landfill Sites Selection For Visakhapatnam City Under Vision 2020 Using GIS And AHP, International Journal Of Contemporary Research And Review, Volume 09, Issue 06, PP 20181-20194.

Dara P K, Reddy T B (2017): A Study on Municipal Solid Waste Management In Visakhapatnam City, International Journal Of Advanced Research (IJAR), PP 1448-1453.

Detailed Project Report on Municipal Solid Waste Management for Visakhapatnam (2016): Feedback Infra Pvt. Ltd. and Eco Save Systems Pvt. Ltd, Andhra Pradesh Urban Finance & Infrastructure Development Corporation, PP 8-264.

District census handbook, Visakhapatnam (2011).

Goswami U, Sarma H.P (2007): Strategies for Urban Solid Waste Management: A Review, Volume 13, Issue 2, PP 255-257.

14

Road Traffic Congestion and its Environmental Challenges: A Study in Vishakhapatnam City, Andhra Pradesh, India

Mouli Sarkar[1] *and Dr. Indrajit Roy Chowdhury*[2]

Abstract: Ramakrishna Beach road is the intersection point of three roads. So the traffic congestion is very high as well as vehicular emission. The research paper has been based on measurement and monitoring of roads traffic congestion at this location. Transport has become very important part of daily life and especially for development of the city. Rk beach road is facing some level of congestion which is effect on human health as well as environment. In the area we find various congestion problems which have been based on degree of measurement and monitoring on the traffic signaling system, illegal car parking and the population of the area gradually increasing day by day. As a result the passengers and commuters cannot reach in their work place on time. Local people faced many problems while walking. By reducing traffic jam, decreasing vehicular emission this city can play a very important role for the state as well as it can be also helpful for the locale people and environment.

Keywords: *Traffic jams, Measurement, Economic*

[1]Former post graduate student, Department of Geography and Applied Geography, University of North Bengal, Darjeeling, West Bengal, India. Email: moulisarkar500@gmail.com

[2]Assistant Professor, Department of Geography and Applied Geography, University of North Bengal, Darjeeling, West Bengal. Email: ndrjt.roychoudhury@gmail.com

development, Vehicle, Congestion

14.1 Introduction

In Visakhapatnam, there are 57.53 lakhs of Motor vehicles in different categories in Andhra Pradesh state. Where two wheelers 65.12%, three-wheelers 34.09% and more than four wheelers 12% respectively. From being loved for its open roads and cleaner atmosphere to being cursed for its congested roads and polluted airs, Visakhapatnam's changing landscape has certainly given us plenty to worry about in the recent times. If the current trends of traffic in Vizag are anything to go by, the citizens seem to be in for some tough times ahead. While the upward trend of vehicle sales might be a reason for the issue, experts also cite improper regulatory systems as a prime cause. With the number of vehicles in the city on the rise, the lanes appear to be getting busier and cramped for room ever than before. It is estimated that around 6000 new vehicles hit the city's roads each month and with the roads not being spacious enough to accommodate them, the situation keeps getting worse.

To reduce traffic congestion, the Vizag police are in initialize one-way rule at some main locations of the city, just like how it is implemented on beach road. At some of the main roads in the city, the officials want to replicate the rule and also, rectify some flaws in the rule imposed at the Vizag shore. (YO VIZAG- city exclusive magazine & portal).

14.2 Area of Study

Visakhapatnam is a coastal, port city, often called "The Jewel of the East Coast", situated in the of Andhra Pradesh, located on the eastern shore of India, nestled among the hills of the Eastern Ghats and facing the Bay of Bengal to the east. It is the administrative headquarters of Visakhapatnam District and is also home of the Eastern Naval Command of the Indian Navy.

14.3 Objective of the Study

The major objectives of this research work are enumerated below:

a) To evaluate the major causes in traffic congestion of the city.
b) To know the traffic scenario of the city.
c) To develop more suitable plan regarding the traffic condition.

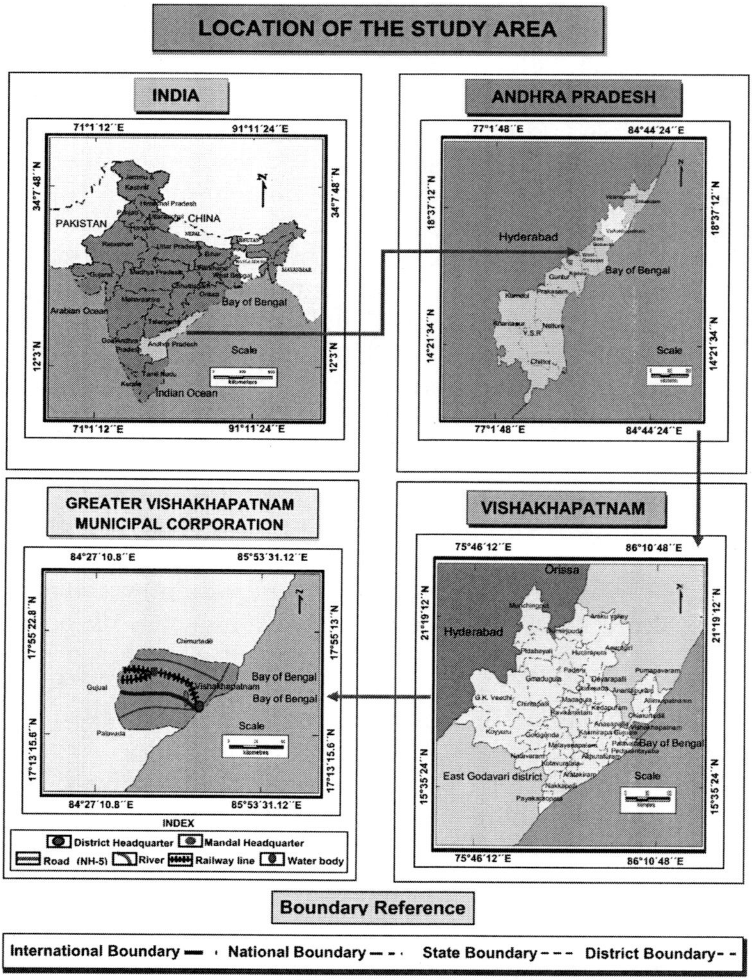

Fig. 1

Source: Oxford school of ATLAS and Vishakhapatnam urban development authority

e) To know the ideas of city development plan of the smart city Vizag.
f) To state the traffic volume of every approaching road of Vizag traffic intersection point.

14.4 Database and Methodology

Primary Data: Data collected by the investigator himself/ herself for a specific purpose.

Secondary Data: Data collected by someone else for some other purpose (but being utilized by the investigator for another purpose).

This research work is based on both primary and secondary data collection from different sources. Primary data mainly source in household, traffic and drivers. And also secondary data given by the RTO office and library. On the basis of primary data where represent the diagram like pie, bar, column, age pyramid etc. Many of digitized thematic maps, location map, and transport map are generally given by the both municipality office in Vishakhapatnam. Many numbers of local newspaper for helping the research of study which makes the work to easy.

A structure questionnaire was used to collect the data from the respondents, respondent's survey, traffic officers survey and driver survey data. 100 household with 20 drivers and 20 traffic police is used for survey with simple random sampling techniques.

14.5 Transport Communication

The city commuters prefer city buses and auto rickshaws as the primary mode of transport, followed by the two wheelers and cars. Road and rail are preferred for long distance commuting and are supported by Dwaraka bus station and Visakhapatnam railway station respectively. It also has sea and air travel infrastructure such as, Visakhapatnam Port and Visakhapatnam Airport. Here Road transport sector of Visakhapatnam is discussed below-

Road Transport: The APSRTC Visakhapatnam Region operates city, district and inter-state bus services from Wanaka bus station. There are more than 600 city buses being run in over 150 routes. Apart from buses, there are about 25,000 auto rickshaws plying on the city roads which provide intermediate public transport as of 2013, the percentage of transport mode shares in the city are, 18% buses, 9% autos, 15% two wheelers, 2% cars and 55% non-motorized transport (bicycles and pedestrians). NH16 a major highway and a part of the Golden Quadrilateral system bypasses the city during the 2016-17 fiscal year.

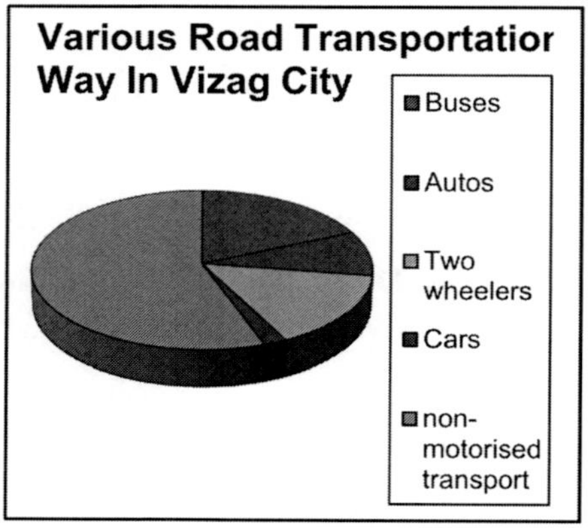

Fig. 2

Source: AP transport department

14.6 Scenario of Traffic Congestion in Vizag City

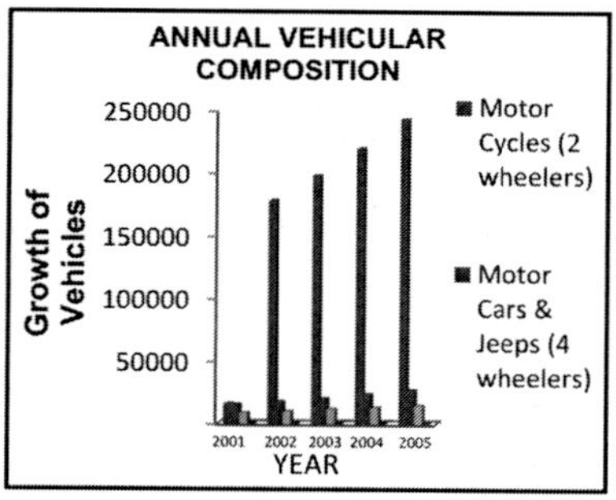

Fig. 3

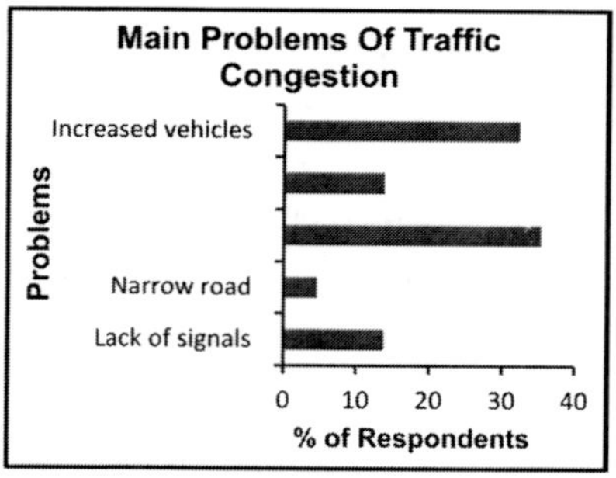

Fig. 4

Source: AP transport and APSRTC, Vishakhapatnam

The diagram (Fig. 3) stated the annual vehicular composition of Andhra Pradesh which shows the rapidly increase of vehicles of the city. The growth of motor cycles (2 wheelers) increasing in a high rate whereas, the growth of

APSRTC is very low in compare to all the vehicles. Commensurate with the growth in population, the number of vehicles also grew at a rapid pace within the urban area. The private transportation has also become the preferred mode of transportation in Visakhapatnam. The growth of cars/jeeps has grown up at an annual growth rate of 8% and that of two wheelers 10.5% over the last decade. The deficiency in frequency of APSRTC buses and non-coverage of suburban train services is one of the reasons for the growth of private vehicles. Overall, there is an attitudinal shift of people to use private vehicle rather than public transport.The (Fig. 4) stated that 35.38% respondents facing main problems because of traffic jams created main problems of reckless driving of vehicles, whereas 32.31% respondents facing problems of increased vehicles, followed by 13.85% because of lack of signals, 13.84% poor traffic managements and 4.62% because of narrow roads. Therefore almost 36% people facing problems of reckless driving of the vehicles.

14.7 Consequences of Road Traffic Congestion

The transport safety is the important component of traffic and transportation mechanism. About 10% of the accidents (Fig. 5) were fatal and remaining 90% were injurious. It was observed that about 40% of the accidents occurring in the city involve pedestrians as the victims. This can be attributed to the poor pedestrian facilities in city road network The fatal accidents involving pedestrians were observed to occur during the road crossings. It was observed that the maximum

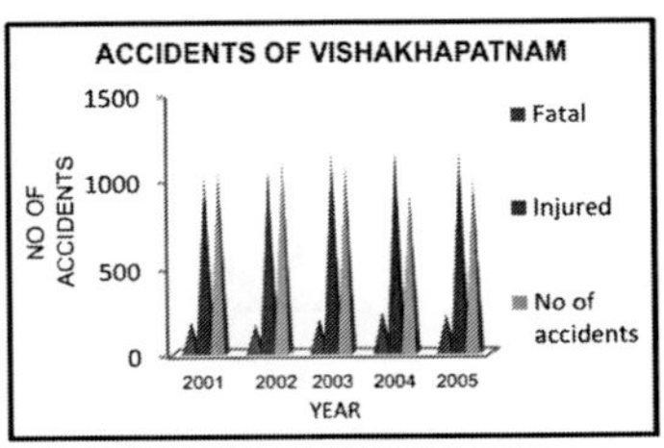

Fig. 5

Source: AP transport and APSRTC, Vishakhapatnam

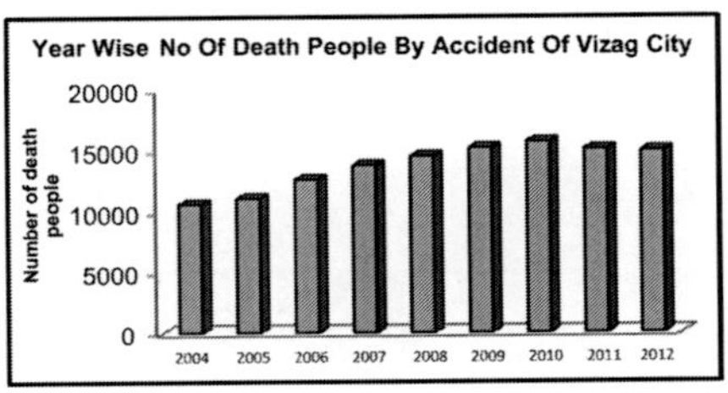

Fig. 6

Source: Secondary Data, Census, 2011

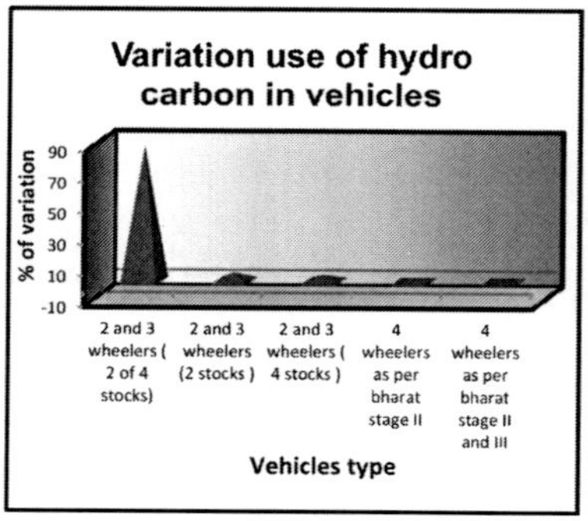

Fig. 7

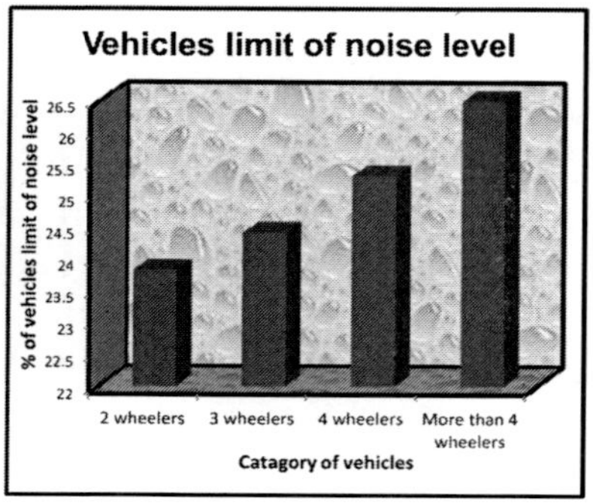

Fig. 8

Source: AP transport and APSRTC, Vishakhapatnam

accidents occurred.

The information stated that, from 2004 to 2010, no. of death people was rapidly increased, where as 2011 and 2012 Was the decreased time of death people by the accidental case.

The figure (Fig. 7) represents the variation use of hydro carbon in vehicles in Vishakhapatnam. Where we can see that higher % in 2 and 3 wheelers (87%) where as 5% in 2 and 3 wheelers (2 stocks) and low in 4 wheelers that is 1.45%. The figure (Fig. 8) represents the vehicles limit of noise level in Vishakhapatnam. Where high % in >4 wheeler that is 26% followed by 25% in 4 wheelers. And low in 3 wheelers that is 24%. So above all discussion we conclude that variation

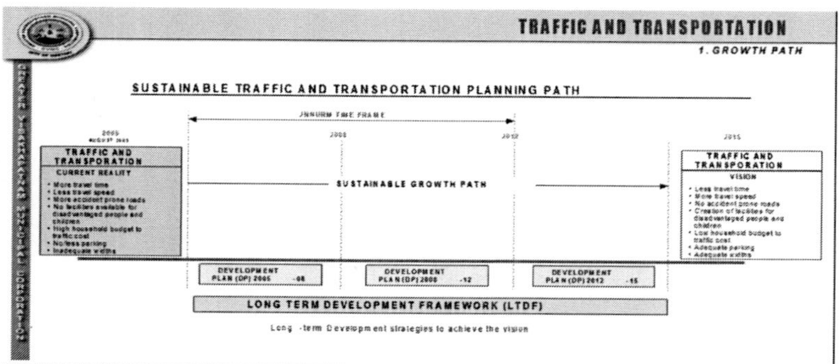

Fig. 9: Sustainable Traffic and Transportation Planning Path

Source: Vishakhapatnam city development plan

of use Hc and noise level are control in this city.

14.8 Government Initiatives about Reducing Traffic Congestion

Table – 1

Goals, Service Outcomes for Different Horizon Years

Vision Indicators	Time Frame			
	2005-06	2011	2016	2021
Road network as % of total area	6%	13%	16%	17%
Accessibility to the disadvantaged/ physically challenged	……	Pilot projects completed	This factor included in all new T & T projects	This factor included in all new T & T projects
Share of public transport	20%	25%	40%	55%
Rail transport as share of total public transport MRTS	0%	3%	10%	25%
Average speed-km/h	15	20	25	25
Side-walks length to total road length	3%	40% of the require-ment	70%of the require-ment	90%of the require-ment
Road accidents		Reduced by 25%	Reduced by 50%	Reduced by 70%
Usage of alternative fuels	Pilot initiated	15%	25%	40%
Environmental Up gradation (SOx, Nox, TSPM levels)	…….	Within acceptable limits	Within acceptable limits	Within acceptable limits

Source: Visakhapatnam city development plan

14.9 Measuring Congestion Level at Beach Road of Vizag City

Determination of road congestion level: There are varieties of indicators for the measurement of congestion. In case of Beach Road traffic intersection point, seven indicators are taken for analysis which can directly assess the severity level of road congestion. These are as follows–

Degree of Congestion: Several indicators have been incorporated to measure the degree of congestion level at beach road in Vizag. Therefore, several transport geographers have contributed various formulas to measure the degree of congestion.

1. **Delay rate (DR) and Travel Time Index (TTI)** – The initial concept of delay rate was developed by Lomax .et. al (1997) based on travel rate. In a simplified way, delay rate is the difference between the time required to cross a specific distance with the CCA through a TIP during peak and off peak period. In other words it is the difference between actual travel time (second per km) and acceptable travel time (second per km). Here, acceptable travel time denotes the minimum time that can be required to cover the specific distance on a traffic free road. Higher DR value indicates more congestion level with in the road stretch.

And the TTI was proposed in the urban mobility report (Shrank and Lomax, 2005). It is expressed by comparing travel time in free flow condition and during peak period on a fixed road segment through a TIP. It represents the peak period travel time is how much greater than free flow travel time. Higher than TTI, higher will be the severity of congestion on a road segment or of a TIP.

Delay Rate: Travel rate during peak period -Travel rate during off peak period.

Travel Time Index: Peak period travel time/ free flow travel time

Table – 2

Name of The Road	Travel Rate During Peak Period (In Sec)	Travel Rate During Off Peak Period (In Sec)	Delay Rate	Travel Time Index
Towards Submarine	420	180	240	2.333

Towards Dolphin point	780	270	510	2.889
Towards the City	1260	390	870	3.231

Source: Collected and Computed by The author

From (Table – 2) it has been identified that , towards the city has maximum delay rate due to huge difference in travel rate during peak period and off peak period while towards submarine delay rate is low due to less congestion. The TTI rate has maximum towards the city than others area. And TTI rate is low towards submarine.

2. Quality of Traffic Transmission Index – It is defined as a function of average speed and the number and sum of speed changes (Levinson and Lomax, 1996). On a free flow, usually the average speed of a car is high and number of gear changes is low. The total number of speed changes and the differences between maximum and minimum speed should also below a freeway. On the contrary, congested roads experience frequent gear changes and differences in speed in a higher order. Here high Q index value represents less congestions and vice-versa.

Q Index = KS/DSÖf

(k=1000, S= average speed, ΔS= Difference between Maximum and minimum Speed, $\sqrt{f}$= No of Speed Change per km)

Table – 3

Name of The Road	S (Average Speed)	DS (Diff B/w Max and Min Speed)	f (No. of speed change /km	Q Index
Towards Submarine	50	20	12	721.688
Towards Dolphin point	60	31	17	469.424
Towards the City	38	40	20	212.426

Source: Collected and Computed by The author

The Table – 3 depicts the degree of resistance of a free flow of a car on congested road. The relationship between the congestion and Q Index is inversed. The more the value of Q Index the less the congestion on the road. So towards the city the frequent change of speed per km is high whereas, the change of speed is less towards the submarine and dolphin point.

3. **Lane-Length Duration Index** – It is measure of extent and durations of freeway congestion as developed by Cottrell (1991) in a study of congestion in 35 urban areas. The LLDI value of each urban area is the sum of the product of congested freeway lane length (in km) and duration of congestion (in seconds) for individual road way segment and is calculated in a modified way.

LLDI – Congested lane length *Duration of congestion

Table – 4

Name of The Road	Congested Lane Length (In Metre)	Duration of Congestion (In Sec.)	LLDI
Towards Submarine	136	195	26520
Towards Dolphin point	204	362	73848
Towards the City	388	294	114072

Source: Collected and Computed by The author

The LLDI is high towards the city which indicates high congestion in the city whereas, the rate is low towards the submarine which means the congestion is less.

4. **Modal Mix Index (MM)** – It is simple number of variety of modes (both passenger goods) moving on a particular road stretch. A road way having limited number of modal types has comparatively less congestion. But roads having all the variety of small to large vehicles without any specific road way maintenance cause severe congestion.

Table – 5

Name of The Road	Total Vehicles	Type of Vehicles
Towards Submarine	1697	4
Towards Dolphin point	1859	5
Towards the City	12721	6

Source: Collected and Computed by The author

Here the type of vehicle indicates congestion level of a city. A road way having limited number of modal types has comparatively less congestion. Towards the city the type of vehicle is more so the congestion is more towards the city whereas, towards the submarine and dolphin point the amount of congestion is less due to less number of vehicle.

5. **Road Area (RA)** – It is an area of the selected road segment approaching to a particular mode within the CCA. Here road length and road widths arte measured separately for each road segment to get the area and an idea of estimated carrying capacity of the roads.

RA – Length of the road (a) * Width of the Road (b)

Table – 6

Name of The Road	Length of the Road in metre (a)	Width of road in metre (b)	RA (in sq metre)
Towards Submarine	84	12	1008
Towards Dolphin point	230	12	2760
Towards the City	205	8.5	1742.5

Source: Collected and Computed by The author

14.10 Measurement of Temperature and Humidity in the Beach Road

Relative humidity is a measure of the water vapor content of the air at a given temperature. These 2 diagrams show the relationship between temperature and humidity in Vizag city (duration of measurement Fig. 10-5.15pm & Fig. 11-8.35pm). The highest of the 1 hour was 28.4°C at 4.30pm and humidity was 53.3% at 5.15pm whereas the lowest temperature was

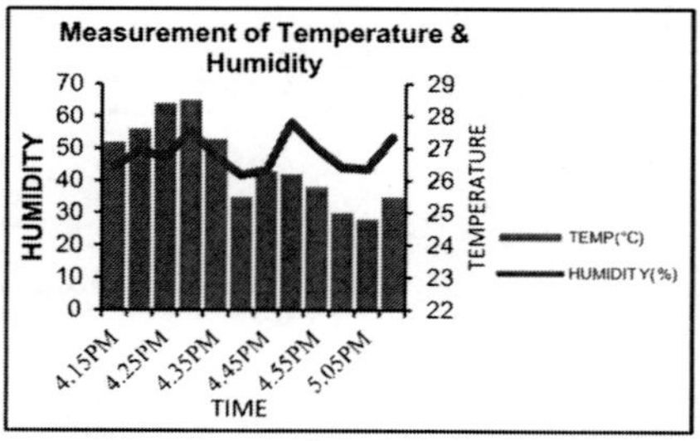

Fig. 10

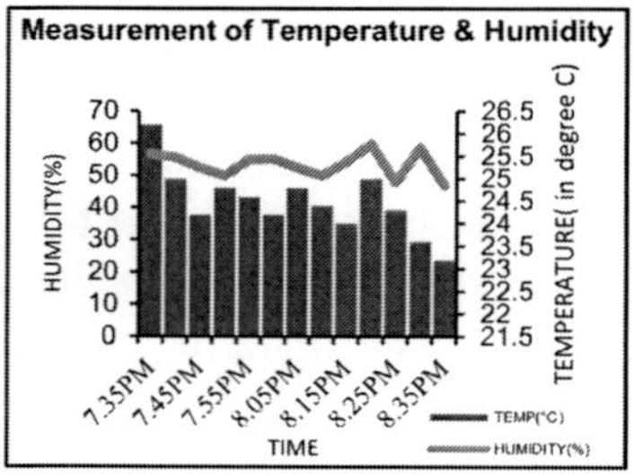

Fig. 11

Source: Calculated and Computed by the author

24.8°C at 5.05pm and humidity was 41.7% at 4.40pm.

The highest of the 1 hour in the 2nd diagram was 26.2°C at 7.35pm and humidity was 59.8% at 8.20pm whereas the lowest temperature was 23.3°C at 8.35pm and humidity was 47% at 8.35pm.

14.11 Measurement of Noise in the Beach Road

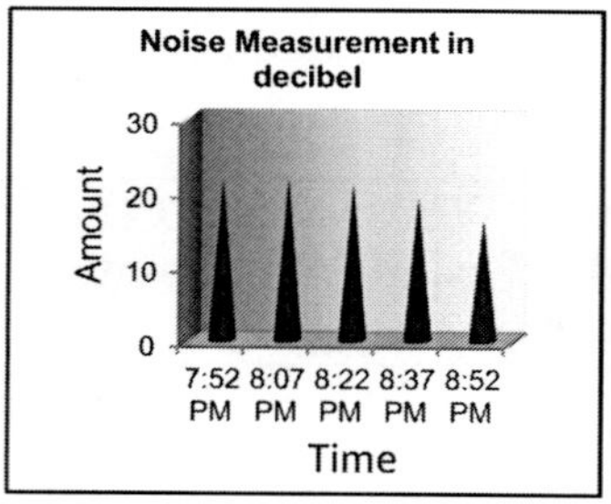

Fig. 12

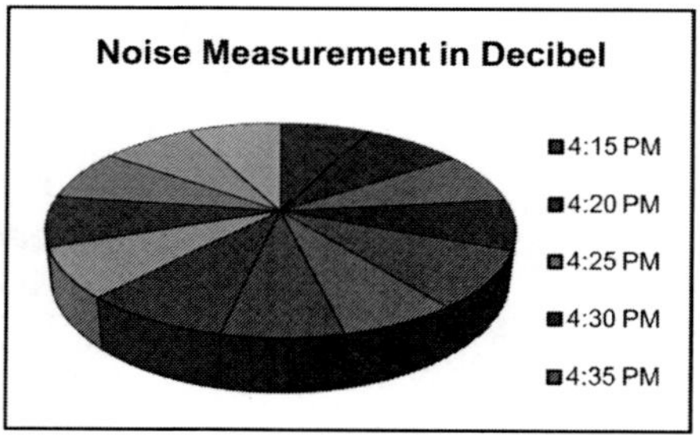

Fig. 13

Source: Calculated and Computed by the author

The figure pointed out that 7.32% noise occurred at 4:15 PM, which is indicate 60.7 decibel noise, 8.1% noise occurred at 4:20 PM, which is indicate 62.4 decibel noise, 7.7% noise occurred at 4:25 PM, which is indicate 67.1 decibel noise, 7.58% noise occurred at 4:30 PM, which is indicate 63.8 decibel noise, 8.71% noise occurred at 4:35 PM, which is indicate 62.8 decibel noise, 6.89% noise occurred at 4:40 PM, which is indicate 72.2 decibel noise, 7.13% noise occurred at 4:45 PM, which is indicate 57.1 decibel noise, 8.57% noise occurred in between 4:50 PM and 4:55 PM, which is indicate 59.1 decibel noise, 7.49% noise occurred at 4:55 PM, which is indicate 71.1 decibel noise, 7.66% noise occurred at 5:00 PM, which is indicate 62.1 decibel noise, 7.65% noise occurred at:05 PM, which is indicate 63.5 decibel noise, 7.65% noise occurred at 5:10 PM, which is indicate 63.4 decibel noise, 7.66% noise occurred at 5:15 PM, which is indicate 63.5 decibel noise.

14.12 Transport Network Analysis (Connectivity)

Connectivity Measurement

1. **Alpha Index (a) = e-v+1/2v-5**

(Here, e= No of edges, v= No of nodes)

= 180–90+1/2*90-5 = 0.52

The value of alpha index ranges between 0 to 1. The calculated value is 0.52. so it indicates moderate connectivity.

2. **Beta Index (b) = e/v**

(Here, e= No of edges, v= No of nodes)

= 180/90 = 2

The value of Beta index ranges between 0 to 100. The calculated value is 2. So it indicates less connectivity.

3. **Gamma Index (g) = e/3(v–2)**

(Here, e= No of edges, v= No of nodes)

=180/3(90-2) = 0.68

The value of Gamma index ranges between 0 to 1. The calculated value is 0.68. So it indicates well connectivity.

4. **Eta Index (e) = m/e**

(Here, m= total route distance, e=no of edges)

= 220/180 = 1.22

The value of Eta index ranges between 0 to 1. The calculated value is 1.22. So it indicates well connectivity.

5. **Theta Index (q) = m/v**

(Here, m= total route distance, v=no of nodes)

=220/90 = 2.44

The value of Theta index ranges between 0 to 1. The calculated value is 2.44. So it indicates well connectivity.

6. Cyclometric Number (μ) = e-v+g

(Here, m= total route distance, v=no of nodes, g=gravity value)

=180-90+1 = 91

The value of Beta index ranges between 0 to 100. The calculated value is 91. So it indicates very well connectivity.

14.13 Findings of the Study

1. Most of the respondents can't reach their destination in accurate time, even often they are facing the problem of traffic block.
2. Very few respondents can used their mobile phone for emergency purpose, where are up to 60% respondents can't used mobile phone while they driving, mainly mobile phone using during driving time is the main reason of road accident. In that case & this case related purpose vizag city is the under of more traffic rules & regulation, and accidental matter can happen little much.
3. That most of the respondents are interested to transportation related job, most of the driver's are engaged up to 5 years. Followed by very few driver's can overtaking to another car for various reason purpose. In this busy road it's another cause of road accident.
4. According to the Andhra Pradesh transportation rule. Most of the respondents are checked their problems of vehicle very frequently & some time. So they are always careful about their vehicle. Followed by they are using the various part of vehicle in different time, such as drivers can drive in night time, they has always used their cars upper and deeper light for reducing the road accident.
5. Most of the respondents given road tax and registered their vehicle followed by if any respondents could nor reissued of their license, without invalid license car driving is a punishable influence, so most of the respondents can reissued their driving license.

6. In this city there are 95% road safety awareness & measures for reducing the any types of road accident. Followed by, those measures are adopted for avoid the traffic jam and growing the smooth function of roads.
7. We got there are no flyover bridge for avoid the road accident but flyover is under of construction in various place in Vizag city, and it's one of requirement for road jam and crossing the road.
8. Lastly we said that, well improvement of traffic police Vizag is developing rapidly and right now accidental case is not happening on the road.

14.14 Problems of Traffic Congestion

1. With increase number of vehicles in the city on the rise, the lane appears to be getting busier.
2. Lack of parking space is found in the main city for traffic congestion.
3. Lack of traffic signals at several places near beach road has been creating jams in the day time
4. Large amount of old vehicles where mainly use diesel that increases high amount of black and white fume.
5. In some parts of the city the traffic police don't work properly which leads to congestion in the road.
6. Some peoples are suffering mental problem in road way.
7. Some auto driver use low quality of vehicular technology which leads to air pollution.
8. Delay, which may result in late arrival for the employment, meetings, education, resulting in lost business or other personal losses.
9. There is no express way available for the ambulance and fire controls, in some cases blocked traffic may interfere with the passage of emergency vehicles travelling to their destinations where they are urgently needed.
10. Higher chance of collisions due to tight spacing and constant stopping and going in the main city.
11. Stressed and frustrated motorists, encouraging the aggressive driving which may leads to accidents.

14.15 Suggestions

1. Improvement of public transport system to discourage use of private vehicles.
2. Parking spaces should be increased to avoid traffic congestion in the Vizag city.
3. Increase of traffic point bar reduces the congestion in the beach side road.
4. To reduce the air pollution, plant more greenery in road side properly.
5. Use of high technology in the vehicles reduces the emission of black and white fume.
6. Creating of some vehicle free zones near the tourism spots can make the traffic flow stable.
7. Provision of bicycle pathways.
8. Increase of Traffic police can reduces the congestion in the road.
9. Optimize the traffic light management.
10. Use CCTV in every road to monitor road condition.
11. Build flyover to reduce the pressure of congestions.
12. Close parking in the main road.

14.16 Conclusion

At the end of the chapter it can be concluded that in Vizag, we find daily passengers, shop owners, drivers are facing different problem of congestion and pollution. Illegal car parking, maintain problem of traffic police, no divider etc are main problems especially in Vizag. This problem has been improved day by day, so we should prefer some management strategies for the betterment of the traffic congestion. And it should prefer a healthy environment for citizens and their future generations.

References

Gopala Raju, S.S.S.V. (2011): Vehicular growth and its management: Visakhapatnam city in India- A case study, Indian Society for Education and Environment (ISEE),

Page no: 903-906, Vol- 4.

Kumar Lohia, Sanjab : Development of Urban Public Transport Infrastructure and Services In India- Initiatives, Challenges and Potentials For International Cooperation, Ministry of Urban Development Government Of India, Page no: 302-308, Vol- 3

Kumar Darapu, Srikanth Satish (August 2013): Air Pollution In Visakhapatnam -An Overview, International Journal of Civil Engineering (IJCE), Page no: 11-14, Vol- 2

Rama Krishna Tvbps, Reddy Mk, Reddy Rc, Singh Rn And Devotta S (2006): Modelling of Ambient Air Quality Over Visakhapatnam Bowl Area, Indian National Science Academy, Page no: 55-61, Vol- 1

Tolkach Denis, Pearlman Michael & King Brian, (2012): 'Key Implementation Factors in Transport Corporation'; Transport research, Page no- 55-70 vol-37